EXCELLENCE
IN
CHARACTER

By Dr. Robb Thompson

Excellence in Character
ISBN 1-889723-45-2
Copyright © 2004 by Robb Thompson
Family Harvest Church
18500 92nd Ave.
Tinley Park, Illinois 60477

Editorial Consultant: Cynthia Hansen
Text Design: Lisa Simpson

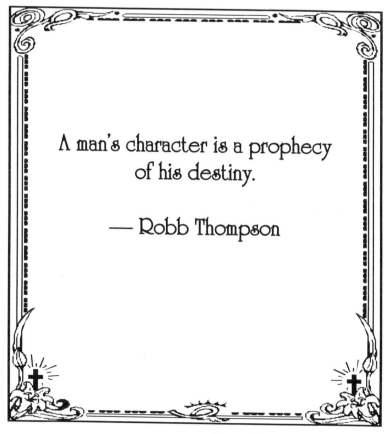

A man's character is a prophecy
of his destiny.

— Robb Thompson

TABLE OF CONTENTS

FOREWORD

This book, *Excellence in Character,* touches a nerve in each one of us, for how often have we faced the temptation to ignore character and just do and say the convenient thing? Dr. Robb Thompson points out correctly and accurately that there are always penalties, sometimes later rather than sooner, for ignoring God's absolutes.

Ultimately, there is no right way to do the wrong thing. Both in the home and out of the home, extending all the way into the world of business and government, we as believers need a renaissance of values that will set us apart and cause others to rethink their own standards. The Christian Church *must* take the lead and reaffirm the biblical mandate to **"buy the truth, and sell it not..."** (Prov. 23:23 *KJV*).

Dr. Peter J. Daniels
President and Founder
World Centre for
Entrepreneurial Studies
Strathalbyn, South Australia

INTRODUCTION

I am interested in foundations.

I want to know what lies underground, hidden beneath the surface. I want to see what type of foundation a person has in his life before I ever hear about the wonderful things he says he can do.

If you are a parent, you are probably well aware of what I'm talking about. During your children's growing-up years, you spend most of your time underground, working on the foundation of their lives. No one can really see what you're building inside them during those crucial years, but *you* know. You're building the foundation of *character.*

The greatest need in the Body of Christ lies in this arena of character, for character is the foundation upon which all of life is built. Too many Christians spend all their time building their lives on an uncertain foundation of compromise and mediocrity — only to find out later that their foundation cannot hold.

Without a strong, solid foundation of God's principles undergirding our lives, everything else we attempt to build or accomplish will eventually crumble and fall. In fact, *any breakdown in life can almost always be traced back to a breakdown in character.*

This is why it is so important that we embrace *principles*, not *people*, in our walk with God. That means we prize principles above relationship. We refuse to break a scriptural principle, no matter what person might come into our lives and try to persuade us otherwise. We don't show favoritism. We don't tolerate double standards in our lives. We don't say it's acceptable for one person to do something but not acceptable for someone else to do it. We live our lives according to what *God* thinks, not according to what we think or what anyone else thinks.

In this book, we're going to explore in depth what it takes to be a person of excellent character. But before we do, I urge you to take the time to ask yourself these questions:

- *Which principles define me as a person?*

- *What are the unseen ideals that invisibly guide my life?*

- *What are the non-negotiable issues for me as a person — the principles I will not break?*

- *Are my ethics guided by the Word of God — or by the convenience of the moment?*

That word "ethics" refers to the code of conduct by which we live; the discipline of duty and obligation; or the behavior that governs our lives. As we focus on building a foundation of godly ethics and scriptural principles in our lives, we of necessity will build a foundation of excellent character. That foundation will keep us on the road to our God-given destiny long after those who thought they were going somewhere fall by the wayside in defeat.

So where do you go from here? The answer to that question is entirely up to you. God tells you in His Word who you are. He gives you the opportunity to be all that He has created you to be. But the outcome of your life will be based on how much you embrace of what God says about you — and how strong you build your foundation.

One more thing — it's important to realize that your life is lived before people, not in isolation. Therefore, as you dismantle your life and then rebuild it on a strong foundation of character, you must learn how to do it in front of the people who have watched you and helped bring you to where you are today. Don't try to go through this process alone, tucked away in some hidden corner.

You simply can't stay the way you are if you want to achieve what God has planned for your life. You must be willing to change on a daily basis; otherwise, you will always be a person who lives by *theory* rather than by *productivity.*

As we look at the ingredients of godly character in this book, I urge you to be honest with yourself. If you want to be all that God has called you to be, look for the weaknesses in the mortar of your own foundation so you can begin to rebuild it into something that is solid and secure. Make the decision to start pursuing excellent character every single day of your remaining time upon the earth. You'll find that once the character issues are straightened out in your life, everything else will begin to fall in line!

Robb Thompson

CHARACTER: THE FOUNDATION OF EXCELLENCE

One night I sat watching a program on the Discovery channel, not knowing that I was about to receive tremendous insight into the value system of man on this earth. The program was about a tribe in the deep part of West Africa that had some very strange customs. The men of the tribe had come together to build a hut for one of the men who was getting married. There was one small problem, however — the man didn't have a bride-to-be yet! He didn't know who his bride was, but he was building her a hut!

The interpreter asked the man, "Do you know where your wife will come from?"

The man replied, "I had hoped to go to another tribe and bring home a wife. But my father has asked me not to marry outside our tribe, for he does not know what foreign customs the woman would bring with her. *I will honor my father's wishes.*" (That last statement alone gives us profound insight into the caliber of the man who was speaking!)

Then the interpreter asked, "But what type of attributes are you looking for in a woman?"

The man replied, "The number-one attribute I am looking for is *a woman of good character.*"

That primitive West African man had more sense than most people I have met with PhDs! However, later I did read about a certain group of men who would agree with that West African man. The book entitled *The Millionaire Mind* includes a survey that was taken in which both middle-class men and millionaires were asked, "What kind of woman are you looking for when you marry?" The number-one attribute the middle-class men said they were looking for was *good looks.* On the other hand, the number-one attribute on the millionaires' list was *good character!*

I find it very interesting that an American millionaire and a tribal West African man would both come to the same conclusion! Both understood that long after good looks are not so good anymore, long after certain areas of our bodies begin to sag and shape themselves differently, good character still remains.

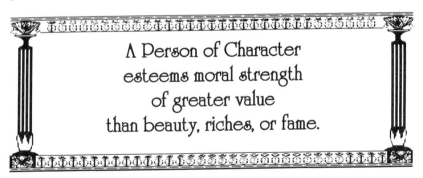

A Person of Character
esteems moral strength
of greater value
than beauty, riches, or fame.

But just what *is* character? Character is the summation of the principles we have down on the inside by which we live our lives. It is the mental and moral attributes, whether good or evil, that define us as individuals.

Good character refers to the virtue, the self-discipline, and the honorable constitution an individual possesses. It also denotes moral strength. When a person possesses this quality, he refuses to be moved away from principle, no matter what anyone says or does. The Scriptures tell us that this kind of strong, godly character is very precious in the sight of God.

The truth is, many people are looking for others of strong character with whom to associate. In fact, people often make good character a prerequisite for access into their lives when they are scouting for a spouse or looking for a good friend.

But I'm actually more interested in discovering the kind of character a person possesses *himself.* That knowledge will tell me much more than knowing the kind of character he requires from others in order to be in his presence!

Anyone who is searching for a person of excellent character knows that such a person is indeed a rare treasure in this world. As Proverbs 20:6 says, **"Most men will proclaim each his own goodness, but who can find a faithful man?"** Even Solomon knew that a faithful person was very difficult to find. He understood that it is easier for people to go with the flow than to stand against the tide and do what is right.

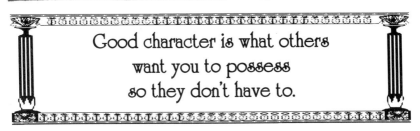

Good character is what others
want you to possess
so they don't have to.

I relate to Solomon's lifelong search for people of character. I have learned through the years that a person who wants to remain irresponsible needs others around him whose good character compels them to be responsible. That way he will always have someone to bear the load he should be carrying himself.

But I cannot care what someone else says or does to me; I must live my life before God. I must be faithful to God, no matter what. Even if that person acts unfaithfully toward me, he will still be the beneficiary of my walk with God.

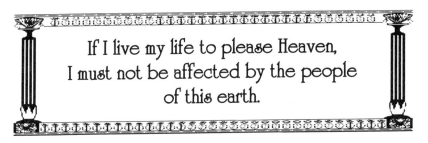

If I live my life to please Heaven, I must not be affected by the people of this earth.

I live by principle, not by feelings. That is the only way I know how to live. I can do anything I have to do without emotions getting in my way, because I have determined never to violate the principles by which God requires me to live my life.

It was after I made the commitment to live my life in this manner that I came to realize how many Christians believe more in the spiritual walk of another who demonstrates character than they believe in their own walk with God. They have allowed circumstances to determine the outcome of their lives; therefore, they cannot trust what they might do in a given situation. On the other hand, they *can* trust what the person with strong character will do. They know he will live by his principles, no matter what.

So why is a person of character so rare? Because everything that is good in life has a down side. There is a price to pay for pursuing excellent character. No matter how great you are in the eyes of people who are on the outside, your family members understand what it has taken for you to get where you are. They are the ones who have to endure the pain. They are the ones who have to go through the hard years with you when you are being molded through the rejection, the pressures, and the difficulties that build your character.

People may look at you and say, "I would sure like to have your life." But how many of those same people want to pay the price you have had to pay in your pursuit of excellent character to get where you are?

Nevertheless, the prize is always greater than the price, for nothing good can ever be built in our lives without good character. Character affects every area of our lives — our decisions, our words, our actions, our attitudes, our goals, and our relationships. If we do not fix our character before we attempt to work on anything else in our lives, we will only experience failure after failure. We will begin to build, but it will get knocked down. We will build, but someone else will steal it from us. We will build, but all our efforts will come to nothing.

Yet we live in a society where character flaws are not only ignored, but too often they are even celebrated. Very few people want to confront the character problems in their lives. As a result, they keep building their businesses, their careers, their marriages, and their families on a faulty foundation that eventually will cause everything dear to them to crumble and collapse.

How do you avoid that pitfall in your own life? First, you must realize this principle:

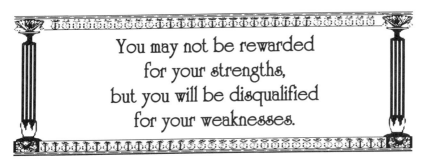

You may not be rewarded
for your strengths,
but you will be disqualified
for your weaknesses.

A chain is only as strong as its weakest link. It might be a huge, 1,000-link chain with 999 super-strong links and only one weak link. But that chain will not be qualified because of its 999 strong links; it will be disqualified because of its single weak link.

Just consider what would happen if that huge chain was used in international tractor pulls by the man who has been the champion for ten straight years. Suppose this champion had been using that same chain for all those years, and now he decides, *This chain has worked great all these years; there really isn't any need to check it this year before the tractor pull.*

So the tractor pull begins. The champion is delighted to see that he is competing against a man whose chain is miniscule compared to his huge chain. Both of them begin to pull. The champion pulls with all his might, waving confidently at the crowd as his tractor moves past his opponent's. But as he continues to put pressure on the chain, the one weak link suddenly breaks, and that huge chain snaps in half!

Meanwhile, the competitor just chugs along a few inches at a time. His chain doesn't look like it could pull the heavy tractor another inch, but still he keeps moving forward, little by little, until he finally reaches the finish line a half hour later.

The competitor's winning strategy is one from which we could all gain a valuable lesson: *Using a chain with no weak links, he pointed himself in the correct direction; then he determined never to quit until he had reached his desired destination.*

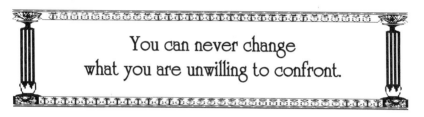

You can never change
what you are unwilling to confront.

We will continue to lose the race in our own lives as long as we seek to be rewarded for our good points while refusing to recognize our weaknesses.

Too often people complain to those over them in authority, "You never see anything I do that is right. All you ever do is pick on my weak points. You need to start emphasizing my *good* points!"

But those in authority would do those individuals a disservice if they followed that advice, because that is not how it works in life. We are not rewarded for our strong points; we are rewarded for our lack of weak points, for it is our weaknesses that disqualify us from being promoted to the next level.

The truth is, if we are everything God wants us to be according to the Scriptures, in His eyes that is normal, not something unusual to be celebrated. When we ask the people in our lives to talk only about our strong points, that immediately closes the door to any discussion about our weak points. But that amounts to a false balance in life, and Proverbs 11:1 (*KJV*) says, **"A false balance is abomination to the Lord, but a just weight is his delight."**

People who refuse to recognize their weak points seldom take responsibility for their own mistakes and failures. Instead, they look for others to blame for the pain they have created in their own lives.

If we need help in order to get over a weakness, we should not be afraid to go to someone we can trust and get help. However, we must first be willing to repent. We cannot just dismiss the issue by saying, "Well, I guess I made a mistake." That is the very reason we have been disqualified in the past. And until we recognize, confront, and conquer our weaknesses, we will just keep wondering why we are not celebrated.

That's why it is my constant desire to focus on constructing the foundation of character, for I have found that everything in life rests squarely on that foundation.

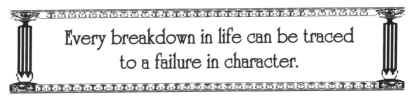

Every breakdown in life can be traced
to a failure in character.

Every failure — whether in marriage, in one's personal habits, at the job, or in the church — can be traced back to a breakdown in character, almost 100 percent of the time.

This explains why some ministers are not able to minister effectively for the Lord. They have allowed themselves to change from being ministers in the likeness of Moses, who was faithful in all his house, to ministers such as Aaron, who transformed a relationship with God into a religion. But Christianity was never designed to be a religion. Christianity is a living relationship with God that is birthed through His Word.

In Deuteronomy 10:12 and 13, God gives us the basic requirements for developing that vital relationship with Him:

> "**And now, Israel, what does the Lord your God require of you, but to fear the Lord your God, to walk in all His ways and to love Him, to serve the Lord your God with all your heart and with all your soul,**
> **and to keep the commandments of the Lord and His statutes which I command you today for your good?**"

We are to fear the Lord, walk in His ways, and love and serve Him with all our hearts and souls. But we don't do this for the good of someone else or for the good of an organization. God said we are to embrace His commands and decrees for our *own* good. Why is this so?

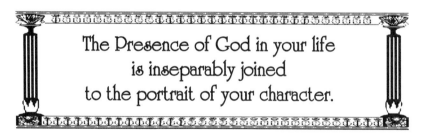

The Presence of God in your life
is inseparably joined
to the portrait of your character.

If we want to understand how God works in our lives, we must also understand that His ability to move on our behalf is directly linked to the kind of character we demonstrate as we walk through life. The hand of God cannot work in our lives by our mishaps or our mediocrity. The hand of God can only work in our lives to the extent that we are willing to receive the Word of God so we can bring forth a spiritual child within us. And that which holds the incorruptible seed of God's Word to the wall of the womb of our spirits is *character*.

That's why so many people continually suffer through spiritual miscarriages. This is also the reason many Christians seem to be continually believing the Word but never seeing God's promises manifested in their lives. Believing that the Word is true is not enough. If godly character isn't holding a person's faith to the womb of his spirit — the place where God-given dreams originate — he may stand for a little while, but eventually he will experience a setback, and his lack of character will cause his faith to blow up in his face.

Character has the ability to hold something firmly without releasing and letting it go. Character not only believes God's Word, but afterward it believes its own word as well.

I can believe in my word because I believe God's Word. I can walk as a righteous man who will swear to his own hurt and never change because I trust Him. I have seen how God is true to His Word in every situation. And because I have seen Him come through in the past, I can therefore know that I can trust myself.

This is how we are to walk on this earth. This is what God requires of us.

Yet so many Christians live their lives by emotion rather than by principle, despite the fact that emotions do not make good decisions. In fact, emotions make mistakes almost every time! By getting emotional and expressing their negative feelings, people take pressure off themselves, at least in the short term. But at the same time, they cause others to back away from them. And in the end, the pressure returns sevenfold, for the root cause of their problem has never been dealt with or eliminated from their lives.

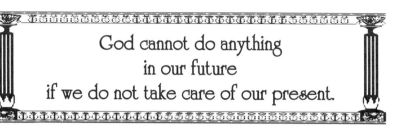

God cannot do anything
in our future
if we do not take care of our present.

People who live by their emotions often want to know what God is going to do with them in the future. But they haven't come to terms with this basic principle of character.

There is no bright future for us if we refuse to confront the weaknesses in our character, for as soon as we arrive at tomorrow, it will be renamed "today" — complete with the same problems that are keeping us in our present mess.

That is why you must fix where you are right now. You have to ask the needed questions and find out what must be fixed in your life before you can be promoted to the next level. After applying that knowledge and making the necessary changes, you must then ask more of the right questions so you can move further along the road toward excellence.

But we must not ask questions about tomorrow if we are not challenging our standards of today. First, we must examine our *present* beliefs and actions — discovering what is hindering our walk with God and then taking the necessary steps to deal with those weaknesses. As we do, the questions of tomorrow will take care of themselves. As Jesus said in Matthew 6:34 (*NLT*), "**...Don't worry about tomorrow, for tomorrow will bring its own worries. Today's trouble is enough for today.**"

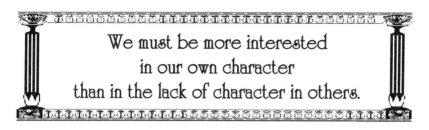

We must be more interested
in our own character
than in the lack of character in others.

As we look for those "weak links" in the chain of our character, we need to continually keep this principle in mind. Jesus clearly states this same principle in Matthew 7:3-5 (*NLT*):

> "And why worry about a speck in your friend's eye when you have a log in your own?
>
> "How can you think of saying, 'Let me help you get rid of that speck in your eye,' when you can't see past the log in your own eye?
>
> "Hypocrite! First get rid of the log from your own eye; then perhaps you will see well enough to deal with the speck in your friend's eye."
>
> **Matthew 7:3-5 *NLT***

I am supposed to concentrate on what I need to do to build my own character rather than focus on how those around me demonstrate a *lack* of good character. God doesn't want me go around giving others a report card on their character. He is much more interested in asking me to examine my own life and give *myself* a character report card!

God never tells us to search the Scriptures to find out what is wrong with other people. He tells us to search the Scriptures to find out what is right with us because we are in Christ. And after we have gotten the beam out of our own eyes — after we have suffered the pain of eliminating our own character flaws — we'll discover that the faults we saw in others really weren't so bad after all.

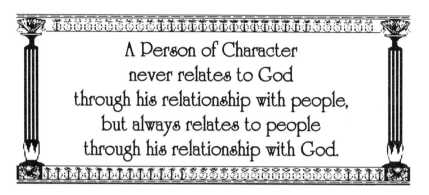

A Person of Character
never relates to God
through his relationship with people,
but always relates to people
through his relationship with God.

In other words, other people are to be the beneficiaries of our relationship with God. Jesus put it this way in Matthew 25:40: "**...Assuredly, I say to you, inasmuch as you did it to one of the least of these My brethren, you did it to Me.**"

What does this principle mean when applied to my everyday life?

- The way I treat others is the way I treat God.

- The way I love others is the way I love God.

- The way I disrespect you is the way I disrespect God.

- The way I keep my word to you is the way I keep my word to God.

- If I don't keep my word to you, I haven't kept my word to God.

- If I don't show love to you, I don't show love to God.

- If I don't submit myself to those whom God has placed over me, I haven't submitted myself to God.

Life is real simple when you understand this principle. You don't have to deal with people on the level of their actions or words. Instead, you deal with them the way God has told you to deal with them in His Word.

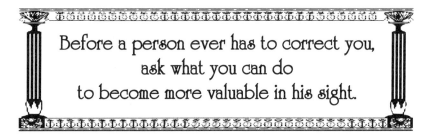

Before a person ever has to correct you,
ask what you can do
to become more valuable in his sight.

As a person who wants to excel in character, you should make every effort to discover the changes you personally need to make in any of your important relationships in life.

- Go to your employer to find out what you can do to become more valuable to him.

- If you are married, go to your spouse and find out how you can better perform as the wife or husband God has called you to be in that marriage relationship.

- If you are a son or daughter, go to your parents and find out how you can become more pleasing and more obedient to them.

Make it your aim to display excellent character in a greater way every day of your life.

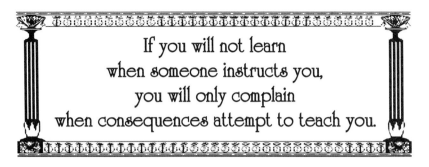

If you will not learn
when someone instructs you,
you will only complain
when consequences attempt to teach you.

What are some of the factors in life that help us strengthen our character? Romans 5:3,4 (*NLT*) gives us one answer:

> **We can rejoice, too, when we run into problems and trials, for we know that they are good for us — they help us learn to endure.**
> **And endurance develops strength of character in us, and character strengthens our confident expectation of salvation.**

I don't know about you, but this passage of Scripture was a tough one for me to accept when I first found out about it. Notice what Paul says here. Because of our faith, Christ has brought us to a place of highest privilege where we now stand, confidently and joyfully looking forward to sharing God's glory. We can therefore rejoice when we run into problems and trials, knowing that they are good for us.

"Wait a minute!" you may protest. "You mean that problems and trials are *good* for me?"

That is exactly what Paul is saying here. In fact, one of the worst things that could ever happen to you in life is to never have any problems!

Now, please understand — God doesn't *want* us to have any problems. He wants us to learn without problems.

But because we so often don't allow ourselves to learn our needed lessons the easy way, the unseen eternal laws find a way to make sure that we learn!

What do I mean by that? If we refuse to learn without problems, problems are going to come to us — and those problems *will* teach us. You see, problems don't forgive; they put their knee on our neck until we bow. Personally, I want to bow by choice, not by being run over!

Nevertheless, Paul said we can rejoice when trials and problems come to us because those trials will help us learn to endure. Verse 4 (*NLT*) explains why that lesson is so important: **"And endurance develops strength of character in us, and character strengthens our confident expectation of salvation."**

Verse 5 (*NLT*) also reveals a very important aspect of this principle: **"And this expectation will not disappoint us. For we know how dearly God loves us, because he has given us the Holy Spirit to fill our hearts with his love."**

Notice that God never expects *us* to manifest what *He* doesn't!

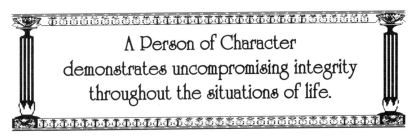

A Person of Character
demonstrates uncompromising integrity
throughout the situations of life.

The words *character* and *integrity* are intimately connected. The Hebrew word for "integrity" is *tom* or *tome*, from the root word *tamam*. It means *completeness; prosperity; innocence; fullness; uprightness at a venture*. It also carries the meaning of being *whole, upright, made perfect and entire, lacking nothing.* The dictionary tells us that integrity refers to *moral soundness or purity, uprightness of character,* and *honesty.*

Integrity, then, is the uncompromising desire to do what is right according to the highest standards of behavior in every situation, regardless of circumstances. It implies an inflexible adherence to this high standard of values and code of excellence.

Integrity is also a person's inward attributes, motives, and character qualities of godliness that outwardly manifest as moral and ethical excellence. It is uprightness and purity in the very essence of a person and speaks of a pure, untouched singleness of heart with no pretense or duplicity. A person of integrity maintains a trusting, unquestioning posture toward God that is very childlike in nature — the attitude and quality of character that Jesus referred to in Mark 10:15:

> **"Assuredly, I say to you, whoever does not receive the kingdom of God as a little child will by no means enter it."**
>
> **Mark 10:15**

A good scriptural definition for integrity is found in Micah 6:8 (*NLT*), which proclaims the common call and assignment of every Christian believer:

> **...O people, the Lord has already told you what is good, and this is what he requires: to do what is right, to love mercy [kindness, favor, loyalty], and to walk humbly with your God.**

Integrity transcends age, race, religion, education, gender, and personality. And according to Proverbs 23:7, integrity originates and flows from the heart: **"For as he thinks in his heart, so is he...."**

Why does the Lord require that we walk as people of integrity? Because it is only through the building of integrity into our lives that we can reach our full potential and fulfill the plan that God designed for us from the foundations of the earth:

"For I know the plans I have for you," declares the Lord, "plans to prosper you and not to harm you, plans to give you hope and a future."
Jeremiah 29:11 *NIV*

Sadly, this present generation has no real knowledge about integrity. If we look back at the direction society has taken over the past several decades, we can see why this is true. Situational ethics was birthed in the '80s. This mentality says, "If an action is good for me at the time a particular situation arises, it is acceptable as long as I don't hurt anyone else." Thus, it's all right for me to lie to you when you ask me a question if telling the truth means I'm going to get caught.

That is the kind of situational ethics the children of the '80s learned as they grew up. Then in the '90s, that idea was taken further until many began to claim that there is no absolute right or wrong at all.

The poisons of moral relativism and situational ethics have continued to infect our culture through the '90s and up to the present. As a result, we have witnessed an alarming deterioration in ethics and integrity. As society has accepted the lie that there is no absolute right or wrong, more and more people have become actively engaged in lying, cheating, stealing, fraud, extortion, pornography, etc. This disturbing trend of declining ethics is most pronounced in today's youth — the citizens and policy-makers of tomorrow.

I want to share a recent report I read, released in October 2002 by the Josephson Institute of Ethics as part of their National CHARACTER COUNTS! Week.[1] This report reveals that teens are much more likely to cheat, lie, and steal than they were just a decade ago. The Institute's president, Michael Josephson, said this:

> The evidence is that a willingness to cheat has become the norm and that parents, teachers, coaches, and even religious educators have not been able to stem the tide. The scary thing is that so many kids are entering the workforce to become corporate executives, politicians, airplane mechanics, and nuclear inspectors with the dispositions and skills of cheaters and thieves.

Here are some statistics to help you get a better idea of the direction our modern society is going in the area of character:

- *Cheating:* In the decade from 1992 to 2002, the number of high school students who admit they cheated on an exam in the past year increased significantly from 61 percent to 74 percent.

- *Shoplifting:* From 1992 to 2002, the number of high school students who admit they stole something from a store in the past twelve months increased from 33 percent to 38 percent.

---

[1] Following a benchmark survey in 1992, the Josephson Institute has conducted a national survey of the ethics of American youth every two years. The Institute is a 501(c) (3) nonpartisan, non-profit organization based in Marina del Rey, CA. The CHARACTER COUNTS! Coalition is a project of the Institute.

- *Stealing from parents:* The number of students who admit stealing from a parent or relative increased from 24 percent in 1992 to 28 percent in 2002. In addition, 25 percent of students with personal religious convictions said they stole from parents — the same percentage as for honor students!

- *Lying to parents:* The increase in young people who admit to lying to their parents is substantial, from 83 percent in 1992 to 93 percent in 2002.

- *Lying to save money:* In just two short years, the percentage of students who say they sometimes lie to save money increased dramatically, from 36 percent in 2000 to 46 percent in 2002.

- *Lying to get a job:* In just two years, the percentage of young people who say they have lied in order to get a job increased 9 percent, from 28 percent in 2000 to 37 percent in 2002.

- *Ideas concerning ethics:* In the past few years, the cynicism of young people has increased substantially. In 2000, 34 percent believed that a person has to lie or cheat sometimes in order to succeed. In 2002, that percentage jumped to 43 percent.

Interestingly, in spite of the high percentages of students who actually lie, cheat, and steal, 79 percent of them agreed, "It's not worth it to lie or cheat because it hurts your character." There seems to be a major "disconnect" between the integrity that students *think* they have and the integrity they actually *demonstrate* in their actions!

Some may believe that "rebellious teens" represent the low end of the ethical scale in our society. But when we look at some statistics from what might be called the "high end" of the scale, we discover the same alarming decline in ethical values:

- In a nationwide survey, 37 percent of males between the ages of 18 to 24 admitted that they had visited sex websites on the internet. Almost 18 percent of those who identified themselves as Christians and 18 percent of married men also admitted viewing these sites. According to the Nielson Net ratings, 17.5 million surfers visited porn sites from their homes in January 2000 alone — a *40-percent increase* since September 1999![2]

- 40 percent of pastors have visited a porn website; more than a third have done so in the last year.[3]

- At least 20 percent of American adults (male and female, Christians and non-Christians) have looked at a sex site online. The ratio is the same for Christians; one in five people in the pews have looked at pornography on the internet.[4]

James 1:22-25 (*NIV*) has something to say about this kind of ethical "disconnect":

Do not merely listen to the word, and so deceive yourselves. Do what it says.

---

[2] "Zogby/Focus Survey Reveals Shocking Internet Sex Statistics," *Legal Facts: Family Research Council*, vol. 2, no. 20, 3/30/00.
[3] *Christianity Today* magazine, Carol Stream, Illinois, 2001.
[4] "Citizens' Alert Email Newsletter," Focus on the Family, March 22, 2000.

Anyone who listens to the word but does not do what it says is like a man who looks at his face in a mirror

and, after looking at himself, goes away and immediately forgets what he looks like.

But the man who looks intently into the perfect law that gives freedom, and continues to do this, not forgetting what he has heard, but doing it — he will be blessed in what he does.

Lack of integrity is rampant and at times applauded in today's world. Nevertheless, it is nothing that we haven't already been warned about in the Scriptures (1 Tim. 1:3-11; 4:1-7; 6:3-5; 2 Tim. 3:1-5; 2 Peter 2:1-22). You'll find that these passages of Scripture are brimming with words that describe a society destitute of integrity — words such as:

- False

- Godless myths

- Lawbreakers

- Rebels

- Ungodly

- Sinful

- Unholy

- Adulterers

- Perverts

- Liars

- Perjurers

- Deceiving

- Conceited

- Envy

- Strife

- Malicious talk

- Evil suspicions

- Slanderous

- Treacherous

Practices that were once unheard of or considered shameful have now become the norm, such as:

- Needing more than a handshake in order to do business with someone.

- Retaining lawyers to find the loopholes and get us out of contracts we no longer want to honor.

- Declaring bankruptcy (*see* Ps. 37:21).

- Theft and embezzlement.

- Not only locking our doors and windows (unheard of not so long ago!), but also installing elaborate security systems in our homes and businesses.

- And the list goes on and on.

We have an additional problem in America when it comes to character, because we have the money to cover up sin. We can get ourselves out of problems just by paying our way out of them. We want to buy our way out of taking care of the elderly, so we build convalescence centers. We want to buy our way out of drug addiction, so we build halfway houses. We want to buy our way out of having unwanted children, so we allow doctors to do abortions.

But we can hide from our sin and buy our way out of problems for only so long. Money covers up reckless irresponsibility for only so long. America is still the greatest country the world has ever seen. But the truth is, we are living off the character and integrity of our great-great-great-great-grandparents. As a nation, we are not getting what we deserve at this point in our history; we're getting what our ancestors deserved. They paid the price for good character, sowing seed for a future harvest of prosperity and blessing they would never live to see.

In Ecclesiastes 8:11 (*NIV*), it says, **"When the sentence for a crime is not quickly carried out, the hearts of the people are filled with schemes to do wrong."** This is the state of affairs in our modern-day society. We have made a lack of character acceptable and have become quite adept at taking shortcuts.

For instance, the judicial branch of our government has been bombarded by an onslaught of precedence over the past several decades. We are no longer a country that lives according to the Constitution of the United States. We are a country that lives according to the previous judgments of men who were placed in their positions as judges. As a result, certain things are now considered legal in our country that our forefathers would never have tolerated, for these practices violate the very principles that once produced a people largely known for their strong character. And as Psalm 11:3 says, **"If the foundations are destroyed, what can the righteous do?"**

This lack of character in modern society extends even into the Church. Today most Christians live their lives based on their relationships with other people, not based on their relationship with God. They look for ways to get back at someone who has wronged them; then they seek to justify their behavior by blaming it all on the other person.

You may say, "Yes, but you don't know what that person did to me — and he's a Christian!"

I can just imagine what that person did, because I know Christians can sometimes act worse than the world when they hold a grudge. More than likely that person was mean to you. Maybe he treated you like a dog or gossiped about you. But whatever he did, God still expects you to respond to him with godly character.

Jesus warned us in Mark 13:5 (*NIV*), "**...Watch out that no one deceives you.**" But how many believers are ignoring this warning today, aimlessly drifting along while denying the dangers and refusing the responsibility for discernment and watchfulness in these perilous times?

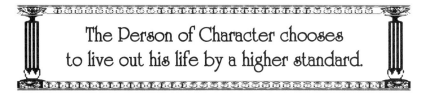

The Person of Character chooses to live out his life by a higher standard.

I'm telling you, it is time that we as the Church get back to our foundation and begin to embrace once more the commands and the decrees of God! It's time to search out what character and integrity really are and to understand the character traits by which we are to live our lives.

Isaiah 59:19 says, "**...When the enemy comes in like a flood, the Spirit of the Lord will lift up a standard against him.**" The common biblical application of the word "standard" referred to a flag, banner, or sign used as a rallying point around which the troops gathered and from which they attacked an enemy. Today the word "standard" refers to an established and recognized criterion of excellence; a beginning point; a bottom line; a foundational principle or value *from which a person refuses to back up.*

God has chosen to use His high standards (His Word or His principles) in our lives as a flag, a banner, or a sign over us. His Word is a rallying point *around which* we must gather for protection from Satan. It is also a rallying point *from which* we can effectively attack and defeat the enemy.

God's Word is also our established and recognized criterion of excellence and integrity. When the enemy attacks our families like a flood, *God will call us to a higher standard.* He will call us to "raise up" our standards to a higher level of integrity, purity, holiness, reverence, commitment, obedience, service, and excellence. That higher standard then becomes a new bottom line, from which we are never to back up.

Each of us must make a choice. If we say no to this higher standard, we will opt out of being changed into the image of Christ according to Second Corinthians 3:18:

> **But we all, with unveiled face, beholding as in a mirror the glory of the Lord, are being transformed into the same image from glory to glory, just as by the Spirit of the Lord.**

But if we say yes to this higher standard, we will immediately tap into greater *protection* from the enemy and greater *power* to defeat the enemy.

The Holy Spirit is calling us to stop compromising the standards by which God has called us to live in the past. The apostle Peter clearly warned us of the dangers of compromise with the world in Second Peter 2:20 (*NIV*):

If they have escaped the corruption of the world by knowing our Lord and Savior Jesus Christ and are again entangled in it and overcome, they are worse off at the end than they were at the beginning.

God is also calling us to protect and maintain our *existing* standards. Along that line, Paul exhorts us in Philippians 3:16 (*NIV*), **"Only let us live up to what we have already attained."**

Peter warns us that we can only do this as we stay vigilant:

Therefore, dear friends, since you already know this, be on your guard so that you may not be carried away by the error of lawless men and fall from your secure position.
2 Peter 3:17 *NIV*

Finally, the Holy Spirit is calling us to pursue change and maturity, to eagerly embrace ever-higher standards as we grow in God. That is what Paul was talking about in Philippians 3:13,14 (*NIV*):

Brothers, I do not consider myself yet to have taken hold of it. But one thing I do: Forgetting what is behind and straining toward what is ahead,
I press on toward the goal to win the prize for which God has called me heavenward in Christ Jesus.

We are all in a spiritual race, and each of us should be pressing toward the finish line that lies before us. After all, the prize is the very thing for which God has called us heavenward in Christ!

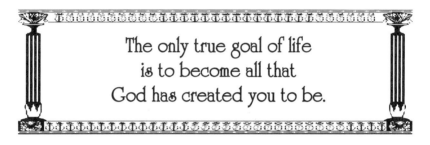

The only true goal of life is to become all that God has created you to be.

In Matthew 5:48 (*AMP*), Jesus stated the high calling you are to pursue in life as a child of God:

You, therefore, must be perfect [growing into complete maturity of godliness in mind and character, having reached the proper height of virtue and integrity], as your heavenly Father is perfect.

God has called you to be a person of character, of integrity, and of strong moral dignity. However, you are the one who must set that standard for your life. You must choose to be the kind of person described in Psalm 15:4, **"...who swears to his own hurt and does not change."**

You *can* make that decision. You can determine, "I will always keep my word. If I said I would do it, I will do it."

Now, I understand that there are rare exceptions when you cannot keep that commitment. Perhaps the person to whom you gave your word acts dishonorably. In that case, you cannot keep your word to a dishonorable person because that dishonorable person won't be satisfied with what you said in the beginning. He will always require more from you than you would ever want to give.

But except in such rare cases, determine to keep your word, no matter what. Do what you say you are going to do. Pay your bills on time. Get out of unsecured debt as quickly as possible. Ask for forgiveness when you offend someone. Do what is right in every situation.

"Yes, but I don't like the way that person treated me!"

How that other person treated you is not the issue. Just do what *you* are supposed to do, and God will honor your decision to walk as a person of character.

Character is the foundation. Without it, you will never succeed in your other pursuits, for that foundation applies to every realm of life you could ever encounter.

- In marriage, character is gentleness.

- In the home, character is respect.

- In business, character is integrity.

- In society, character is courtesy.

- In the workplace, character is diligence.

- In sports, character is fairness.

- In relationship, character is kindness.

- Toward the victors in life, character is shared joy.

- Toward the victims in life, character is protection.

- Toward those who do wrong, character is resistance.

- Toward the less fortunate, character is a hand up.

- Toward the strong, character is trust.

- Toward the repentant, character is restoration.

- Toward yourself, character is the willingness to hear the truth.

- Toward God, character is reverence, love, and commitment.

So determine to be *all* that God has called you to be. Pursue excellence in character with all your heart, your mind, and your strength. Start building an enduring foundation that will uphold God's highest and best in every arena of your life!

PRINCIPLES FOR PURSUING CHARACTER, THE FOUNDATION OF EXCELLENCE

☆ **A Person of Character esteems moral strength of greater value than beauty, riches, or fame.**

☆ **Good character is what others want you to possess so they don't have to.**

☆ **If I live my life to please Heaven, I must not be affected by the people of this earth.**

☆ **You may not be rewarded for your strengths, but you will be disqualified for your weaknesses.**

✫ You can never change what you are unwilling to confront.

✫ Every breakdown in life can be traced to a failure in character.

✫ The presence of God in your life is inseparably joined to the portrait of your character.

✫ God cannot do anything in our future if we do not take care of our present.

✫ We must be more interested in our own character than in the lack of character in others.

✫ A Person of Character never relates to God through his relationship with people, but always relates to people through his relationship with God.

✫ Before a person ever has to correct you, ask what you can do to become more valuable in his sight.

✫ If you will not learn when someone instructs you, you will only complain when consequences attempt to teach you.

✫ A Person of Character demonstrates uncompromising integrity throughout the situations of life.

✫ The Person of Character chooses to live out his life by a higher standard.

✫ The only true goal of life is to become all that God has created you to be.

NOTES:

THE CHARACTER OF GOD: OUR EXAMPLE

So where do we start in our search for the ingredients of good character? How do we discover the character traits we are to develop in our lives? The answer is simple. We must look to the ultimate Example of character — the God who redeemed us and made us new creations in Christ.

The Character of the Father

The first thing to understand about God is that He is good. Surprisingly, this is one of the most difficult truths for many people to grasp: that the Father is always good. He is *always* the Giver of good and perfect gifts.

> **Every good gift and every perfect gift is from above, and comes down from the Father of lights, with whom there is no variation or shadow of turning.**
>
> **James 1:17**

Don't ever let yourself get confused about this issue when others are wondering whether or not God was behind some calamity or tragedy. God gives only *good* gifts. Satan is the thief who kills, steals, and destroys (John 10:10).

James 1:13 makes this point very clear: **"Let no one say when he is tempted, 'I am tempted by God'; for God cannot be tempted by evil, nor does He Himself tempt anyone."** We might say, "But that isn't what I've been taught at my church." That's the reason God gave us a Book — so other people couldn't lie to us about Him! We need to stop listening to other people's opinions about the Word and start spending time searching the Scriptures for ourselves so the Holy Spirit can lead us into all truth.

Throughout the Bible, the message of God's goodness is proclaimed. As the psalmist said in Psalm 34:8, **"Oh, taste and see that the Lord is good; blessed is the man who trusts in Him!"**

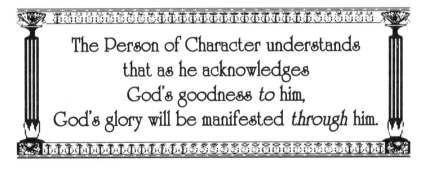

The Person of Character understands
that as he acknowledges
God's goodness *to* him,
God's glory will be manifested *through* him.

The goodness of God was also the theme at the dedication of God's temple:

> **Indeed it came to pass, when the trumpeters and singers were as one, to make one sound to be heard in praising and thanking the Lord, and when they lifted up their voice with the trumpets and cymbals and instruments of music, and praised the Lord, saying: "For He is good, for His**

mercy endures forever," that the house, the house of the Lord, was filled with a cloud,

so that the priests could not continue ministering because of the cloud; for the glory of the Lord filled the house of God.

2 Chronicles 5:13,14

Notice the divine sequence:

1. First, we come to the understanding that God is good.

2. Then the cloud of God's glory comes and fills the house of God.

Today our bodies are the temple of the Holy Spirit (1 Cor. 3:16). Only as we firmly establish the truth that God is good in our hearts will we begin to experience the "cloud of God's glory" and walk in His Presence on a daily basis.

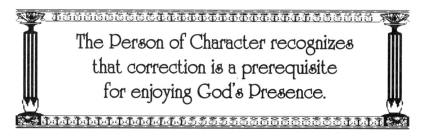

The Person of Character recognizes that correction is a prerequisite for enjoying God's Presence.

Second, God is holy. In Isaiah 6:3, the prophet Isaiah relates a vision in which he saw the Lord sitting on His throne and angels standing above it, crying out to one another, **"...Holy, holy, holy is the Lord of hosts; the whole earth is full of His glory!"**

Then in verse 5, Isaiah says, **"So I said: 'Woe is me, for I am undone!'..."** Before we truly comprehend the holiness of God, we are prone to think we don't need

Him. But once we receive a revelation of His holiness — when we discover just how wonderful and how perfect He is — that is the moment we finally recognize our utter need for Him. We realize that in reality, we are nothing without Him.

That's why the song "This Is How We Overcome" means so much to me. I was at such a low point in my life when God turned my mourning into dancing and made this valley sing. The moment I saw His holiness and His glory, all of a sudden I was changed from the inside out. That lingering edge of pride and arrogance was removed from my life. Everything changed the moment I saw the holiness of God. All I wanted to do was to yield myself to Him and allow Him to make me what He wanted me to be.

Until we truly see the Lord in His holiness, we won't understand how He works in our lives. When something good happens to us, we might *hope* that it is a result of God's work in our lives and not just the result of our own efforts; but at the same time, we wouldn't want Him to interrupt our day with an inconvenient word of correction or reproof.

But I've seen the holiness of God, and now I'm always looking for what the Lord has to say to me. I'm always looking to be corrected. God doesn't have to tell me how great I am. He doesn't have to blow any sunshine in my direction, for I know by His Presence in my life that He cares for me.

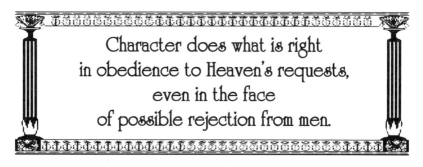

Character does what is right
in obedience to Heaven's requests,
even in the face
of possible rejection from men.

As I said earlier, most people live their lives asking, "Why do you always tell me what I do wrong? Why not tell me all the things I do well?" But as long as people are focused on looking for someone to praise them, they will always be disappointed, for the encouragement of man can be dreadfully deceitful.

I never want to live my life that way. I want to serve and worship God because I love Him. I know Him. I've seen His holiness and His strength. It is His strengths that reveal my weaknesses, and I know that when I am weak, then I am strong in Him.

Third, God is faithful. We can trust in His absolute faithfulness to perform every promise He has ever made to us. Psalm 36:5 (*NIV*) tells us that His faithfulness to us extends beyond what our natural minds can even comprehend.

Your love, O Lord, reaches to the heavens, your faithfulness to the skies.

Psalm 36:6 (*NIV*) goes on to give us two more of God's character qualities: *God is righteous and just.*

Your righteousness is like the mighty mountains, your justice like the great deep. O Lord, you preserve both man and beast.

God's plan of redemption through His Son Jesus reveals that He is both a righteous and a just God:

Whom [Jesus] God set forth as a propitiation by His blood, through faith, to demonstrate His righteousness, because in His forbearance God had passed over the sins that were previously committed,

to demonstrate at the present time His righteousness, that He might be just and the justifier of the one who has faith in Jesus.

Romans 3:25,26

Not only is the Heavenly Father entirely just in all His ways, but He is also our Justifier when we put our faith in His Son Jesus.

Fifth, God is loving. John 3:16 says, **"For God so loved the world that He gave His only begotten Son...."** Romans 5:8 confirms this message: **"But God demonstrates His own love toward us, in that while we were still sinners, Christ died for us."** There could be no more potent proof of God's love for us than this. The Father was willing to give the ultimate gift — Jesus, His only begotten Son — so that we might escape the just penalty of our sin and instead live in eternal fellowship with Him.

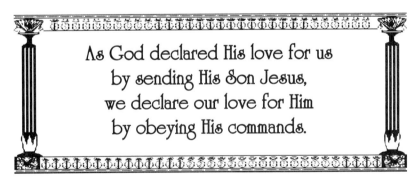

As God declared His love for us
by sending His Son Jesus,
we declare our love for Him
by obeying His commands.

The way we live our lives every day is to be an unspoken testimony of our love for God.

- We declare our love for God by recognizing and thanking Him for the difference He has made in our lives.

- We declare our love for Him by gathering with other believers in the house of God.

- We declare our love for God with our tithes and offerings.

- We declare our love for God by the way we unashamedly raise our hands in our worship of Him.

- We show our love for God by the respectful way we posture ourselves in our relationships with others.

Because we love God, we don't do or say things because of other people. Everything we do and say is a result of our relationship with God. He is the One who is always beside us. He is the One who is our invisible Partner. His Presence can be sensed in everything we do. He hears every word we speak, watches our every action, and continually grades our character.

Why is God so watchful of us? Because He wants to promote us. He wants to give us greater responsibility in His Kingdom. He wants to connect us with other people — people of character who live their lives on a higher level and who can promote us to a higher level as well when we prove ourselves ready.

The Character of Jesus

What about the character of Jesus? First, we must understand that *the Son is the very likeness of the Father.*

Everything the Father is, Jesus is. Whatever character qualities the Father possesses, Jesus possesses.

Hebrews 1:3 reveals this truth about Jesus:

> **Who being the brightness of His glory and the express image of His person, and upholding all things by the word of His power, when He had by Himself purged our sins, sat down at the right hand of the Majesty on high.**

Jesus is the brightness of the Father's glory, the express image of His person. He is the perfect imprint of the Father. Second Corinthians 4:4 (*KJV*) confirms this same truth:

> **In whom** [the lost] **the god of this world hath blinded the minds of them which believe not, lest the light of the glorious gospel of Christ, who is the image of God, should shine unto them.**

Jesus is the express image of God. He wants to be like His Father every day, every moment, and He wants us to strive for that same goal.

Second, Jesus is a Lover. Second Corinthians 5:14,15 (*AMP*) talks about the compelling force of Jesus' great love for us:

> **For the love of Christ controls and urges and impels us, because we are of the opinion and conviction that [if] One died for all, then all died;**
> **And He died for all, so that all those who live might live no longer to and for themselves, but to and for Him Who died and was raised again for their sake.**

John 15:13 verifies the extent of Jesus' love that took Him to the Cross: **"Greater love has no one than this, than to lay down one's life for his friends."** Jesus said, "I'll prove to you that I love you. Just watch what I do, for love can be seen."

We must always remember that love is undeniably linked to our actions, not to our emotions. Jesus showed us that love isn't just a collection of words. Love has to do with our actions and our attitudes, with our posture and our approach toward other people. It has to do with proving our love by demonstrating a true servant's heart and laying down our lives for our brethren.

The Character of the Holy Spirit

Finally, the Bible reveals to us the character of the Holy Spirit. For instance, the Scriptures tell us that:

1. *He is the Spirit of holiness.*

> **...Who through the Spirit of holiness was declared with power to be the Son of God by his resurrection from the dead: Jesus Christ our Lord.**
>
> **Romans 1:4** *NIV*

The Holy Spirit is in the instruction business, for it is His role to give us guidance and direction through every situation of life. However, He always instructs us according to the rules of godly character. He will never give us instructions that violate His own holiness or that are independent of the lines of authority He has established in our lives.

2. *He is the Spirit of truth.*

> **"But when the Helper comes, whom I shall send to you from the Father, the Spirit of truth**

who proceeds from the Father, He will testify
of Me."

John 15:26

"...When He, the Spirit of truth, has come, He
will guide you into all truth; for He will not
speak on His own authority, but whatever He
hears He will speak; and He will tell you things
to come."

John 16:13

The Holy Spirit reveals the truth we need to live victoriously. We never need to make an excuse for the Holy Spirit, for He has never lied to us, nor has He ever let us down. In fact, Titus 1:2 (*NLT*) tells us that God, from whom the Spirit of truth proceeds, is not even capable of lying!

This truth gives them the confidence of eternal life, which God promised them before the world began — and he CANNOT lie.

3. *The Holy Spirit is powerful.*

And Jesus returned in the power of the Spirit into Galilee: and there went out a fame of him through all the region round about.

Luke 4:14 *KJV*

The supernatural power of the Holy Spirit now resides within each one of us, for He has come to live His life through us in a victorious manner. The Holy Spirit wants us to lift up our heads and walk through this life with dignity as ambassadors of Heaven who are filled with divine power. We are not to live as the off-scouring of the world, mocked by others because we say that we believe in God and yet nothing good ever happens for us. Jesus wants us to eliminate all compromise from our lives and to walk as *He* walked on this earth. As we do, we will begin to see the power of the Holy Spirit manifested mightily in our lives.

4. *The Holy Spirit is eternal.*

How much more shall the blood of Christ, who through the eternal Spirit offered Himself without spot to God, cleanse your conscience from dead works to serve the living God?

Hebrews 9:14

Because the Holy Spirit is eternal, we can rest assured that He knows the future and wants to give us insight into *our* future. He wants to tell us about tomorrow.

That means we must stop worrying about the past. There is nothing we can do about yesterday. However, if we will change *today*, tomorrow will be different as the eternal One who lives within us guides us each step of the way, showing us things to come (John 16:13).

5. *The Holy Spirit is creative.*

The Spirit of God has made me, and the breath of the Almighty gives me life.

Job 33:4

You have to know this about the Holy Spirit's character. He is always productive, always creative, always giving life.

6. *The Holy Spirit is a Giver.*

There are diversities of gifts, but the same Spirit.

There are differences of ministries, but the same Lord.

And there are diversities of activities, but it is the same God who works all in all.

But the manifestation of the Spirit is given to each one for the profit of all.

1 Corinthians 12:4-8

From whom do we receive the various manifestations of the Holy Spirit? From the Holy Spirit Himself. He is the Giver of gifts who decides which skills, gifts, and talents each of us possess.

One of the greatest gifts that the Holy Spirit personally imparts is a prayer language that dramatically increases and strengthens our faith. First Corinthians 14:4 (*NLT*) says, **"A person who speaks in tongues is strengthened personally in the Lord...."** This truth is confirmed in Jude 20,21: **"But you, beloved, building yourselves up on your most holy faith, praying in the Holy Spirit, keep yourselves in the love of God...."**

7. *The Holy Spirit is the Source of every desired emotion we are pursuing.*

But the fruit of the Spirit is love, joy, peace, longsuffering, kindness, goodness, faithfulness, gentleness, self-control. Against such there is no law.

Galatians 5:22,23

For instance, *the Holy Spirit is the source of our joy.* Psalm 16:11 says, **"You will show me the path of life; in Your presence is fullness of joy; at Your right hand are pleasures forevermore."**

Also, the Holy Spirit gives us the necessary love we need for others. Romans 5:5 says, **"Now hope does not disappoint, because the love of God has been poured out in our hearts by the Holy Spirit who was given to us."**

As we study the character of God, we see the standard we are to follow in our own pursuit of excellent character. God is good; He is holy; He is faithful; He is loving; He is true; He is righteous and just in all His ways.

All these divine character qualities provide the blueprint that leads us to excellence of character in our own lives. However, it is up to us to make that blueprint come alive, as we work on constructing a solid *foundation* of character — little by little, brick by brick — in preparation for undergirding the God-given dreams we are called to fulfill in this life.

PRINCIPLES REGARDING THE CHARACTER OF GOD

✭ The Person of Character understands that as he acknowledges God's goodness *to* him, God's glory will be manifested *through* him.

✭ The Person of Character recognizes that correction is a prerequisite for enjoying God's Presence.

✭ Character does what is right in obedience to Heaven's requests, even in the face of possible rejection from men.

✭ As God declared His love for us by sending His Son Jesus, we declare our love for Him by obeying His commands.

NOTES:

_____

_____

_____

NOTES:

REAPING THE HARVEST OF GODLY CHARACTER

To excel in character, you must come to the place where you recognize Jesus' absolute lordship in your life. That means Jesus is the One who makes your decisions from this point on. His Book is your decision-maker, even when the world thrusts its pain upon you.

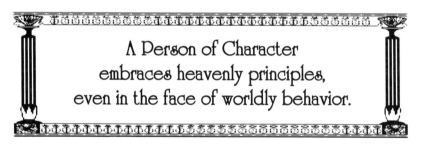

A Person of Character embraces heavenly principles, even in the face of worldly behavior.

As you embrace Jesus as Lord of your life, the tide will begin to turn for you, and divine favor will start flowing in your direction. But realize this: You simply cannot embrace Jesus without embracing His Word, for Jesus and His Word are one.

Some people say, "Well, I love Jesus, but I don't read the Bible."

But how can we love someone, yet not want to be with that person? Whom do we love more — ourselves or God?

Look at what Jesus said in Luke 6:46 (*NIV*) about this subject: **"Why do you call me, 'Lord, Lord,' and do not do what I say?"** In other words, Jesus is asking us, "How can you say that you love Me when you won't listen to what I tell you?" The answer is simple: *We cannot!*

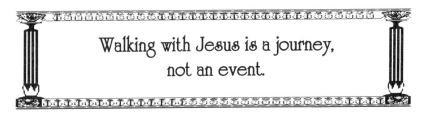

Walking with Jesus is a journey, not an event.

Second Timothy 3:16 says that God gave us His written Word because it is **"...profitable for doctrine, for reproof, for correction, for instruction in righteousness."** Notice in particular the phrase "instruction in righteousness." That divine instruction is not an overnight process. It takes time to learn how to walk in righteousness. However, the summation of the principles by which you live your life — the extent to which you act on what is right, even when it hurts — will determine how much righteousness you walk in on a daily basis.

Joseph is a good example of a man of principle whose strong character caused him to walk in righteousness, no matter what anyone else said or did. But Joseph didn't learn how to walk as a man of principle overnight. He endured many difficult challenges along the way as God tested his character.

Joseph was a man whom God loved and to whom God had given two visions when he was still a teenager. In the first vision, eleven sheaves of wheat, representing Joseph's brothers, bowed down to his sheaf. In his second vision, eleven stars and the moon, representing the brothers and Joseph's father, bowed down to Joseph's star.

But Joseph made a mistake: He talked about the visions with his brothers. (Sometimes it's just better to keep quiet and allow the word that God has given you to unfold in His way and timing.) As a result, Joseph caused himself a lot of heartache when his brothers' simmering jealousy and bitterness boiled over, causing them to plot together to rid themselves of their youngest brother once and for all.

But God's hand was still on Joseph even when his brothers sold him as a slave to some Egyptian traders. A higher purpose was at work behind the scenes.

> **Moreover He [God] called for a famine in the land; He destroyed all the provision of bread.**
> **He sent a man before them — Joseph — who was sold as a slave.**
> **They hurt his feet with fetters, he was laid in irons.**
> **Until the time that his word came to pass, the word of the Lord tested him.**
>
> **Psalm 105:16-19**

Until the time came for God to fulfill His word to Joseph, the Lord tested his character to see if he would do right in every situation. In every challenge, Joseph passed the test, and the day came when God promoted him to the second-highest position in all of Egypt.

> **The king sent and released him, the ruler of peoples set him free.**
> **He made him master of his household, ruler over all he possessed,**

to instruct his princes as he pleased and teach his elders wisdom.

Psalm 105:20-22 *NIV*

Whether we realize it or not, God is testing every one of us at this very moment. Will we do what is right, or will we do what we want to do? Will we do what is convenient and easy to do, or will we do what *God* wants us to do? When we pass one test, it is only to enter another one.

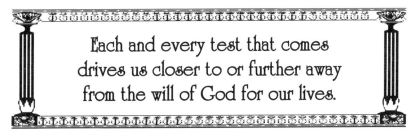

Each and every test that comes drives us closer to or further away from the will of God for our lives.

We will eventually reap the harvest of whatever seeds we have sown. But God believes in us so much that He expects us to make right choices all the time. Meanwhile, the devil is attempting to pervert the law of sowing and reaping in our lives, using it for his own evil purposes.

The enemy wants us to sow seeds of bad character so that we will reap a harvest of negative consequences and then point our finger at God and say, "Lord, You didn't come through for me!" Proverbs 19:3 (*NLT*) talks about this particular deception: **"People ruin their lives by their own foolishness and then are angry at the Lord."** Meanwhile, the devil sits back and laughs as we blame God over our own failure to sow the right seeds of integrity and godly character.

But as we determine to become people of character, we will avoid this trap of the enemy. We just need to stay continually aware that God's Word is testing us every day. God believes that everything written in His Word about us is absolutely the truth. He so believes in us that He doesn't sit around thinking about or writing down all that we have done wrong. Instead, He says, "What I've written in the Book is what is true about you."

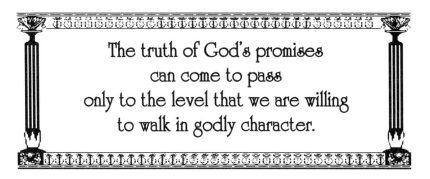

The truth of God's promises
can come to pass
only to the level that we are willing
to walk in godly character.

As we believe God's words and act on them in obedience, our lives will eventually portray what His Word says about us.

Think back to Joseph for a moment. Even when the Egyptians put Joseph in chains and clamped an iron collar around his neck, Joseph still would not compromise his character. The devil may have been testing Joseph with that iron collar, but God was testing him with His Word.

Every moment of every day, your life is being tested as well. On the positive side, God is testing you in order to get you into position for promotion. On the negative side, the devil is testing you in order to destroy your life, using everything negative he can find to throw at you.

So in one sense, God and Satan desire the identical thing for you: to draw you into the universal law of sowing and reaping so you can reap from the seeds you have sown. That law is universal; it will be in operation as long as the earth remains. God cannot break or overturn that law in your life. There's nothing He can do to change it except by performing a miracle.

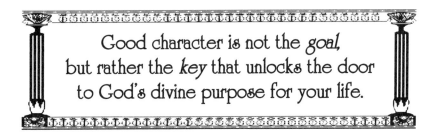

Good character is not the *goal,* but rather the *key* that unlocks the door to God's divine purpose for your life.

But we're not supposed to live by miracles. We are supposed to change the natural course of our lives by sowing seeds of obedience and godly character. For whatever seeds we sow, good or bad, that is the kind of harvest we will reap.

Many Christians say, "It doesn't matter what I do; God will bless me anyway." But that isn't true. If God blessed sin, He would violate His own character.

That's the issue, friend — *character.* How long are you willing to stand? Are you willing to live for the rest of your life under the pressure that comes from holding fast to everything God has said in His Word about you?

As long as you're willing to stand, the door for promotion will remain open. Yes, you may face trials and tribulations. But even in the midst of adversity, you will continue to rise to ever-higher levels of excellence, as long as you don't stop sowing the right seed.

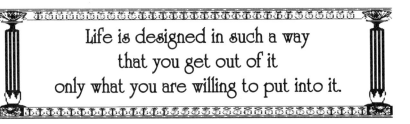

Life is designed in such a way
that you get out of it
only what you are willing to put into it.

This earth is programmed to bring forth what we sow. People or the devil or circumstances may try to stand in our way, but nothing can stop God from causing our harvest to come forth. All we have to do is put our seed in the ground and then leave it there, no matter what winds of adversity blow against us. As we do, we'll find that this universal law works not part of the time, but *every* time.

The problem is, we live in a microwave society in which everyone expects instant answers. Too often we wonder and waver because things don't happen as quickly as we think they should. As a result, we stand in danger of canceling out our rightful harvest with our own doubt and unbelief!

Proverbs 12:14 has something to say about this universal law of sowing and reaping: **"A man will be satisfied with good by the fruit of his mouth, and the recompense of a man's hands will be rendered to him."** Remember, this is a law that God Himself cannot break; otherwise, He would be a covenant-breaker.

I'm referring to the covenant God made with Noah when He put the rainbow in the sky and said, "I will never destroy the earth by water again. And as long as the earth remains, seedtime and harvest, cold and heat, summer and winter will never stop" (*see* Gen. 8:21-9:17). At that moment, God declared that the earth — including the life of every person born on this earth — would be governed by the law of sowing and reaping as long as there *was* an earth.

Consequently, it is imperative to understand that *it is our character that causes the recompense of our hands to come to us.* If our character is good, then good will come into our lives from the good deposit we have made. If our character is bad, that evil deposit will bring forth evil fruit in our lives as a result of the law of sowing and reaping. We may think that we are getting away with the sowing of bad seed and that God will still bless us anyway. But how can we expect to reap a harvest of blessing from seed we have never sown? There isn't a farmer in the world who thinks he can do such a thing.

Some Christians go around claiming, "Praise God, I'm blessed!" But how many seeds of blessing are those people sowing? How can they expect people to love them when they disrespect others?

"Well, I'm not really sowing very much, but I'm blessed."

The truth is, those Christians are going to have a blow-out in a couple years — *if* they last that long! Then they'll wonder why God didn't come through for them. But the reason why is simple: Those people never became the farmers of their own fields!

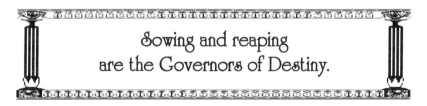

Sowing and reaping
are the Governors of Destiny.

Consider the example of the Egyptian Pharaoh during Moses' time. Remember, both God and the devil wanted to pull Pharaoh into the law of sowing and reaping. At that time, Pharaoh had a choice. He could have said to the Israelites, "Listen, go worship God. You need to be free. You have sown all these years, and now you are owed your freedom."

But Pharaoh didn't do that. Instead, he said, "You can go away for three days. But after you have worshiped, I want you to come back here. Men, leave your wives and your kids when you go and worship. That's the only way I can be sure you will come back."

Thus, Satan drew Pharaoh into the negative side of the law of sowing and reaping. Pharaoh spoke his desire when he said to the Israelites, "No, I'm not going to let you go." That was the seed he chose to sow. Pharaoh would not help the people of God.

This same process continued throughout the ten plagues. Yet the day came when God brought the Israelites out of Egypt with silver and gold (Ps. 105:37). In fact, by the time the ninth plague had come and gone, the children of Israel had begun to borrow from the Egyptians for their journey into the wilderness to worship God. The Israelites asked the Egyptians for their gold, their silver, their fine spices and perfumes, their valuable possessions — and the Egyptians were giving them whatever they asked for!

What was happening? The Israelites' long-overdue wages for all their labor, held back by the Egyptians for four hundred years, were finally being released. The Israelites had sown in a foreign land for four hundred years. They were just picking up their check!

But the Israelites' harvest didn't stop with the loan of Egyptian silver and gold. They also experienced supernatural debt cancellation when the Red Sea opened, allowing them to cross, and then crashed down upon Pharaoh's army. With the Egyptian army gone, no one was left to go after the Israelites and repossess their rightful wages.

So we see that both God and the devil drew Pharaoh into the law of sowing and reaping. First, God gave Pharaoh an opportunity to set His people free and to bless them on their way out. But Pharaoh refused, choosing instead to sow more of the same bad seed that had been sown for four hundred years against the Israelites.

Some of that evil seed had been sown years ago when Moses was just an infant, and Egypt's ruler ordered all the Israelite male babies to be drowned. Now it was decades later, and Pharaoh sowed some more bad seed when he and his army pursued the Israelites after deceiving them into thinking they were free to go. As a result, he and all his men were drowned in the Red Sea. The time had come for Egypt to reap what it had sown.

Let me give you a similar modern-day example. In 1970 when abortion was passed as law, thousands of babies began to be aborted. The number of aborted babies is now more than 41 million.

Those babies who were aborted in 1970 would be over thirty years old today. Now there is a national debate about the fact that the Social Security system is in trouble. But think about all the lost revenue that would have been deposited into Social Security by the millions who have been aborted since the early '70s. The very people who passed the law to kill unborn children will not be taken care of in their old age largely as a result of that decision!

Make no mistake, friend — the law of sowing and reaping is supreme in the universe. Don't ever fool yourself into believing that you won't reap what you have sown.

But what about a biblical example of someone who chose to sow the right seed? Let's look at a man named Abimelech in Genesis 20. This is the account of the time Abraham and Sarah traveled to Egypt because of a famine in the land. While they were in Egypt, Abraham was afraid that someone was going to kill him in order to take his beautiful wife. So he and Sarah made a covenant together that she would tell everyone she was his sister and not his wife. That was in fact partially true, since they had different mothers but the same father.

Once again, we see both God and the devil attempting to draw a person into the law of sowing and reaping for diametrically opposed purposes. It began with Abimelech, the king of Gerar, taking Sarah to be his wife after hearing that she was only Abraham's sister. But then in the middle of the night, God came to Abimelech in a dream and said, "Abimelech, if you touch that woman, you'll be a dead man in the morning, and everyone around you will die as well."

Abimelech said, "But, Lord, you would actually destroy an innocent nation?"

The Lord replied, "If you touch her, you're a dead man."

So Abimelech waited until dawn and then called for Abraham. When Abraham stood before him, Abimelech asked, "Why didn't you tell me that Sarah was your wife, not your sister?"

Abraham said, "Because I was afraid."

"Well, you might be afraid, but I was going to be dead!"

Satan tried to draw Abimelech into the law of sowing and reaping for his destruction by coaxing him, *Take her; take her; take her.* Abimelech took Sarah, but then before he could have sex with her, God showed up and said, "Here's your way out."

That's the way God is; He always gives a person a way out. That way out is called *repentance*, and it is the choice of good character.

For some reason, Abimelech's character would not allow him to take Sarah physically; he himself wasn't even sure why until after he had that dream from Heaven. Afterward, Abimelech continued to make decisions according to his character. Instead of getting angry at Abraham and Sarah, Abimelech blessed them with gifts and gave them access to the best of his land. As a result, the Bible says that God healed Abimelech, his wives, and his maidservants (Gen. 20:17). Because he chose to act according to his good character, Abimelech's entire household was blessed!

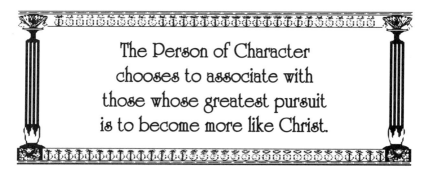

The Person of Character
chooses to associate with
those whose greatest pursuit
is to become more like Christ.

But then the Bible says that this man Abimelech had a similar encounter with Rebekah because Abraham's son Isaac told the same lie! Isn't it interesting how both sin and righteousness are passed down from generation to generation!

Isaac came to live on this same man's property with Rebekah (*see* Genesis 26). Abimelech's men saw Rebekah and said, "Wow! What a beauty!" When they asked Isaac about her, he told them, "She is my sister" in order to save himself. (This time, though, it wasn't even a partial truth!)

Later Abimelech witnessed Isaac and Rebekah showing physical affection to each other in public. So Abimelech brought in Isaac and confronted him with his deception.

"That woman is your wife. Why did you say she is your sister? One of my men could have lain with her and brought great guilt upon our nation!"

Isaac's answer sounded very familiar: "Because I was afraid."

But just as he had blessed the father, Abimelech now blessed the son. Isaac was allowed to remain and farm in Abimelech's land.

Now, you need to understand something about Isaac. He wasn't a farmer; he was a shepherd. Farmers and shepherds didn't even get along because the sheep always ate the crops. But the Bible says that for one year, Isaac became a farmer and prospered greatly in the land.

The terrain surrounding Abimelech's home was mountainous and very steep. Nevertheless, the Bible says that Isaac, the shepherd-turned-farmer, sowed his seed in that land and within the period of one year, received back a hundredfold (Gen. 26:12)!

Why did that happen? Because Isaac was sowing in a righteous man's field!

When you sow in a righteous man's field, you don't even have to know what you're doing. You just need to know that *he* knows what *he* is doing. That's why it is so important to find people of character you can trust with whom to associate. Sadly, in this day and age, that isn't always easy to do.

In First Corinthians 15:33 (*NLT*), Paul refers to people of poor character who foolishly say, **"...If there is no resurrection, 'let's feast and get drunk, for tomorrow we die!'"** Paul goes on to warn us, **"Don't be fooled by those who say such things, for 'bad company corrupts good character.'"**

I sometimes enjoy reading books that were written at least a hundred years ago. Once I get past the Queen's English, I often begin to see the author's depth of character, even when I have never heard of the individual before.

Sometimes I read the speeches of Abraham Lincoln or Winston Churchill, and I am struck by the wisdom and strong character exhibited in some of the statements they made. The same is true when I read the works of some of this country's forefathers. As I read, I compare their words to the present generation, and I think, *My Lord, how things have changed! Instead of thinking it strange when we find a person who doesn't have character, we think it's strange when we find a person who does!*

I'm not so interested in the number of degrees a person might have. I want to know what he has done in life to develop his character. When I see someone break the back of generational curses, then I take notice.

I remember one woman who stood up during a meeting and said, "I'm a fifth-generation welfare recipient, but I just want to let everyone know that I'll never be on welfare again."

That woman changed the future forever for herself, for her children, and for her country when she made that courageous stand and said, "No more. Those days are over." I respect a person like that. Those are the kind of people I want to associate with during my time on this earth.

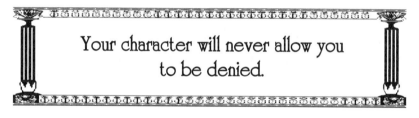

Your character will never allow you to be denied.

Consider Ruth. Ruth, although a Moabitess, chose to travel to Israel with her mother-in-law, Naomi, after they had both lost their husbands. Once in Israel, Ruth allowed herself to be mentored by Naomi.

Naomi told Ruth about the kinsman-redeemer whose name was Boaz. Boaz was a rich, older man, and Ruth wasn't necessarily attracted to him. But she listened to Naomi's counsel concerning what would help them better their lives and leave their future generations with a tremendous heritage.

Growing up as a Moabitess, Ruth had probably witnessed many people offering their children as human sacrifices to the god Molech. Yet Ruth became part of the genealogy of the Lord Jesus Christ. As someone born in a Gentile nation, she normally would not have been allowed that honor. But because of her internal strength and good character, Ruth was put in that genealogy because her good character would not be denied.

Your character will not allow you to be denied. It will compel people to deal with you. When you walk in a room, some will think, *Why does this person irritate me so?* They won't be irritated because you've done something wrong. They will be irritated because you are a person who does what is right. And if you are the one in charge, they will be irritated because they won't be able to get away with their own faulty character choices now that you have entered the scene and said, "That is not the way it's going to be as long as I'm here."

What did Ruth do to become qualified for the genealogy of the coming Messiah? For one thing, she chose to follow her mentor's wise counsel. In Ruth chapter 3, Naomi told Ruth what to do in order to find favor in the eyes of her kinsman-redeemer.

In essence, Naomi told Ruth, "Don't bother the man while he's eating or drinking. Don't become a nuisance to him. Don't nag him or jump his case. Just watch yourself, and keep your character right. Never, never, never, push yourself into the life of Boaz, Ruth. Instead, this is what you must do. Wash yourself, and put on perfume. Wait until he goes to sleep; then uncover his feet, lay down, and wait until the man wakes up."

Ruth did exactly what Naomi told her to do. That next morning, Boaz awoke to find his lovely kinswoman lying at his feet.

And he said, "Who are you?" So she answered, "I am Ruth, your maidservant. Take your maidservant under your wing, for you are a close relative."

Then he said, "Blessed are you of the Lord, my daughter! For you have shown more kindness at the end than at the beginning, in that you did not go after young men, whether poor or rich.

"And now, my daughter, do not fear. I will do for you all that you request, for all the people of my town know that you are a virtuous woman."

Ruth 3:9-11

Notice what Boaz says to Ruth in verse 11: "...I will do for you all that you request...." Women often say, "He never does what I want to do." But all a woman has to do is what Ruth did, and they will get whatever they want from their man!

Boaz said, "Anything you want, I will do for you. You name it, and it's yours. Everything you require, I will do." He went on to tell Ruth, "Everyone in this town knows that you are a virtuous woman."

This, then, is the reason Ruth became part of the genealogy of Jesus: *She gained that place of honor because of her strength of character, which would not be denied.*

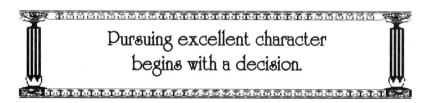

Pursuing excellent character
begins with a decision.

The journey that led to Ruth's place of honor in the genealogy of the coming Messiah started with her decision to act as a woman of character in a foreign land. Character always starts with a decision. You must determine that you *will* be a person of character, no matter what anyone else says or does. When things get hard, you must choose to stand on the principles in God's Word rather than throw in the towel and give up.

So don't spend your time thinking about whether the character of other people is good or bad. Be more interested in building your own good character than you are in meditating on the lack of character in others. Give them the liberty to straighten out their own lives.

Meanwhile, evaluate the condition of *your* character. Think about who you are, what you think about, and what you do and say in your daily life. Then allow the Holy Spirit to reveal any areas of needed adjustments. As you do, I promise you — a day will come when the seeds of godly character you have chosen to sow will produce an abundant harvest of honor and blessing in your life beyond what you could ever ask or imagine!

PRINCIPLES FOR REAPING
THE HARVEST OF GODLY CHARACTER

⭐ **A Person of Character embraces heavenly principles, even in the face of worldly behavior.**

⭐ **Walking with Jesus is a journey, not an event.**

⭐ **Each and every test that comes drives us closer to or further away from the will of God for our lives.**

✯ The truth of God's promises can come to pass only to the level that we are willing to walk in godly character.

✯ Good character is not the *goal*, but rather the *key* that unlocks the door to God's divine purpose for your life.

✯ Life is designed in such a way that you get out of it only what you are willing to put into it.

✯ Sowing and reaping are the Governors of Destiny.

✯ The Person of Character chooses to associate with those whose greatest pursuit is to become more like Christ.

✯ Your character will never allow you to be denied.

✯ Pursuing excellent character begins with a decision.

NOTES:

_____

_____

_____

_____

_____

_____

_____

NOTES:

THE CONSEQUENCES OF BAD CHARACTER

As people go through life, many don't realize the consequences that result from their actions. They don't understand that the decision they make today could forever change their own lives, their family's lives, and the lives of several generations to come.

Studies have been conducted that actually traced through an entire family tree the consequences of one individual's poor choice, such as the decision to start drinking alcohol, abusing drugs, or engaging in sexual promiscuity. When an individual makes a bad decision like that, he may think it is all over as soon as he completes the deed. But it is *not* over, because the effect of that single poor choice often continues to produce an evil harvest long after that person is dead and gone.

For instance, I once read about a woman who made a poor choice that started her down a path leading to a life of immorality and sin. This woman's descendants included a number of prostitutes, alcoholics, and lower middle-class people — all as a result of the bad decision that this one woman had made.

In contrast, I also read of a gentleman who decided to give his life to Christ and live a holy life before God. It was this man's fervent desire to live in sincerity and truth according to the Word of God, and he determined that he would never allow anything to deter him from that goal.

The fruit of this godly man's decision to follow Christ could be seen in the lives of his descendants. From his family line came a number of professors, preachers, and inventors whose creative ideas for inventions came directly out of the wisdom and revelation of God.

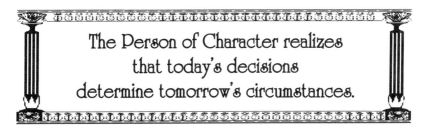

The Person of Character realizes
that today's decisions
determine tomorrow's circumstances.

Think about that principle for just a moment. How have your past decisions brought you to where you are today? If you made some poor choices in the past, what right choices can you make today that would help you get your life back on track?

To help us answer these questions for our own lives, we need to turn to the Word. As we examine a chronological timeline in the lives of specific biblical characters, we will see the kind of consequences that occurred as a result of their decisions.

The Consequences
Of Adam's Wrong Choice

Let's begin with Adam's decision. The Bible says that Adam actually walked and talked with God face-to-face every day. The Bible doesn't tell us for how long Adam was by himself on the earth, but we know that he wasn't living a lonely life. How can a person be lonely who talks with God face-to-face on a daily basis? How can he be lonely when everything in the world belongs to him? (You see, we only become *convinced* that we are lonely when the enemy persuades us to not value what we have been given.)

God asked Adam to do two things: *to dress* and *to keep* the garden. God also gave him one thing *not* to do:

> **And the Lord God commanded the man, saying, Of every tree of the garden thou mayest freely eat:**
>
> **But of the tree of the knowledge of good and evil, thou shalt not eat of it: for in the day that thou eatest thereof thou shalt surely die.**
>
> **Genesis 2:16-17 *KJV***

At that moment, Adam had a choice to obey or disobey. Then God said, "It isn't good for a man to be alone. He needs someone to help him be My expression in the earth, so I'm going to make a helper for him."

So God laid Adam on the ground, put him to sleep, and then removed a rib from his side. From that rib, God formed a woman. Interestingly, the Bible does not say God breathed life into her; it just says He brought her to the man alive (Gen. 2:22). In other words, the first woman was born alive the same way our children are born alive. However, she was born as an adult. She did not grow up; she was born mature. There is no other human being that can really be compared with this first woman whom God made especially for His man.

Adam took one look at this beautiful creature and said, **"This is now bone of my bones and flesh of my flesh; she shall be called Woman, because she was taken out of Man"** (Gen. 2:23). Adam was obviously impressed with God's handiwork! However, Adam grew to love the woman more than he loved God. This was the reason behind Adam's wrong decision that led to such terrible consequences — not only for himself, but for all of mankind.

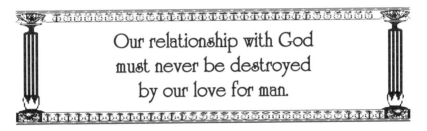

Our relationship with God
must never be destroyed
by our love for man.

Many of us have experienced negative consequences in our lives as a resulting of doing the same thing Adam did. We have made decisions based on our love for another person even when those decisions violated our love for God.

Too often we make the mistake of remembering this principle only when we want to go a different direction than authority wants us to go when making a decision. That's when we claim, "I can't allow another individual to usurp my relationship with God." But we forget that God has established an authority structure on the earth for both our *protection* and *provision*.

There will be situations that arise and questions presented to us in life that we are not necessarily prepared to handle. But if we will listen to the authority God has placed in our lives, we can come through each situation safely as we receive the wisdom we need.

A vivid example of what happens when a person doesn't listen to the proper authority can be seen when the serpent came to tempt the first man and woman to disobey God. Notice to whom the serpent asked the question, *"Hath God said?"* (Gen. 3:1). He didn't address that question to Adam, but to the woman.

Why? Because Satan knew that the question wasn't hers to answer; it was Adam's. The enemy knew that a person must never attempt to take authority over something that God has not made him or her responsible for.

Adam had been given the responsibility to be God's representative on the earth. We know that to be true because of the ease with which the woman was deceived by the serpent's words. She took of the forbidden fruit because she saw that **"...the tree was good for food, that it was pleasant to the eyes, and a tree desirable to make one wise..."** (Gen. 3:6).

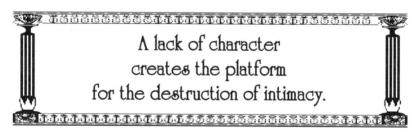

A lack of character
creates the platform
for the destruction of intimacy.

So what did Adam do when Eve partook of that which God had forbidden? Instead of siding with God, Adam immediately sided with the woman. And at the precise moment he partook of the fruit, the eyes of both of them were opened, and they knew they were naked. Later when they heard God's voice coming to them in the cool of the day, they made aprons out of fig leaves to cover their loins, for sin had created immediate withdrawal from intimacy. They also attempted to hide from God because they no longer wanted to be transparent with Him.

This is the test you and I face every day in the area of character. Are we going to be transparent with God and others, or are we going to look for ways to hide from intimacy by covering up our lack of character?

Let's look at the larger implications of Adam's choice to align himself with Eve rather than with God. Romans 5:12 (*KJV*) tells us the nature of the ultimate consequence:

Wherefore, as by one man sin entered into the world, and death by sin; and so death passed upon all men, for that all have sinned.

Can you imagine how Adam must have felt walking away from the Garden of Eden? If he looked back at what he was leaving behind, he saw the angel with the sword standing between him and the Garden he had once been called to dress and to keep. Now he would never be allowed to enter that Garden again.

What must Adam have been thinking? Did he think that God had been too hard on them or that God didn't love them anymore because He had turned them out of the Garden? Or did Adam realize that it wasn't God's lack of love at all that had caused this sad turn of events, but rather the consequences of their own lack of character?

Every one of the problems that you and I are facing right now — whether it be a generational curse, a disease, financial lack, feelings of insecurity, or low self-esteem — all these negative things are the result of Adam's poor character. He chose to love the woman more than he loved God.

Whenever you put a person before the Word of God in your life, you will be disappointed every time. So don't allow your focus to be on another person, on other people's failures, or on what others did or didn't receive. Just focus on what God said in His Word, and you'll make the right decision every time.

Now let's consider Cain and Abel. The disagreement between these two brothers was over the tithe, a principle that God had already established. That disagreement resulted in murder.

> **And in process of time it came to pass, that Cain brought of the fruit of the ground an offering unto the Lord.**
>
> **And Abel, he also brought of the firstlings of his flock and of the fat thereof. And the Lord had respect unto Abel and to his offering:**
>
> **But unto Cain and to his offering he had not respect. And Cain was very wroth, and his countenance fell....**
>
> **And Cain talked with Abel his brother: and it came to pass, when they were in the field, that Cain rose up against Abel his brother, and slew him.**
>
> <div align="right">Genesis 4:3-5,8 <i>KJV</i></div>

One man brought to God what God wanted; the other man brought to God what *he* wanted to bring. When God rejected Cain's offering, Cain became enraged that Abel had been favored over him. The dissension became so great between the two men that the elder brother suddenly rose up and killed his younger brother.

Do you realize that as a consequence of Cain's action, the earth never saw the offspring of Abel's character? All that was ever seen was the offspring of Cain's character. Thus, mankind has had to live not only with the consequences of what Adam did, but also with the consequences of what Cain did when he murdered his brother.

That is the way it works in this life. My character matters to you. Your character matters to me. What we do in this life matters greatly, for our actions produce consequences far beyond the small circle of our own lives.

What King Saul Lost Through a Lack of Character

Let's talk about a young man named Saul, who was so humble that he wouldn't even approach the man of God without an offering (1 Sam. 9:6,7). The prophet Samuel anointed this young man as God's chosen king. Later, however, the pressure of that position influenced Saul and as a result, his character changed. And when God gave Saul his first big assignment — to utterly destroy the wicked Amalekites — he chose to love the people more than he loved God (*see* 1 Samuel 15).

After the battle, the prophet Samuel came to Saul, and Saul told him, "I've done everything God wanted me to do. I have utterly destroyed the Amalekites."

Samuel asked, "Then what is this bleating of sheep and lowing of oxen that I hear?"

"Oh, that? Well, the people wanted to keep the best of the sheep and oxen for an offering to the most High God."

Samuel replied, "Does God desire sacrifice more than He desires obedience?"

Finally, Saul admitted, "All right, I made a mistake. So pardon my sin, and let's get on with the sacrifice."

But it was too late for Saul to save himself from the consequences of his non-compliance to God's command. The prophet declared, "**...You have rejected the word of the Lord, and the Lord has rejected you from being king over Israel**" (v. 26).

Did you ever sense that God was getting ready to move on your behalf — but then your breakthrough never materialized, and you wondered why? This account of Saul's poor character choice may provide insight into the reason.

Saul doesn't even demonstrate a willingness to right the wrong he had committed. This is also one of the greatest indictments against us as God's people.

We should all consider Saul's story in light of our own lives, evaluating our character and the times we ourselves have made compromises that produced negative consequences. And as we do, we should realize this: The tests we face in our lives today are nothing compared to the tests we will one day face when we attain the place God wants to take us in Him.

The Consequences
Of David's Sin

What about David? David was a man after God's own heart, the pastor of Israel who brought his people back to God. But one day he did not do what God told him to do. Instead of going to battle with his men, he stayed home. And while he was home, he went out on his rooftop and looked down upon a woman bathing. Then he went out to look on her the next day and the next — until his desire grew so ferocious within him that he took his friend's wife for himself (*see* 2 Samuel 11 and 12).

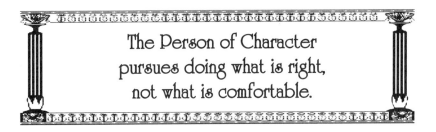

The Person of Character
pursues doing what is right,
not what is comfortable.

David understood what his poor character choice meant. He knew he couldn't walk with God and have that woman. But David refused to listen to the Holy Spirit and went his own way. As a result, he was out of fellowship with God for an entire year. Finally, God sent the prophet Nathan to bring David to repentance. David did repent, but he still lost his newborn son by Bathsheba as a consequence of his sin.

Many times we don't really know what is wrong in our lives until someone comes and tells us what is wrong. We don't recognize what's happening until someone loves us enough to tell us the truth. But the question is, will we listen and respond to that wise instruction when it is given to us?

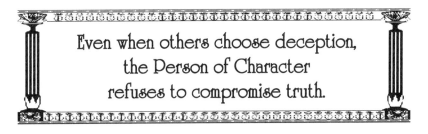

Even when others choose deception,
the Person of Character
refuses to compromise truth.

Why is it that most people back away from telling someone else the truth? Because most of the time when a person is told the truth, he rejects the one who came to him with the truth.

We have to remember that there is one person we can never help: *the person who doesn't accept the Bible as his final authority.* Instead of listening to what the Word has to say, a person who fits this description will try to drag us into an argument. And even though he may take in biblical knowledge, he will produce no fruit.

But we were never called by God to preach *against* something; we were called to speak the truth. We should never compromise or back away from the truth, for that truth may be God's way of escape for someone caught in the devil's snare.

The Bible gives us an example of a man who caused many negative consequences because he didn't speak the truth to a person who needed to hear it. The man's name was Ahithophel, David's chief advisor and one of his closest friends. In fact, Ahithophel and David had been friends from their youth.

David also had a son named Absalom. Absalom was a handsome man who had always been popular with the people. Absalom knew all the right things to say to look like he was wise. But in reality, Absalom was actually denying and rebelling against his father (*see* 2 Samuel 15).

As the years passed, David had to do certain things as a king that other people didn't understand, and Absalom was right there to take advantage of the moment by drawing people's allegiance away from David and unto himself. Even Ahithophel, David's best friend, was deceived by Absalom. David's wisest counselor actually went over to Absalom's side and, as a result, almost destroyed David's kingship.

David wrote Psalm 55 at the time he was facing opposition from Absalom and Ahithophel, two of the people he loved most:

> Day and night they go about on its walls; iniquity and mischief are in its midst.
> Violence and ruin are within it; fraud and guile do not depart from its streets and marketplaces.
>
> Psalm 55:10,11 *AMP*

I want to talk to you about guile for a moment. Guile occurs inside an individual when the seat of his life has become crooked. So when Jesus said concerning Andrew, "This is an Israelite in whom there is no guile" (John 1:47), Jesus meant, "This man is straightforward; he speaks only the truth."

On the other hand, a person with guile is a fraudulent person, a double-talker. He may talk well of you to your face, but behind your back he will leave little hints of doubt about you. He may not say anything overtly negative, but somehow he finds a way to plant seeds of distrust about you in the minds of others. This was what Absalom did in his father's relationship with Ahithophel — until finally Absalom succeeded in pulling Ahithophel away from David, his best friend.

David's grief over Ahithophel's betrayal can be seen as we read on in Psalm 55:

> For it is not an enemy who reproaches and taunts me — then I might bear it; nor is it one who has hated me who insolently vaunts himself against me — then I might hide from him.
> But it was you, a man my equal, my companion and my familiar friend.

We had sweet fellowship together and used to walk to the house of God in company.

Let desolations and death come suddenly upon them; let them go down alive to Sheol (the place of the dead), for evils are in their habitations, in their hearts, and their inmost part.

As for me, I will call upon God, and the Lord will save me.

Evening and morning and at noon will I utter my complaint and moan and sigh, and He will hear my voice.

He has redeemed my life in peace from the battle that was against me [so that none came near me], for they were many who strove with me.

God will hear and humble them, even He Who abides of old — Selah [pause, and calmly think of that]! — because in them there has been no change [of heart], and they do not fear, revere, and worship God.

[My companion] has put forth his hands against those who were at peace with him; he has broken and profaned his agreement [of friendship and loyalty].

The words of his mouth were smoother than cream or butter, but war was in his heart; his words were softer than oil, yet they were drawn swords.

Cast your burden on the Lord [releasing the weight of it] and He will sustain you; He will never allow the [consistently] righteous to be moved (made to slip, fall, or fail).

Psalm 55:12-22 *AMP*

Consider what would have happened to Absalom had Ahithophel gone to the younger man and told him, "Absalom, don't do this. You're making a mistake, Son." Perhaps Absalom would have listened to his father's chief advisor and repented of his plan to betray his father. We'll never know, because Ahithophel chose the way of poor character when he gave in to his own pain and Absalom's deceptive ways that turned him against his best friend.

The Consequences
Of Jacob's Deception

Now consider the life of Jacob. God gave a word to Rebekah while she was still pregnant, telling her that the elder brother would serve the younger (Gen. 25:23). But later when the boys had grown into men, Jacob wanted to make that word from God come to pass on his own; he didn't want to wait and allow God to make it happen. This lets us know that there was something crooked in Jacob's character that had yet to be straightened out.

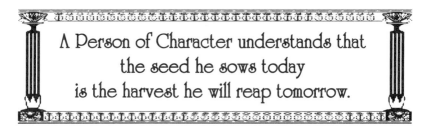

A Person of Character understands that
the seed he sows today
is the harvest he will reap tomorrow.

So Jacob lied to his father and cheated his brother out of his birthright; then he ran away to his uncle Laban's house. But the seeds of deception that Jacob sowed to obtain the birthright would later reap a harvest of consequences that would adversely affect him the rest of his life. After falling in love with Laban's younger daughter

Rachel, Jacob found himself in the tent on his wedding night with the older sister Leah! He had married the wrong woman, and there was nothing he could do to change that. But Jacob still wanted Rachel, and he was willing to give seven more years of service to Laban in order to win her as his wife.

Through the years to come, Rachel heard the words of love that Leah never heard from Jacob. Leah only heard words of resentment from her husband. And no matter how hard she tried to please Jacob, he was never pleased, for she represented nothing but deception to him. Leah was a woman scorned, never to enjoy the acceptance and love of the man she married.

But what if Jacob had rejoiced in the birthright of Esau, his brother? What if Jacob had allowed God to bring His word to pass in his life instead of trying to make it come to pass on his own? It is likely that Esau, after being blessed by Isaac, would have followed his grandfather Abraham's example and sent someone to his relatives' house — the house of his uncle Laban — to find a wife for him. Who would that wife have been? The girl who was meant for Esau was *Leah* — the first-born daughter for the first-born son. Just imagine how different Jacob's life and the lives of those closest to him would have been if he had done things God's way!

The same principle holds true in our own lives. How many negative things have happened in our lives because of our own lack of character? How many negative consequences have we suffered just because we wouldn't listen to wisdom and choose the right course?

Personally, I'm sure my life would have been different if I had made some better choices in the past. I wouldn't have gone through so many times when I felt like I was walking up to Heaven backwards, wondering if I was ever going to make it!

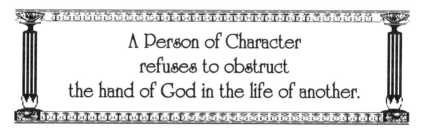

A Person of Character
refuses to obstruct
the hand of God in the life of another.

The Bible says that a person is no longer a son but a bastard, or an illegitimate son, if he refuses to be trained in godly character (Heb. 12:8). There are serious consequences for those who insist on remaining stubborn and unteachable. If we refuse to be trained in character, life will become a torture to us.

However, it is a testament to God's infinite mercy that He even uses the consequences of our wrong choices to get us back on track with His plan for our lives. That is why we make a grand mistake when we attempt to stop God's Word from working in people's lives in the arena of consequence.

We must make the quality decision not to stand between another person and the consequence of his action. Now, that may be difficult to do at times. Our greatest desire may be to stop the pain that someone else is going through. But if that person never experiences the painful consequences of his poor character choices, he may never learn that he needs to stop disobeying God.

The same thing is true in the natural realm when a wife tries to stop her husband from disciplining the children. As the husband gets ready to spank a disobedient child, the wife cries, "No, no, don't do that! Don't hit him!"

"But this kid needs a good dose of discipline on his behind!" says the father.

"No, no, no, don't do it!" So the wife stands between the children and their father, thus preventing them from experiencing the consequence of their actions so they might learn to obey.

In the same way, we as Christians often stand between the Heavenly Father and His sons and daughters. We need to get out of the way and let God deal with His children!

Remember, the Bible says that if we are without chastisement, we are illegitimate sons. If God isn't dealing with us about becoming more obedient in every area of our lives, we are not His children. Thank God, our Daddy loves us! We can know that because He is dealing with us all the time!

One of our biggest failings as Christians is that we try to fix the lives of people who have been disobedient to God. We have to learn the difference between helping a person who is down and attempting to circumvent the hand of God in that person's life.

I won't stop consequences from coming to another person. Now, I can take authority over the devil's strategies in his life, but I won't necessarily attribute his negative consequences to the devil. That person may have sown some bad seed in the past, and he may very well be reaping his own negative harvest. If so, I can't stop that harvest because God is smarter than I am. He knows that if I stand between that person and his consequence, it won't be long before he's in the same jam all over again.

Many of us have made this mistake with our children. We keep trying to erase any future reaping of consequences from our children's lives. But when we do that, we're stopping their Heavenly Father from dealing with them.

When we as parents don't take our rightful position in the disciplining of our children, our Heavenly Father will step in to do it for us by allowing them to reap the negative harvest that disobedience brings. We need to be very careful that we don't try to prevent these consequences; otherwise, we actually stop the Heavenly Father from being able to deal with our children in a way that can produce lasting change. And if we continue to tolerate sin and rebellion in our children over a long period of time, we stand in danger of seeing the day come when they **"...will suddenly be destroyed — without remedy** (Prov. 6:15 *NIV*).

None of us want to see our children destroyed. We all want our children to be blessed. But we must realize that they can only be blessed as they learn to follow God's way of blessing, *not* ours.

It's our responsibility to teach our children what we must learn ourselves: *Lack of character reaps a negative harvest.* There is no substitute for character — *none!*

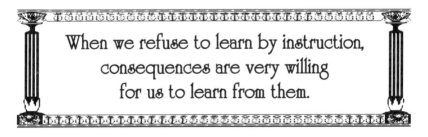

When we refuse to learn by instruction,
consequences are very willing
for us to learn from them.

A lack of character is the reason that in years gone by, the lives of several tremendously gifted men of God ended hideously. We have often discounted the greatness of these fallen ministers because of the way their lives ended; yet no one can deny that they accomplished great things for the Kingdom of God in their earlier years.

So why did their lives end the way they did? Because of a lack of character. They refused to live their lives in a principled manner. Thus, they made themselves open game for the enemy, who always comes to steal the Word and destroy everything good in a believer's life.

This is what Jesus was talking about in His parable about the sower:

> **But the ones on the rock are those who, when they hear, receive the word with joy; and these have no root, who believe for a while and in time of temptation fall away.**
>
> **Now the ones that fell among thorns are those who, when they have heard, go out and are choked with cares, riches, and pleasures of life, and bring no fruit to maturity.**
>
> **Luke 8:13,14**

People who fit in these two categories may look like they are in the promised land of their inheritance, but they are not actually eating the fruit that the promised land has to offer them. And there is one primary reason they "bring no fruit to maturity": *They lack strength of character.* This can all be summed up by the following principle:

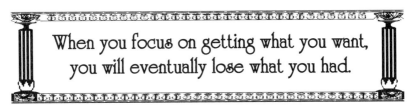

When you focus on getting what you want, you will eventually lose what you had.

Once you start recognizing the consequences of bad character, it is easy to see why character is such an important issue to God. In fact, it's more important to Him than faith or the doctrines of prosperity and healing.

Our character needs to be the very first thing we deal with in our lives. As we strive to train our own flesh and live as people of excellent character, we'll discover the pain of fighting to overcome the strongholds that have held us for so long. But we'll also discover that the pain is well worth it as we begin to experience a whole new category of consequences — the harvest of *godly* character. That is the harvest God designed for us to reap all along, for it is the one that brings blessing and wholeness and increase to every area of our lives!

PRINCIPLES REGARDING THE CONSEQUENCES OF BAD CHARACTER

✶ The Person of Character realizes that today's decisions determine tomorrow's circumstances.

✶ Our relationship with God must never be destroyed by our love for man.

✶ A lack of character creates the platform for the destruction of intimacy.

✶ The Person of Character pursues doing what is right, not what is comfortable.

✶ Even when others choose deception, the Person of Character refuses to compromise truth.

✶ A Person of Character understands that the seed he sows today is the harvest he will reap tomorrow.

✮ A Person of Character refuses to obstruct the hand of God in the life of another.

✮ When we refuse to learn by instruction, consequences are very willing for us to learn from them.

✮ When you focus on getting what you want, you will eventually lose what you had.

NOTES:

_____

_____

_____

_____

_____

_____

_____

_____

_____

_____

_____

_____

_____

_____

NOTES:

THE FIRST STEP TO EXCELLENCE IN CHARACTER

Most Christians live and die without ever comprehending what actually happened to them when they came to Jesus. As a result, they spend their entire lives struggling with yesterday. They never grasp the truth that Jesus already set them free from the person they were before they were born again.

But you can't live in this unenlightened state if you want to walk in the character of God. Something happened to change you from the inside out on the day you came to Jesus. You received a new nature; you became a new creature in Christ. Now you need to understand who you are so you can live in a manner that is worthy of the One who gave you new life in Him.

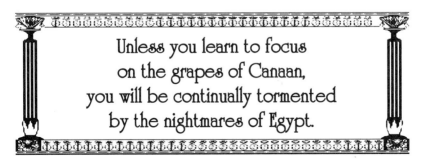

Unless you learn to focus
on the grapes of Canaan,
you will be continually tormented
by the nightmares of Egypt.

That was one thing I understood after I came to Christ: *God had given me a new life.* I didn't accept Jesus as my Savior because someone beat me in a debate or because it was the fashionable thing to do. In the years before I made that decision, I made fun of the Gospel. I analyzed it; I criticized it; I turned my back on it. But then after all that foolishness, I bowed my knee to Jesus because I knew He was the only Truth. Everything else I had ever pursued had led me down a dead-end alley of lies. Now that I knew *the* Truth, I wanted only one thing: *to pursue the new life Jesus had given me with everything I had within me.*

But I soon found out that even though I was born again, I still had to deal with *me* every day. I didn't need deliverance from demons at that point — I needed deliverance from myself! I'd think, *Why am I like I am? Why do I have to put up with this earthen vessel when I have a treasure inside me that can change the world?*

That dilemma may sound familiar to you, so let me share what I discovered as I searched for answers to my questions. I tried to find out who had been talking to me every day for all those years before I got saved. What were the things that had determined my life and made me the way I was? And how could I begin to change into the man God had recreated me to be?

To begin with, we have to understand some facts about our natural lives on this earth. In this natural realm, there are certain "determinisms" — in other words, certain factors that determine the outcome of our lives. The first is *genetic determinism*; the second is *psychological determinism*; and the third is *environmental determinism.* These three forces are called determinisms because without death, there is no escape from them. We are going to be the way we're going to be because these three factors will make sure that it happens.

Genetic Determinism

First, let's talk about genetic determinism. All your physical attributes — brown eyes or blue eyes, short or tall, thickset or thin — were given to you by the genetic determinism of your parents, your grandparents, your great-grandparents, and your great-great-grandparents. All these people in your family line have helped make you who you are.

But much more than physical attributes can be passed down from generation to generation. On the negative side, a propensity to contract certain diseases or to be bound by certain strongholds can also be passed down.

Your life is actually a culmination of approximately four hundred years of family history, for Numbers 14:18 says that the sins of the fathers are passed down unto the third and fourth generations. That means every sin, every problem, and every stronghold that your ancestors struggled with have been passed down from generation to generation, and over the years you have had to deal with them in your own life. To say it another way, the temptations and the wrong desires that torment you at times are the manifestation of four generations of sin. They are all a part of this issue of "genetic determinism."

Your forefathers may or may not have ever been able to overcome the sins, habits, or diseases that troubled them. Nevertheless, defeat does not have to be *your* story. You have a choice to make — a choice that is absolutely essential if you are ever going to live as a person of character.

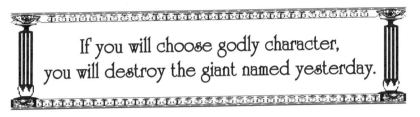

If you will choose godly character,
you will destroy the giant named yesterday.

It is of the utmost importance that you break the power of yesterday in your life. You must determine to go beyond and do more than those who have come before you. You don't have to live the way your daddy and your momma lived. You don't have to be the way your teachers taught you to be in school. You have been made a new creature in Christ. You have a new Father, and according to Titus 3:5, that new Father "re-engineered" you!

Not by works of righteousness which we have done, but according to His mercy HE SAVED US, THROUGH THE WASHING OF REGENERA-TION and renewing of the Holy Spirit.

You are a new creature in Christ; your past has been wiped away. But you won't enjoy the benefits of that fact until you start *acting* like a new creature!

It is up to us to make sure that we break the back of our genetic determinisms by the power of the Holy Spirit. We must destroy those bad habits and strongholds that were passed down to us through our genes so we are free to live as people of excellent character.

Of course, that isn't what the world says. Whereas the Bible says sin is passed down to the fourth generation, the world just says that a person is "predisposed" to a certain lifestyle. For instance, some say, "Oh, people who are homosexual just have a different kind of a gene." No, those are not genes causing people to live as homosexuals; those are evil spirits assigned to individuals and even to entire family lines.

Let's talk about alcoholism for a moment. Suppose a son has parents who are both alcoholics, but he grows up never dealing with the issue in his own life. Then later his dad dies, and suddenly the adult son is dragged into alcoholism! Why is this? Because that evil spirit left the father's body at the moment of death and came over to the son.

Here is something you should know about spirits that are assigned to a particular family: These evil spirits won't necessarily deal with each generation. They may try to trick people by skipping a generation. Or a particular individual may resist a particular stronghold of the flesh and cause it to become very weak in his life — only to have it turn up again in the next generation.

You may have known someone to whom bad things kept happening, and you could never figure out why. Perhaps it was just time for the harvest to come from the bad seeds planted in that family line.

We are all in a race against time, friend. What we do, what we think, how we act, and the way we treat people will always produce a harvest — if not in our lives, then in the lives of our children. That means someone has to pay the price so our children can live free of all the generational baggage — and that someone should be each one of *us*!

Psychological Determinism

Second, you must deal with your own personal psychological determinism. According to Proverbs 23:7, you are what you think: **"For as he thinks in his heart, so is he...."**

We may say, "I don't believe that's true. I'm more than just a product of whatever I think!" But it doesn't matter what we believe about this truth; we still have to deal with it.

This concept of psychological determinism is the very thing that slammed me around and beat me up in my mind until Jesus came into that mental institution in 1975 and changed my life. He delivered me from my own psychological determinism overnight. Then He began to teach me how to stay delivered utilizing that same principle, *as I think in my heart, so am I* — only this time I learned how to do it based on the Word.

Consider these questions to determine your own psychological determinism:

- What do you allow your mind to dwell on?

- What do you let yourself listen to?

- What are the things that most influence your life?

- Who is the person who has most influenced your life?

Many times when people try to think of the individuals who have most influenced their lives, they say, "Oh, that would be my mom. She has influenced me so much." Or they say, "The person who most influenced me was my wonderful teacher in the third grade."

No, the person who has influenced you the most just so happens to be the one who is controlling your mind right this second with the hurt, disappointment, or offense he or she has caused you. That is what you are dwelling on; therefore, that is your psychological determinism, for it is the issue you have been mulling over and over in your mind while doing what you can to believe God.

Thank God, He has provided us with deliverance through Jesus Christ from our psychological determinisms! But before we talk about that, let's discuss the third factor that determines the outcome of our natural lives: *environmental determinism.*

Environmental Determinism

Our environmental determinism is where we live and the circumstances that surround us throughout our lives.

Do you realize that in this country today, there are people who live and die in a one-mile radius? They think they have everything they need inside that one mile, so that's as far as they ever go.

As I was growing up, my mom didn't want me to go past 63rd Street. But I can remember how I was always looking toward 59th Street — always looking for an escape from the less-than-perfect environment I was living in.

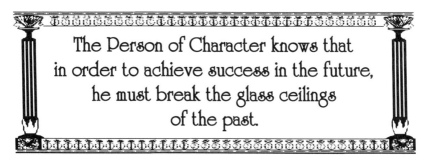

The Person of Character knows that in order to achieve success in the future, he must break the glass ceilings of the past.

Many people spend their whole lives looking for greener grass on the other side of the fence. They become what I call "excusiologists" because they try to use their genetic and environmental background as their excuse for not achieving success in life. For instance, they might say:

- "I had a difficult childhood."

- "I'm not of the favored race."

- "I've never had enough money."

- "I was born on the wrong side of the tracks."

These excuses can go on indefinitely, but they always reflect the attitude of the excusiologist: "All these circumstances are just wrong, wrong, wrong, wrong, wrong. If only they were right, everything would be different for me."

But as children of God, it doesn't really matter where we came from or what color we are. There are advantages and disadvantages to every genetic and environmental background. We just need to become sensitive to the Holy Spirit so we can understand *our* advantages. Then as we are diligent to walk as people of character, we'll be prepared to walk through the doors of opportunity that God opens for us in life.

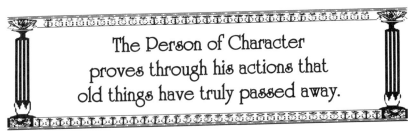

The Person of Character
proves through his actions that
old things have truly passed away.

As I said earlier, the reason these three factors are called *determinisms* is that there is no escape from them without death. But in Second Corinthians 5:17, the Bible lets us know that natural death is not our only escape from these forces that begin to govern our lives from the moment of birth:

Therefore, if anyone is in Christ, he is a new creation; old things have passed away; behold, all things have become new.

When we received Jesus Christ as the Lord of our lives, we became new creatures. Those old sinful habits and carnal thought patterns that absolutely controlled our lives before we were born again no longer have any right to rule and reign. This is why there is as much power in understanding that our old life is dead and gone — *not* just altered or revised — as there is in understanding that we have a new life in Jesus.

I have found that there are basically two types of believers in the modern Church. First, there are those who are willing to put to death the old life but never embrace the new. Many denominational churches fit in this category. Second, there are those who embrace the new life but never put to death the old. Sadly, this second category describes a large portion of those who call themselves Charismatic believers.

We Charismatics love to embrace our new life in Jesus, but too often we just won't put that old man to death once and for all. We just aren't willing to say, "That is sin, and it isn't a part of my life anymore. I refuse to do that any longer."

To me, it is interesting that the very things God calls sin and tells His people not to do, modern society has made into diseases. For instance, alcoholism is now labeled a disease, and even Christians sometimes use that definition to justify their drinking habits. As long as these Christians can get enough people around them to agree with them that their actions are acceptable, it doesn't matter to them what God has said.

But Ephesians 5:18 says, **"And do not be drunk with wine, in which is dissipation; but be filled with the Spirit."** What is a person to do if he wants to get rid of that "gene" of alcoholism? God provides the answer: He is to *be filled with the Holy Spirit.* When a person purposes to do things *God's* way, nothing is too hard to deal with.

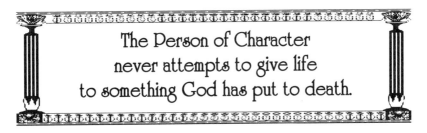

The Person of Character
never attempts to give life
to something God has put to death.

The book of Romans is the greatest document that has ever been written for our Christian growth. In Romans 6:6 (*NIV*), the Bible tells us this: **"For we know that our old self was crucified with him...."** I can tell you from personal experience that this particular verse, when believed and acted upon, is of inestimable value to us in our pursuit of excellent character.

So many Christians still struggle with yesterday — with sins and habits that held them captive before they were born again. Many of these same people try to justify where they are in their spiritual walk because deep down inside, they are unwilling to repent of and forsake their sin.

But the Bible says that our old self was *crucified* with Jesus in the new birth. Our old nature that wants to sin is already dead. That is very good news for us, because death is our only escape from those determinisms we looked at earlier. When we count our old man as dead and begin to walk in the newness of life that Jesus has purchased for us, we break the power of those strongholds that have held sway in our lives for so long!

I like the way the *New Living Translation* says it in Romans 6:6:

> **Our old sinful selves were crucified with Christ so that sin might lose its power in our lives. We are no longer slaves to sin.**

I like to say it like this: "My old sick self was crucified with Him. My old poor self was crucified with Him. My old angry self was crucified with Him. Everything from my old life was crucified with Him. Anything that reminds me of that guy who used to live here before Jesus came died with Him!"

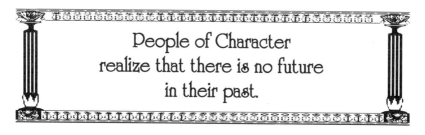

People of Character
realize that there is no future
in their past.

If we are going to walk in the character of God, we must live according to this truth every day of our lives. But to do that, we also need to understand the principle found in Second Corinthians 5:7: **"For we walk by faith, not by sight."**

I don't care what I look like to other people. It does not matter what anyone else says about me. I only care about what God says, for only His Book contains the truth about who I am.

You, too, must hold fast to the truth about who you are. The Bible says your old sick self has been crucified with Jesus. Your old poor self, your old confused self, your old guilty self has been nailed to the Cross with Him!

"But you just don't know the pressure I'm under and the temptations I face. It's too much to bear sometimes!"

I like what W. Clement Stone, the wealthy tycoon and philanthropist, said when one of his fourteen secretaries came in and said, "Mr. Stone, we have a big problem on the East Coast."

Stone replied, "Wonderful. Problems make me strong. Give it to me."

That's an excellent attitude for us all to adopt in life! Too many of us are either running from the problems we see in ourselves, or we are trying to deny that those problems even exist. But we need to first admit that we have a problem with counting our old nature as dead; then we must go to the Bible to find out what God says about it. Nothing but His Word will give us the answers we must have to walk in a manner worthy of Jesus in this life.

Galatians 2:20 (*KJV*) is another important scripture about who we are in Christ:

I am crucified with Christ: nevertheless I live; yet not I, but Christ liveth in me: and the life which I now live in the flesh I live by the faith of the Son of God, who loved me, and gave himself for me.

The *Laubach Translation* says it this way: **"Christ took me to the cross with Him, and I died there with**

Him...."[5] If Jesus took us to the Cross with Him and we died there with Him, why do we keep trying to raise from the dead something that God says stinks? Why would we attempt to be something in our own natural strength or inject into our lives something of this natural world when God said that this world is passing away? As Second Corinthians 4:16 says, "...**Our outward man is perishing, yet the inward man is being renewed day by day.**"

Romans 6:1 asks a pointed question along this line: "**What shall we say then? Shall we continue in sin that grace may abound?**" The answer to that question is an emphatic *no*. Remember, we enter the grace of God by faith, which includes the newness of life and all God has provided for us that we didn't work for, earn, or deserve. All of this is ours to enjoy — *if* we would just believe.

In the same chapter, the Bible tells us what we must do to enjoy the newness of life: "**Likewise you also, reckon yourselves to be dead indeed to sin, but alive to God in Christ Jesus our Lord**" (v. 11).

You should do this every day of your life. Tell yourself with your own mouth so your ears can hear it: "I am dead to sin, but I am alive to God through Jesus my Lord. Therefore, I will not give my mind or my body to that which would cause me to go backwards. I will only give my mind and body to the things that add value to my life in God!"

This is the first step to walking in the character of God. This is also the answer to the question, "Why do so many Christians experience defeat and a breakdown in character in their lives?" Christians suffer a breakdown in character when they don't reckon themselves as dead

---

[5] Frank C. Laubach, *The Inspired Letters in Clearest English* (Nashville: Thomas Nelson, Inc., 1956).

to sin and alive unto Jesus. Instead, they continue to allow yesterday to control them and to dictate their direction in life.

That *never* has to describe you, friend! Romans 6:14 tells you so in no uncertain terms:

For sin shall NOT have dominion over you, for you are not under law but under grace.

You are no longer under the law that brings condemnation and guilt. God's grace has now become your new set of rules. But you must put this truth to work in your life on a daily basis by giving yourself a daily dose of affirmation from God's Word.

I suggest that you make yourself a set of confession cards that affirm who you are as a new creature in Christ. Speak those truths out loud boldly and often. Then whenever problems and temptations arise throughout the day, you will find it much easier to act according to who you are in Christ instead of according to how your flesh feels at the moment.

Tell yourself again and again until the truth of your words sinks deep down in your heart:

✳ "I am a new creature in Christ. Old things are passed away, and all things are become new. I do not boast in anything or anyone except the Cross of my Lord and Savior Jesus Christ, through whom the world has become a dead thing to me. I am dead to the world, for my old self has been crucified with Him, and it is no longer I who live but Christ lives in me. The life I now live in this world, I live by faith in the Son of God, who loved me and gave Himself for me."

This is the way to break the power of yesterday in your life. This is the way to walk in newness of life. You must focus only on what *God* says about you.

God says that you are born of Him and therefore can overcome the world by your faith (1 John 5:4). He says that sin shall not have dominion over you (Rom. 6:14). He says that you *can* walk in holiness, just as He is holy (1 Peter 1:15).

Once you have made these truths alive and active in your heart, you have taken the first step toward becoming a person of excellent character. After all, you now know that every time you choose to do what is right, no matter what the cost, you are only acting according to who you really are!

PRINCIPLES FOR THE FIRST STEP TO EXCELLENT CHARACTER

✫ Unless you learn to focus on the grapes of Canaan, you will be continually tormented by the nightmares of Egypt.

✫ If you will choose godly character, you will destroy the giant named yesterday.

✫ The Person of Character knows that in order to achieve success in the future, he must break the glass ceilings of the past.

✫ The Person of Character proves through his actions that old things have truly passed away.

✫ The Person of Character never attempts to give life to something God has put to death.

✫ People of Character realize that there is no future in their past.

NOTES:

Self-Control:
The Key to Walking
In Excellence

Virtually everything in life runs on an operating system, a set of commands that tells its host what it can or what it cannot do in its present configuration. Computers are like that. Every computer has an operating system on which it runs.

In the same way, we need to understand that there is an operating system — a way in which things run — to everything in our lives. There isn't any area of our lives that is inexplicable or that lacks an "owner's manual." And if we will embrace the rules that run the particular system in which we are pursuing excellence, we will reach our goal every time.

Many people run their lives on a faulty operating system. They have the idea that opportunities for promotion in life just "happen" for some and don't happen for others.

That is one of the first myths we have to throw out of our minds on our way to building a foundation of character. The truth is, the lack of open doors of opportunity in our lives is sometimes an indication of an underlying problem.

Someone might seem like a person of good character to the outside world but show a completely different side of himself when he goes home. This person's life will not produce the open doors he needs in order to become what God wants him to become. You see, when a person is one way on the outside and another way on the inside, it's only a matter of time before life catches up with his faulty operating system.

We now know that character is the foundation of a life of excellence. We also know that discovering who we are in Christ is the first step in building that foundation. But is there a character *key* that unlocks the operating system — a character quality that governs and directs every other quality of godly character?

I believe there *is* such a character key, and it is called *self-control*. If we don't possess this vital key, we will find ourselves continually falling short in the pursuit of excellent character. Why is this? Because our own worst enemy to walking in excellence is the *lack* of self-control. This is an enemy we often don't want to deal with or talk about, for it speaks of our unwillingness to hang in there and endure for the long haul.

Far too often, we discard difficult relationships or abort challenging situations right at the point when we are about to win. This was an enemy I had to overcome in my own life. Before I was born again, I would work for a company for a few months and become the employee or the salesperson of the year. But as soon as I found out I had earned that distinction, I would quit! Why? Because there was an operating system of failure inside me that I had embraced. That destructive operating system was set to destroy me, for it continually aborted every good thing that ever came into my life.

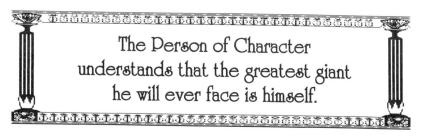

The Person of Character understands that the greatest giant he will ever face is himself.

So how do you pick up the character key of self-control and unlock a new kind of operating system in your life?

First, you have to recognize that your flesh and your spirit are at war against each other. It doesn't matter if you eclipse John the Baptist as a great person in the Kingdom of God. It doesn't even matter if you're the greatest person who has ever been born except for the Lord Jesus. Your flesh is still an enemy of your spirit — it is *never* your friend!

I will prove what I'm saying to you from the Scriptures. Look at what the apostle Paul says in Galatians 5:17 (*NAS*):

> **For the flesh sets its desire against the Spirit, and the Spirit against the flesh; for these are in opposition to one another, so that you may not do the things that you please.**

In verse 16 (*NAS*), the apostle Paul tells us the only way to make sure that the flesh doesn't win this war that is being waged inside us every day of our lives: **"But I say, WALK BY THE SPIRIT, and you will not carry out the desire of the flesh."**

Do you know what stops us from getting in the Word? Our flesh. Our flesh will come up with all kinds of ways to rationalize our neglect of the very thing we need most.

"I think I'll just wait till later to read the Bible."

"I'm just too busy today to read the Bible. I have so much going on."

"I know what I'll do. Tomorrow morning I'll set the alarm for four o'clock and read two days' worth of the Bible!"

It happens every time. *Our flesh tries to convince us to continually put off into the future what we know we need to do in the present.*

But what can we expect to happen when we begin to "walk by the Spirit"? Galatians 5:22,23 gives us a description of the spiritual fruit that will begin to manifest in our lives:

> **But the fruit of the Spirit is love, joy, peace, longsuffering, kindness, goodness, faithfulness. gentleness, self-control. Against such there is no law.**

Notice that Paul calls it "the *fruit* of the spirit." He is only talking about *a* fruit of the spirit, not nine different types of fruit, but he needs nine words to identify this one fruit.

Let's look at some of the characteristics of the fruit we produce from our new nature. The first word Paul mentions is "love," which is the Greek word *agape*. *Agape* gives love regardless of feelings — even if a person doesn't deserve it, even if that person is utterly unworthy of being loved. This word *agape* isn't something we feel at all but rather *a love of reasoning* or *a love of the will*. In other words, when we sit back and consider the consequences of life, we choose to allow love to drive us rather than bitterness or hatred. We choose to love rather than to press for our own ways or try to protect ourselves.

Another characteristic of this spiritual fruit is *joy*. This word "joy" is referring to an *inner gladness* or a *deep-seated pleasure*. A person of joy has a depth of assurance and an inner confidence that continually ignites a cheerful heart. That cheerfulness then permeates both his attitudes and his behavior.

By the time Paul is done describing the fruit of the human spirit, he has listed nine characteristics. Before we talk about the last characteristic, self-control, notice the way Paul summarizes that list: "**...Against such there is no law.**" The *Amplified* translation says, "**...Against such things there is no law [that can bring a charge].**"

No one can bring a charge against a person whose life exhibits love, joy, peace, longsuffering, kindness, goodness, faithfulness, gentleness, and self-control. There is *nothing* negative that anyone can say about an individual who lives his life that way. A person who walks in all nine of these characteristics that make up the fruit of the spirit is someone against whom no one can bring a charge, no matter how hard he or she searches for one.

That is why the apostle Peter said, "**If you are reproached for the name of Christ, blessed are you, for the Spirit of glory and of God rests upon you. On their part He is blasphemed, but on your part He is glorified**" (1 Peter 4:14). Why are you blessed when others unjustly bring a charge against you? Because it brings the Father glory when you bear much fruit. You leave your adversary no recourse but to come against the God whom you honor with your righteous life.

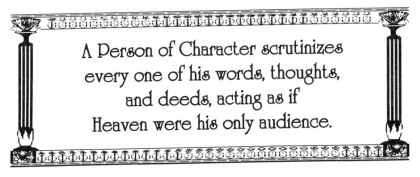

A Person of Character scrutinizes every one of his words, thoughts, and deeds, acting as if Heaven were his only audience.

Now let's look at this ninth characteristic called *self-control*. The word "self-control" means *to master the flesh with all its lusts*. It means *to be strong, controlled, and restrained.*

Let me give you my working definition of self-control — the definition that governs my own operating system in this life. Self-control is *living in the fear of God under the control of the Holy Spirit while loving the Body of Christ.*

I am continually evaluating every one of my actions, thoughts, and words on the basis of this definition. I ask myself, *How will it please my Father? How will it affect my brother? Is God pleased with the way I am thinking about this situation?*

Now, I'm not talking about the renegade thoughts that shoot across our minds like demonic shooting stars. All of us deal with those kinds of thoughts at times. I'm talking about evaluating the thoughts we allow to remain in our minds on the basis of how those thoughts: 1) please God, and 2) affect others.

The latter point is one thing Christians don't really think about a great deal. They often don't have the foresight to consider what the consequences of their actions will mean to another person. They don't weigh out a situation before they act or evaluate how their decisions will affect those around them.

But this evaluation process is absolutely crucial to walking in excellent character. Why? Because as you endeavor to walk in excellence, you will face many opportunities to become disqualified from pursuing the goal. Actually, the devil isn't looking for ways to disqualify you as much as he is waiting for you to disqualify *yourself*. He wants you to pull out. He wants you to draw away. He wants you to say, "I give up — I can't conquer this." *But it is your responsibility to make sure that this never happens.*

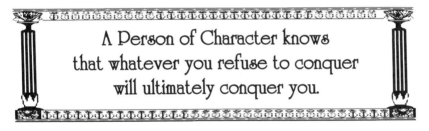

A Person of Character knows that whatever you refuse to conquer will ultimately conquer you.

Consider the example of Jesus. The Bible says He was *led of the Spirit* into the wilderness. Only after Jesus' character was tested and proven in the wilderness did He return in the power of the Spirit to fulfill His divine purpose on this earth (Luke 4:1,14).

In the same way, before you can go forth in the power of the Spirit, you must first go to the wilderness. You don't have to go there the same way Jesus did, because He has already defeated every challenge you could ever encounter in the wilderness. Nevertheless, you will have to face your own wilderness, and that wilderness is *you*. You will have to conquer yourself so the enemy can never succeed in conquering you.

So what do we do when we face a situation in which the devil is working overtime to convince us to disqualify ourselves? What do we do when the temptation seems overwhelming to say, "I can't take this anymore. This is just too much"?

Do you know what I do in those times of intense pressure? I go back to my working definition of self-control. I make sure I am loving the rest of the Body of Christ. I begin to evaluate myself, examining every one of my thoughts, every one of my words, and every one of my deeds.

If I can't find anything I've done or said to disqualify me from attaining the outcome I desire in that situation, I realize that the opposing circumstances did not originate from any bad seed I have sown. The pressure I am facing has come against me to block me from attaining the prize on the other side of this mountain. And since I know there will be no prize if I don't keep blasting through that mountain, I just keep blasting away, pursuing excellence with everything that is within me. I refuse to disqualify myself from what God has for me in any area of my life.

I often think of the sons of the prophets in Second Kings 2 when I'm tempted to give up before I attain the prize. As Elisha and Elisha traveled to the older prophet's final destination where he would be taken up to Heaven in a whirlwind, they first passed through Bethel and Jericho. The sons of the prophets were in both of these cities, and these men knew everything that was going on with Elijah and Elisha. But whereas Elisha followed Elijah all the way to Heaven's chariot, the sons of the prophets remained in the cities — all except for a small group that followed Elijah and Elisha and watched from afar.

Why did the sons of the prophets hold back? Because that was as far as they wanted to go. They had heard from God, but they didn't act on what they had heard. As the saying goes, "they just didn't get it."

Well, I'm tired of "not getting it" in my own life. After all, tomorrow morning is going to be tomorrow morning whether I arrive there in victory or in defeat. So how long am I willing to control myself? *What am I holding on to that is worth the loss of the prize God has set before me?* These are the questions we must all ask ourselves.

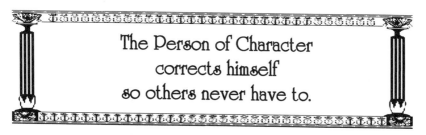

The Person of Character
corrects himself
so others never have to.

In First Corinthians 9:24-27 (*KJV*), Paul explained how he made sure that he never disqualified himself:

> **Know ye not that they which run in a race run all, but one receiveth the prize? So run, that ye may obtain.**
>
> **And every man that striveth for the mastery is temperate in all things. Now they do it to obtain a corruptible crown; but we an incorruptible.**
>
> **I therefore so run, not as uncertainly; so fight I, not as one that beateth the air:**

But I keep under my body, and bring it into subjection: lest that by any means, when I have preached to others, I myself should be a cast-away.

Notice that Paul says that **"...every man that striveth for the mastery is temperate in all things...."** He did *not* say, "Every man that striveth for *mediocrity* is temperate."

In other words, it is only those who are determined to live in excellence who are temperate, or self-controlled. They know that a lack of self-control is the greatest enemy to the pursuit of excellence. Therefore, they live in the fear of God under the Holy Spirit's control while in love with the Body of Christ. They consider every one of their thoughts, every one of their words, and every one of their actions, evaluating how it will please their Father and affect their brother.

I am one of those whose continual desire is to "strive for the mastery" in their walk with God. I learned long ago that I didn't have to stay the way I was in the years before I came to Jesus. But I still had to find out what it would take to get me in a position to be changed. That is what I was hungry to know. At the time, I didn't need an exegetical, verse-by-verse teaching of the New Testament. First, I had to stop drowning in the whirlpool created by my own operating system of defeat. Then I would be ready to hear more.

What do we have to do in order to have our lives changed and rearranged? Paul helped answer this question that burned in my heart in verse 27 (*NIV*). This scripture holds a key to permanent change for each of us so we can make sure that we never disqualify ourselves.

No, I beat my body and make it my slave so that after I have preached to others, I myself will not be disqualified for the prize.

Paul was saying in essence, "Every time my flesh wants to rise up, I slap it back down and say, 'Get back down, flesh! You're not starting that mess again! All of that is over in my life.'"

The apostle Peter provides more biblical instruction on self-control in First Peter 4:1 (*KJV*):

Forasmuch then as Christ hath suffered for us in the flesh, arm yourselves likewise with the same mind: for he that hath suffered in the flesh hath ceased from sin.

Peter is saying in effect, "If you will focus inwardly and deal with those destructive words, attitudes, and emotions that you have spewn out upon others, it will shut off the valve of wrong in your life, because he who has suffered in the flesh will cease from sin. So take an honest look on the inside and deal with those issues that are building a faulty foundation in your life instead of making everyone else pay the price for them."

If I am allowing my flesh to manifest in a certain area, someone else should not have to come and use a spiritual crowbar to pry that problem off my life. It isn't my responsibility to deal with other people's lack of self-control. I have to deal with *me* by establishing my own set of self-control standards. I know that if I will choose to deal with me, God will never have to send someone else to do it.

You may say, "Yes, but you just don't know my situation. You don't know what they did to me and what I've gone through."

Let me tell something from personal experience — the day you learn that God's perspective matters more than how the situations of life affect you is the day you will be free. That will be the day your passions no longer control you; instead, your highest desire will be to embrace God's instruction and walk in His ways.

Why is this? Because he who suffers in the flesh will cease from sin. Instead of imposing his flesh on someone else and making sure that the other person suffers, he deals with *himself*. He gets to the point where he says, "That's it — I'm giving this up! I don't want this in my life anymore!"

I have made that decision in my life. I will not get into a wrestling match with someone else over the areas I need to change. I will deal with myself. I will wrestle with me so others don't have to.

You must do the same. Wrestle with your own shortcomings and weaknesses so no one else has to wrestle with you. Then when you are finished, the only fruit that people will see growing on your "branches" will be love, joy, peace, longsuffering, gentleness, kindness, faithfulness, and self-control!

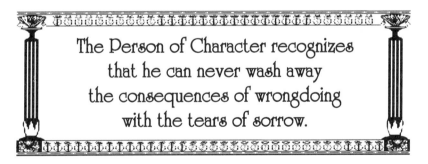

The Person of Character recognizes
that he can never wash away
the consequences of wrongdoing
with the tears of sorrow.

Self-control begins by recognizing that there are consequences for our actions. Of course, we live in a society today where consequences for a lack of self-control are few and far between. But we need to realize that even though society hands out very few consequences for wrong behavior, there are great consequences in the Kingdom of God, and those consequences don't go away.

For instance, Deuteronomy 22:22-24 reveals how serious the consequences were for certain sins under the Old Covenant.

> "If a man is found lying with a woman married to a husband, then both of them shall die — the man that lay with the woman, and the woman; so you shall put away the evil from Israel.
> "If a young woman who is a virgin is betrothed to a husband, and a man finds her in the city and lies with her,
> "then you shall bring them both out to the gate of that city, and you shall stone them to death with stones, the young woman because she did not cry out in the city, and the man because he humbled his neighbor's wife; so you shall put away the evil from among you."

People were actually put to death for specific sins committed under the Old Covenant! They were told, "If you commit this sin, this will be the consequence." Then it was their decision whether they obeyed or disobeyed the Law.

As we saw earlier, the law of sowing and reaping under the New Covenant carries its own message of deed and consequence. Paul explains in Galatians 6:7,8:

Do not be deceived, God is not mocked; for whatever a man sows, that he will also reap.

For he who sows to his flesh will of the flesh reap corruption, but he who sows to the Spirit will of the Spirit reap everlasting life.

We may not want to hear about consequences in this day and age, but the truth still remains — if we let our flesh have its way, it will only be a matter of time before negative consequences manifest. There *will* come a day when the law of sowing and reaping will bring forth the fruit of our choices.

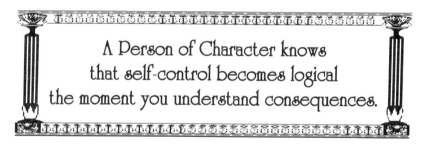

A Person of Character knows that self-control becomes logical the moment you understand consequences.

You have to understand temptation in order to develop self-control in your life. Why? Because when you are aware that temptation comes to cause you to disqualify yourself, you are better equipped to resist the temptation.

James 1:2,3 (*KJV*) says, **"My brethren, count it all joy when ye fall into divers temptations; knowing this, that the trying of your faith worketh patience."** Remember, joy is an inner gladness or a deep-seated pleasure. So when we fall into different temptations, we are to be glad with a depth of assurance and confidence that ignites a cheerful heart and leads to cheerful behavior.

Why can we remain cheerful when facing temptation? Because we don't take it personally. We are aware of the enemy's strategies, and we have already determined that we will not compromise our principles.

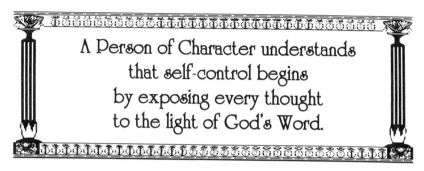

A Person of Character understands
that self-control begins
by exposing every thought
to the light of God's Word.

Self-control begins when we decide to expose our thoughts and feelings to the Word of God before we ever put them out in front of other people. This is what First John 1:7 is talking about:

> **But if we walk in the light as He is in the light, we have fellowship with one another, and the blood of Jesus Christ His Son cleanses us from all sin.**

If I walk in the light as the Father is in the light, I will have fellowship with Him. But that means I have to continually expose my thoughts and feelings to the light of the Word. Then once the Word reveals the true nature of my thoughts and emotions, I have to decide whether or not I want to unload them on the people around me.

It becomes so much easier to exert self-control after spending time in the light. After all, when we are full of the Word, why would we want to put our brothers and sisters in the Lord on red alert just so we can spend a few hours, days, or weeks in the flesh? Why wouldn't we expose our bad attitudes to the Word of God and let the Word correct them before we ever load those bad attitudes on other people?

It is so good to know that God can change who we are before we ever show other people how foolish we can be. I like that about God — He gives us the answers to the test before the test ever comes!

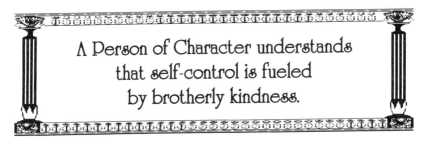

A Person of Character understands that self-control is fueled by brotherly kindness.

The Greek word for "brotherly kindness" is *philadelphia*. Philippians 2:3,4 tells us how brotherly kindness is manifested:

> **Let nothing be done through selfish ambition or conceit, but in lowliness of mind let each esteem others better than himself.**
> **Let each of you look out not only for his own interests, but also for the interests of others.**

How do I consider my brother to be better than I am? It is a choice. I consider what he goes through to be more important to me than what I go through. I don't take what he is going through lightly because I know it is the most important issue in the world to him. Therefore, I control my own emotions and choose to make my brother's concerns the most important issue in the world to me.

The word "philadelphia" is related to the word "philanthropy," which means *giving to the needs of others.* Galatians 6:10 tells us that this is our God-ordained responsibility:

Therefore, as we have opportunity, let us do good to all, especially to those who are of the household of faith.

This means we are called to treat everyone with kindness. However, those in the Church are to get our attention and receive better treatment from us than anyone else.

Too often just the opposite is true. The people we *don't* know are the ones who see our best and get most of our attention. Meanwhile, the people we care about the most are the ones who usually pay the price for all we've already given out to the people in the world!

What a difference it makes in our lives when we make it our top priority to show brotherly kindness toward our fellow believers! As we consider the interests of others as more important than our own, our flesh stops being our motivating force. Instead, self-control becomes our new internal operating system by which every other area of our character is run.

Finally, let's go back to Galatians 5:24 (*NAS*), which tells us the prerequisite for manifesting self-control and the other characteristics that make up the fruit of the spirit in our lives:

Now those who belong to Christ Jesus have crucified the flesh with its passions and desires.

There is a crucifixion that must take place in your flesh so you can let what is inside you come out. You don't have to work at *making* it come out; you must *let* it manifest.

Think about it — have you ever seen fruit that labors to show itself? Do you walk by a peach tree and think, *Those peaches are really working hard at showing up on those branches!* No, fruit is just there. It is an effortless growth process once the right seed is sown, as long as there is adequate soil, water, and light.

So make the decision to count your flesh and its desires as crucified; then pick up the character key of self-control and unlock a new kind of operating system in your life. Begin to sow the right seed as you expose every thought and emotion to the light of God's Word. Come to the place where you decide once and for all that your days of losing are *over*.

You have had enough of giving up right before your victory manifests. You've had enough of trying to win in your own strength. From now on, you are operating as the righteousness of God in Christ. That's the way you're going to start every day, and that's the way you are going to *keep* every day victorious!

PRINCIPLES FOR SELF CONTROL: THE KEY TO WALKING IN EXCELLENCE

✶ The Person of Character understands that the greatest giant he will ever face is himself.

✶ A Person of Character scrutinizes every one of his words, thoughts, and deeds, acting as if Heaven were his only audience.

✶ A Person of Character knows that whatever you refuse to conquer will ultimately conquer you.

✶ The Person of Character corrects himself so others never have to.

✬ The Person of Character recognizes that he can never wash away the consequences of wrong-doing with the tears of sorrow.

✬ A Person of Character knows that self-control becomes logical the moment you understand consequences.

✬ A Person of Character understands that self-control begins by exposing every thought to the light of God's Word.

✬ A Person of Character understands that self-control is fueled by brotherly kindness.

NOTES:

_____

_____

_____

_____

_____

_____

_____

_____

_____

_____

_____

_____

NOTES:

CHAPTER SEVEN

OBEDIENCE: THE CORNERSTONE OF GODLY CHARACTER

Some things are non-negotiables once you decide to walk with God. In other words, you can't bargain your way out of them. There is no way you can tell the Lord, "I don't want to be part of this anymore." It is like sitting on a roller-coaster after it has been released from its starting point. You can't just suddenly decide to get off!

Once we decide to surrender our lives to God, He begins to reveal to us the great blessings He wants to bring to us and the great things He wants to accomplish through us as we walk with Him. But somewhere along the way, the thought should strike us, *Hey, wait a second! I shouldn't just be looking for what I can get out of my relationship with God. What does HE get out of His relationship with ME?*

It is at this point that God begins to teach us about one of those "non-negotiables" in our spiritual walk — the issue of *obedience*. This is the cornerstone to the foundation on which our lives are built. It is also the one area of our character that needs more attention than any other, for if we will give God our obedience, all the rest of the character traits will be easy for us to conquer.

Thankfully, we don't have to learn how to be obedient in our own strength. Philippians 2:13 (*NLT*) says, "**For God is working in you, giving you the desire to obey him and the power to do what pleases him.**" Whether we realize it or not, the familiar inner turmoil we have all felt on the inside is the struggle between what *we* want and what *God* wants for our lives. God is continually working in us to give us the desire to obey Him, and our flesh doesn't like it one bit!

Many people deal with that inner struggle most of their lives before they fully surrender to God. Through the years, they struggle and then surrender. Then they struggle some more, and then they surrender again. This same pattern is repeated again and again and again. These people may not want to admit it, but their problem can be simply stated: *God doesn't hold enough value in their lives to cause them to submit to Him and obey.*

Whenever you encounter those who are disobedient, you'll become aware that they possess some other characteristics that always accompany disobedience. For instance, when you find a disobedient person, you'll also find:

- Rebellion

- Self-will

- Self-centeredness

- An individual who only cares about himself

Sadly, a great many Christians fit this description, for disobedience doesn't have an age bracket. A person can be eighty years old and still be self-willed and disobedient to the Lord.

So let's talk about this all-important cornerstone of godly character. What exactly does the word "obedience" mean?

Obedience refers to *give in to the orders or instructions of the person who has been placed in charge.* It also means *to perform what is required by authority and to abstain from what is prohibited.*

If there is something that is prohibited by my God-ordained authority, I don't need to find out about it. If he says to me, "That isn't good," then that settles it — it isn't good, and I am going to leave it alone.

The first time this principle was ever broken was in the Garden of Eden after God commanded Adam, **"But of the tree of the knowledge of good and evil you shall not eat, for in the day that you eat of it you shall surely die"** (Gen. 2:17).

Then the devil came to the woman and said, "Wait a minute. Has God *really* said that you can't eat of that tree? He just knows that as soon as you eat that fruit, you'll be like Him, knowing good and evil." So the woman listened to the devil's lies and partook of what was prohibited.

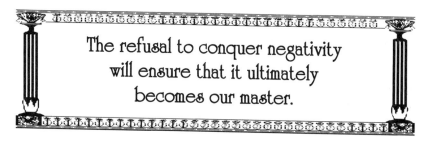

The refusal to conquer negativity
will ensure that it ultimately
becomes our master.

But did you ever wonder how long the devil poured out his barrage of lies to the woman before she acted on what he had told her? How long did he bombard her with his words before she actually listened?

The same is true with us. If we refuse to eliminate negative things from our lives, those negative things will ultimately destroy us, and there will be nothing we can do about it.

Let's look at the Hebrew word for "obey," the word *shama*, to find out what else this word means. *Shama* is a root word meaning *to hear intelligently*. It also means *to consider and consent with contentment; to diligently discern;* and *to perceive with one's ear*.

Because I have determined to be obedient, I don't have to have my own way. I listen; I hear; and I am content to follow through with the instructions I receive. Why? Because I know it is my God-given responsibility to obey. It is also God's desire for me to be pleasing to others.

"To obey" also means *to be submissive to authority; to be compliant;* and *to be dutiful and loyal*. The Greek word for "obey" is *hupakouo*, which means *to be in a subordinate position*. *Hupo* literally means *to place under* or *to place beneath; akouo* means *to hear and understand*. When compounded together, *hupakouo* means *to listen attentively as a subordinate and then conform to the authority's command*.

That is the divine pattern: to listen and then to conform, to hear, and to act. God doesn't ask us our opinion or what we think about His commands. He just expects us to *obey*.

This is where we begin to run into a problem in this modern society. We live in a world where people want to know *why* about everything: "Why do you want me to do that? Why do you want to do it that way? Why, why, *why*?"

How do we get past that problem in our own lives? For one thing, it will help us to better understand a word that is related to obedience — the word *submission*.

The word "submit" is the Greek word *hupatasso*. It actually means *to put oneself under the authority of another*. When you submit, you are turning your will over to the will of another person based on God's delegated authority structure. This is a voluntary action, for you are the one who chooses to be obedient. No one can make you do it. You obey because you want to enjoy the reward that God prepares for the obedient.

Keep this definition in mind as you read the following verses. Each speaks of willingly submitting to those whom God has placed over us in this life:

> **Likewise you younger people, submit yourselves to your elders. Yes, all of you be submissive to one another, and be clothed with humility, for "God resists the proud, but gives grace to the humble."**
>
> 1 Peter 5:5

> **Therefore submit yourselves to every ordinance of man for the Lord's sake, whether to the king as supreme,**
>
> **or to governors, as to those who are sent by him for the punishment of evildoers and for the praise of those who do good.**

For this is the will of God, that by doing good you may put to silence the ignorance of foolish men.

1 Peter 2:13-15

Therefore submit to God. Resist the devil and he will flee from you.

James 4:7

An obedient person has a compliant temperament that easily yields or submits. There is no greater person you can ever be around in your life than a compliant individual. When he wakes up in the morning, he's happy. He's always asking, "What would you like me to do? I want to do what *you* want me to do." When you give him instructions, he says, "Fine, no problem — whatever you want." There isn't anything in the world you wouldn't do for a person like that because it's such a blessing to be around him!

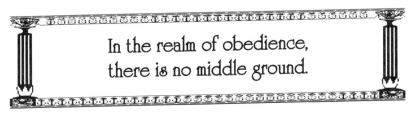

In the realm of obedience,
there is no middle ground.

Often we can find out what something *is* by learning what it *is not*. So let's learn more about obedience by taking a look at its opposite.

On the opposite side of being obedient is a person who is *insubordinate, rebellious*, and *contrary*. This person is also very *willful* and *headstrong*, someone who always has to have his own way. He will wear you down as he pressures you to go his way on a certain subject; then when you finally give in, he'll say, "See? You said I could do it."

The disobedient person is also *recalcitrant*, which means *stubbornly obstinate.* Once this person digs his heels in the ground, you might as well build a monument around him, because he isn't moving! All these negative traits add up to a person who is *ungovernable* and *unruly* — a continual grief to those who are in authority over him.

When I began to look at all these words that describe the disobedient, I was struck by the severity of the words: *insubordinate; rebellious; contrary; willful; headstrong; recalcitrant; ungovernable; unruly.* All of a sudden, Proverbs 29:23 (*NAS*) made more sense to me: **"A man's pride will bring him low, but a humble spirit will obtain honor.**

When a person says that he is his own god, he governs himself. No one tells him what to do. He is willful. He is headstrong. He has an opinion about everything. And his pride will eventually bring him down.

While studying this subject, I came to realize that in the realm of obedience or disobedience, there is no middle ground. There is no place for a person to tell his authority, "Well, that's your opinion. I'm going to do things my way." That would mean a third opinion can enter into a God-ordained authority structure. But in all my years of searching for truth, that is not what I have found to be true.

Nevertheless, that is exactly the way modern society wants it. Second Timothy 3:1-7 aptly describes this world we live in today, for these are the last of the last days.

But know this, that in the last days perilous times will come:

For men will be lovers of themselves, lovers of money, boasters, proud, blasphemers, disobedient to parents, unthankful, unholy,

unloving, unforgiving, slanderers, without self-control, brutal, despisers of good,

traitors, headstrong, haughty, lovers of pleasure rather than lovers of God,

having a form of godliness but denying its power. And from such people turn away!

For of this sort are those who creep into households and make captives of gullible women loaded down with sins, led away by various lusts,

always learning and never able to come to the knowledge of the truth.

Notice that the apostle Paul tells us to *"know this"* about the last days. He is saying, "Have a deep, intimate knowledge of these things. Don't have it proven to you by falling into the enemy's trap." What are we to know? That in the last of the last days, perilous, treacherous, dangerous times shall come.

It is interesting to note that these perilous times will manifest primarily through people's disobedience and lack of character. Let's look briefly at how Paul describes those who live during these perilous times.

First, Paul says, **"For men will be lovers of themselves..."** (v. 2). People will be lovers of their own ideas — of the things *they* want out of life. They will only be interested in what they can get for themselves, not what they can give to anyone else. They won't even be interested in that word "give." That certainly describes the prevailing attitude of our modern-day society, doesn't it?

Paul goes on to say that in the last days, people will be "...**lovers of money, boasters, proud, blasphemers, disobedient to parents, unthankful, unholy.**" Several words in that list spring from *pride*, one of the most dangerous traits of ungodly character a person can possess.

Remember, Proverbs 29:23 (*KJV*) tells us, "**A man's pride shall bring him low: but honour shall uphold the humble in spirit.**" Now, what is God saying here? It's very simple. A person of honor will always be upheld, for that person is a humble person. By contrast, the person who is proud always does everything his own way and isn't interested in what anyone else has to say. A person like that can never be upheld, for a man's pride will always bring him low.

I became well-acquainted with that particular character trait as I was growing up. I can remember the day creditors backed up the truck to our house when I was a boy and took away all our furniture. How does a young boy pretend that he isn't the laughingstock of the block when they just took his family's furniture away? How does he pretend that it means nothing and that it doesn't hurt? *With a façade of pride.* He covers up his feelings and doesn't let anyone see the pain.

From that moment on, he no longer lives as who he really is. Instead, he takes on the image and form of someone he is not. And when others attack him, he begins to react from that imaginary person in his mind. As a result, he becomes very, very distant from his true emotions until finally, he is no longer able to connect with who he is as a person. During this destructive process, he also becomes a very unthankful person for whom nothing is ever good enough.

How do I know all this? Well, I didn't learn it from Dr. Spock! This is the person I had become before that day in 1975 when I became a new creature in Christ.

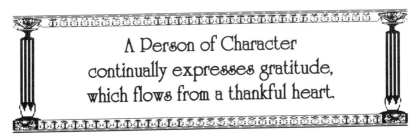

A Person of Character
continually expresses gratitude,
which flows from a thankful heart.

One of the first things I prayed for after I came to Christ was a thankful heart. I never again wanted anyone to feel like he or she owed me anything.

But thankfulness is a rare commodity today, just as Paul said it would be in the last days (v. 2). We live in a country filled with people who think the world owes them something. Rather than seeking to emulate the character and hard work of their predecessors that has produced a prosperous nation, people assume they can just keep reaping from seed sown in past years without ever sowing themselves. As a result, this country has accumulated trillions of dollars of national debt, the price of which someone will have to pay. If this generation doesn't pay the price, the succeeding generations will have to.

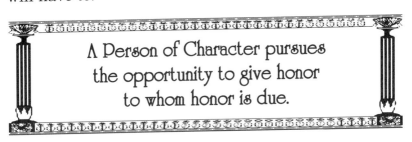

A Person of Character pursues
the opportunity to give honor
to whom honor is due.

If we will take an honest look back through the last few decades of our society, we will discover how much we as a people have rejected wisdom over the years. For instance, to a large extent we have taken honor away from the elderly. Instead of esteeming the experience and wisdom of the elderly, we have gone looking for those who seem more exciting but who don't have a great deal of experience.

Remember, youth is driven by its own desires — by "what's important to me," *not* by "what's important to *us.*" The older generation goes to work early and stays late. They work all the time, and they deal with issues and situations other people would never touch. But youth is interested in its own pleasures and in "what I'm going to get out of this."

But when Americans rejected the elderly, an unexpected outcome, spoken of in verse 2, became the result: People began to stop honoring and thus became disobedient to their parents.

Today's society has paid a heavy price for this lack of honor and obedience. What was called a dysfunctional family twenty years ago is now called a functional family. In fact, if a child has two parents living at home with him, his family is now statistically considered abnormal!

I determined long ago to be an answer to the lack of honor I see everywhere I go. Honor is such an important part of obedience — honor for the elderly, honor for godly wisdom, honor for authority — for it adds value both to the recipient and the individual who chooses to give **"...honor to whom honor is due"** (Rom. 13:7 *AMP*).

Notice the next words Paul uses as he continues to describe people in the last days: **"unloving, unforgiving, slanderers, without self-control, brutal, despisers of good, traitors..."** (vv. 3,4). How do people become traitors? By continually trading what they have for what they think is a better deal.

For instance, someone might think, *If I made a mistake in getting married, I'll just change marriage partners.* Or he might reason, *I made too much of a financial commitment, so I'm going to file bankruptcy.* People who start thinking this way also become headstrong. There is nothing you can say to a person like that, because even if you try to entreat him, he won't listen.

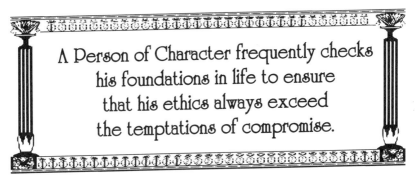

A Person of Character frequently checks his foundations in life to ensure that his ethics always exceed the temptations of compromise.

This "traitor mentality" isn't limited to the world either. Many Christians think this way as well, for their foundation of character isn't pushing them beyond their circumstances.

Whenever our ethics do not exceed our circumstances, we're in greater trouble than we even understand, for our character defines who we are to the outside world. For instance, we should never have to sign a contract in order to ensure that we keep our word.

Do you know why people started writing contracts? Because they were well aware of the lack of ethics in society. Then they started paying lawyers a tremendous amount of money to make certain that all the doors were closed inside their contracts.

Now, it isn't our fault that society has adopted a lifestyle that embraces a lack of character. It only becomes our fault when we become part of the problem. How do we become part of the answer instead? By celebrating character not only in our own lives, but also in the lives of others.

For instance, Christians have only themselves to blame when they allow themselves to become overconsumers, unable to pay for what they buy. People who fit in this category often stop tithing or laying up an inheritance for their children's children, using the excuse, "We have too many bills." But the truth is, they are overconsuming and they need to repent!

Remember this: *To live on credit is to take from our future in order to enjoy in our present that which we believe God will not give us.*

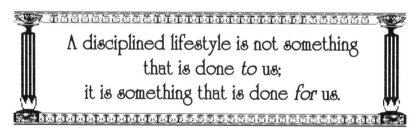

A disciplined lifestyle is not something that is done *to* us; it is something that is done *for* us.

No one can make us disciplined in the way we live on this earth. But when we make God's priorities *our* priorities, we will find all the grace we need to help us push beyond our circumstances and remain faithful in our commitments to God and man.

Think about it — if this truly is the last of the last days, there are multitudes of people in this world who desperately need to come to Christ. That is certainly God's priority, and we need to make it our priority as well. Rather than focus on all our temporal little projects, we need to put our greatest efforts into eternal matters. After all, Heaven will one day be our eternal home, so what Heaven says should matter to us!

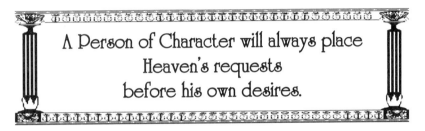

A Person of Character will always place
Heaven's requests
before his own desires.

People who love God don't walk away from what He tells them to do. They don't say, "Well, I love God, but I just want to live the way I want to live."

It doesn't matter how you look at it — if you want more of God, you walk *toward* Him. If you don't want Him, you walk away from Him. It is that simple.

You might ask me, "But haven't you ever backslidden, Robb? Don't you think you ever will — even a little?" Never — not for one second of one day. I know the darkness on the other side, and I'm not going back there!

"Well, then, what do you think I need to do so I can say the same thing?"

Resist the devil, and he will flee from you (James 4:7)! Then make the decision to always, *always* walk *toward* God and not away from Him, no matter what.

God is interested the direction we are going in life. Interestingly, there are people sitting in the bars today who are walking *toward* God and people in the local churches who are walking *away from* Him.

Which way are *you* walking? God is trying to bring you to a place where your relationship with Him is alive and growing every single day, regardless of the circumstances that surround you. So make the decision that walking away from God even for a moment is not an option for you. No matter how you feel, what you think, or what other people say about it, you're going to keep yourself pointed in the right direction — toward the One who saved you, redeemed you, and now holds you accountable to comply with what He says!

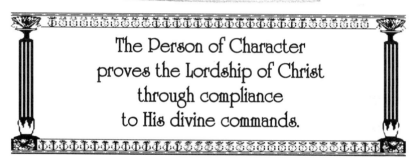

The Person of Character proves the Lordship of Christ through compliance to His divine commands.

There are two philosophies of obedience in this world. Let me use a mental picture to give you an idea of these two ways of thinking.

Three men are standing on the deck of an aircraft carrier. The Sergeant in Arms, who is standing on a level just above the deck, suddenly calls out, "Duck! Hit the deck!"

Two of the men immediately hit the deck. The third man remains standing and looks around, asking, "Why? What's going on?" Suddenly an incoming missile explodes on the deck. The third man who failed to heed the Sergeant's warning is killed by exploding shrapnel. A few minutes later, the other two men who instantly obeyed the warning get up from the deck uninjured.

Let's tie in that illustration to the two philosophies of obedience. First, is the Greek understanding of obedience, which is represented by the third man. He remained standing on the deck asking the question *why*. He was only ready to comply once he understood the answer.

The modern American culture is based on the Greek philosophy of obedience. In this country today, a person asks questions first and then decides if he wants to obey. But back when our country was much more biblically based, people usually didn't have to be asked a second time to do anything. They obeyed the first time because they believed in the integrity of the person who had given them the instruction. This is the Hebrew understanding of obedience. It tells us that a person obeys first, and then he will understand why.

Why is it important to understand these two philosophies of obedience? Because the Bible assumes that you have a close relationship with God and that you submit to Him all the time. For instance, Jesus said in John 10:27, **"My sheep hear My voice, and I know them, and they follow Me."** Then on that basis, the Word gives you directives to instantly obey without question.

If you choose instead to live according to the Greek philosophy of obedience, the day will come when you wish you had learned to instantly obey. The Holy Spirit will say, "Duck!" and while you stand there asking, "Why?" one of the enemy's "missiles" will hit you from behind in an attempt to take you out of your spiritual race.

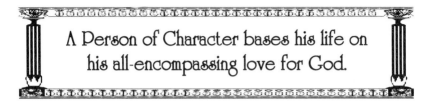

A Person of Character bases his life on his all-encompassing love for God.

There are two secrets to living an obedient life before God, and Deuteronomy 11:1 gives us both of them:

"Therefore you shall love the Lord your God, and keep His charge, His statutes, His judgments, and His commandments always."

First, we are to *love the Lord our God*. The truth is, every choice to obey God in this life is based on our love for Him, for love transcends everything. It is the reason we can stay in difficult situations or continue to deal with difficult people. We love God so much that we are willing to work through any challenge in order to please Him.

My wife Linda is a beneficiary of my love for God. She is very secure because she knows my love for Jesus will keep me pursuing excellent character in a world that is degenerating all around me. It is my love for God that causes me to look the best I can. It is my love for God that causes me to stop at the store and buy her a new dress or a piece of jewelry. I make sure that Linda doesn't want for anything because of my love for God.

Make it your highest priority to cultivate your intimacy with God, for it is your love for Him that will motivate you to obey Him in every area of your life.

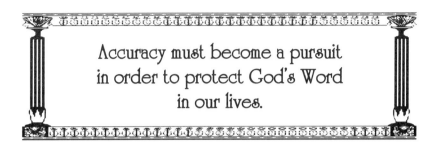

Accuracy must become a pursuit
in order to protect God's Word
in our lives.

Once we understand this principle, we are ready for the second secret to living an obedient life before God: *We are to keep His commandments always.* That word "keep" means *to guard; to protect;* or *to defend.*

We have to understand that accuracy is a continual pursuit. We can't walk with Jesus one day and then the next day live like the devil, only to get up the day after that to live for Jesus again. No, we have to continually protect God's Word in our lives. That's why Proverbs 4:23 (*NAS*) says, **"Watch over your heart with all diligence, for from it flow the springs of life."** The *New Living Translation* tells us, **"...for it affects everything you do."**

I personally can't imagine saying, "God, I love You, but I'm not showing up at church today" or "God, I love You, but I'm still going to get back at that person for what he did to me!" I can't do that. I don't know where to cut off my commitment to God in order to follow my own fleshly desires — and I don't ever want to find out!

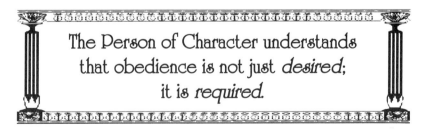

The Person of Character understands
that obedience is not just *desired;*
it is *required.*

Obedience doesn't bless the person to whom we are obedient; obedience is a matter of life or death to you and me. Obedience is the choice we must make in order to live as God designed for us to live on this earth. It isn't an option with Him.

This was God's message spoken through Moses in Deuteronomy 11:26-28:

"Behold, I set before you today a blessing and a curse:

the blessing, if you obey the commandments of the Lord your God which I command you today;

and the curse, if you do not obey the commandments of the Lord your God, but turn aside from the way which I command you today....

"Blessing" is one of the most popular words in the entire Bible; *everyone* wants to be a recipient of God's blessings. However, too many Christians want to get rid of the "ifs" in the Bible. Instead of acknowledging their failure to fulfill the "if" of a divine promise, they make up excuses to explain why they haven't received the blessing.

In this passage of Scripture, God said, **"The blessing, if you obey the commandments of the Lord your God which I command you today; and the curse, if you do not obey the commandments of the Lord your God..."** (vv. 27,28). I may not be very bright, but I can read! God said I would be blessed if I obeyed and cursed if I disobeyed. He declares the same message in the following two passages of Scripture:

"If you are willing and obedient, you shall eat the good of the land;

But if you refuse and rebel, you shall be devoured by the sword"; for the mouth of the Lord has spoken.

Isaiah 1:19,20

If they obey and serve Him, they shall spend their days in prosperity, and their years in pleasures.

But if they do not obey, they shall perish by the sword, and they shall die without knowledge.

Job 36:11,12

If I am willing and obedient, I will eat the best God has to offer me in life. But if I refuse and rebel, I'll be devoured by the enemy. There isn't a great deal of wiggle room in that particular divine edict, so I'd just rather be willing and obedient! Even if others act wrongfully toward me, I will stay willing and obedient because I know that is what Heaven requires of me. On the other hand, if I choose to refuse and rebel, I better get all the enjoyment I can out of my rebellion, because the devil will get the last laugh in my life!

That is why we need to pay close attention to the word "if" whenever we find it in one of God's promises. There is a *big* difference between being devoured and eating the best of the land, and it all depends on what we do with that word "if"!

Disobedience is one of the most destructive things we could ever deal with in life. Proverbs 29:1 sternly warns us of this truth: **"He who is often rebuked, and hardens his neck, will suddenly be destroyed, and that without remedy."**

You have probably encountered this type of person at one time or another. You can talk to him until you are blue in the face, but he will never heed your warning or make the changes that are necessary to get off the path to destruction and onto God's path that **"...shines ever brighter unto the perfect day"** (Prov. 4:18).

In Proverbs 30:17, the Bible says, **"The eye that mocks his father, and scorns obedience to his mother, the ravens of the valley will pick it out, and the young eagles will eat it."** When I read that verse the first time, I thought, *"The ravens of the valley will pluck out the eye of the one who hates to obey? That is definitely NOT a good outcome!"*

What is the principle behind this graphic verse? Our disobedience and willfulness doesn't hurt the person we're disobeying. Our willfulness hurts *us*. We might not like the person we are supposed to obey, but the consequences of disobedience are far worse than the idea of obeying the "unlikable" in life!

I know many people who are destroying their own lives because they have given up on the Word. We already looked at Proverbs 19:3 (*NLT*), which talks about people like this:

> **People ruin their lives by their own foolishness and then are angry at the Lord.**

Initially these people received the Word and by faith walked halfway out on the water. But then they started to listen to that other voice — the voice that says, "You don't need God anymore. You don't need the Word anymore." Finally, they let go of the Word in their hearts. But the moment they did that, they started to sink — and then blamed God for getting wet!

Where does that kind of behavior come from? Too often it arises from a false perception of God's grace. We need to know this about walking with the Lord: Just because we are children of God doesn't mean we can put obedience on the sidelines and never suffer any consequences. As long as we choose to walk in disobedience, we will not enjoy the inheritance God has provided for us through Jesus.

The truth is, it takes a big dose of God's grace to continually submit to Him and to those He has placed in authority over us. First Peter 5:5 talks about this: **"Likewise you younger people, submit yourselves to your elders. Yes, all of you be submissive to one another, and be clothed with humility, for 'God resists the proud, but gives grace to the humble.'"** God resists the man who is his own "I Am," but He gives abundant grace to the person who is willing to obey his God-ordained authority in humble submission.

There are far too many books being written at this time in history that undermine the way God deals with His people through delegated authority. I cannot find any place in God's written Word where He condones this type of dissension.

This statement is very unpopular at best. Nevertheless, the truth remains that two things happen in the Body of Christ today as a result of this type of book:

1. People sell books that only document their rebellion.

2. These same people derail the faith of those who are only novices, as well as those who are unfamiliar with the written Word of God.

Let's look at some biblical examples of men who submitted themselves to God. First, there is the example of Joseph, as we mentioned earlier. Sold into Egyptian slavery by his jealous brothers, Joseph remained obedient and submissive to his master Potiphar, gaining favor in his eyes. As a result of Joseph's submission to his master, God blessed Potiphar and all his household. But later when Potiphar's wife lusted after Joseph, the young man refused to submit himself to her, choosing instead to submit himself to a higher power:

> **"There is no one greater in this house than I, nor has he kept back anything from me but you, because you are his wife. How then can I do this great wickedness, and sin against God?"**
>
> **Genesis 39:9**

As a result of Joseph's choice to submit to a higher power than Potiphar's wife, he ended up in jail. But God was true to His Word, giving abundant grace to this man who chose to walk in humility and obedience in every circumstance. The day came when Joseph was not only freed from slavery and prison but exalted to the second highest position in all of Egypt!

Then there is the example of Daniel. When just a young man, Daniel was taken into captivity by the Babylonians and trained to serve the king. Conducting himself with honor and humility, Daniel came to be respected and honored by his Babylonian masters. Then one day he was commanded to eat food that was not in the Levitical law. So Daniel made an appeal to a higher authority — the Babylonian king. The king had observed how Daniel had obediently submitted himself since his arrival to the Babylonian court. Thus, Daniel gained favor in the king's sight and was permitted to submit himself to God's Law regarding his diet (*see* Dan. 1:8-20).

Then another time, Daniel was thrown in the lion's den because he wouldn't worship the king's graven image. Daniel said, "Look, I am not going to violate the Word of God. I will not do it!" But God shut the mouths of those lions, and in the end, the king sent out a decree, saying, "I command everyone throughout the land to worship the God who delivers Daniel from the power of the lions!" (*see* Dan. 6:26,27).

The same will prove true in your life. When you refuse to go against the Word, you can be assured that God will deliver you!

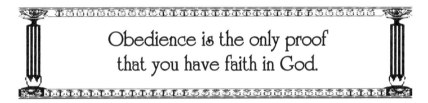

Obedience is the only proof
that you have faith in God.

You have to get it out of your mind that any lack of progress in your life is someone else's fault. No one else can stand between you and God's will for you when you are walking in humble obedience to Him.

Here are some "test questions" to ask yourself to help you determine whether or not you are an obedient person.

1. *Do you obey whatever is requested of you?*

Remember, obedience is based on what God says is right. Compliance isn't based on the way *we* think we should do something.

However, you must never just blindly obey someone who is in authority over you, giving up your personal responsibility to understand the will of God for yourself.

Sometimes people don't want to be responsible for what is going on in their lives. This is the type of person who sometimes says to me, "Pastor Robb, tell me what you want me to do in this situation I'm facing."

But I just reply, "I'm not going to tell you what to do. Do whatever you believe is right. You will anyway, regardless of what is said to you."

I never tell a person what to do. If I did, I would be taking his personal responsibility away from him, and God didn't call me to do that. The most anyone will ever get out of me is what I would do if I were in the same situation that person is facing. Then I leave the door open for that person to tell me what *he* believes is the right thing for him to do.

2. *Do you ask for reasons why when your request is denied?*

When you request something and your request is turned down, do you ask why? If you do, you are flirting with non-compliance and disobedience.

3. *Do you respond immediately when you are given an instruction?*

Or do you say something like, "I'll get to it as soon as I can"? Obedience is stopping what you want to do to fulfill the desire of the person you need to obey.

4. *Do you smile when you are given an instruction?*

Or do you look like you're dealing with an upset stomach? Obedience doesn't just mean doing what you're asked to do; it means *cheerfully* responding to the requests of your authority.

5. *Do you ever give reasons why you cannot do a job?*

Obedience is finding ways to overcome obstacles.

6. *Have you ever had to be reminded to do something you were asked to do?*

Obedience doesn't put off the assigned task according to its own convenience.

7. *Do you ever have to redo a job that you did incorrectly or in mediocrity?*

Obedience is being diligent to correctly follow instructions the first time.

8. *Have you ever complained or thought that the job a superior gave you was stupid?*

Obedience is doing the job now and then understanding later.

9. *Have you ever asked one parent for permission to do something when the other parent already said no?*

This test of obedience may only be a distant memory, but it might help you discover when some seeds of disobedience were first planted!

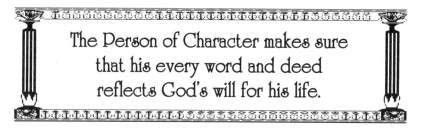

The Person of Character makes sure that his every word and deed reflects God's will for his life.

This principle reveals the ultimate test of obedience: *Are you carrying out every word and deed by God's will or by your own will?* Any words or deeds that are initiated from your own will are expressions of iniquity. In fact, that's what the word "iniquity" means in the biblical sense: doing one's own will with the attitude of "I don't care what anyone else thinks."

This is a crucial test for those who identify with the Charismatic movement. Although this movement has brought forth tremendous truths, it was born in rebellion and in the spirit of Absalom. That challenging spirit still lives in many believers today, keeping them from achieving the fullness of God's plan for their lives.

Charismatic Christians often have no trouble standing in their own righteousness, but they don't seem to understand that the person they are gossiping about is as righteous as they are. They also have no trouble challenging the authority structure of the church, claiming, "God made us all equal in His eyes."

But that isn't true. Every believer is called, but those who stand in ministry offices are chosen by God. A person steps into a ministry office because he has been drafted by the Head of the Church, and Jesus expects everyone who enlisted under that person's authority to willingly submit and obey!

Charismatics also don't like to hear about suffering. But personally, it doesn't bother me when a person wrongs me personally and the offense doesn't involve anyone else. I don't care. I'm just thankful to the Lord that I can be worthy of suffering for His Name's sake.

Suffering is painful, and it takes character to endure it. But God's Kingdom will be born inside of us as we obey Him *in the midst of* challenge and conflict, not by *running away from* it.

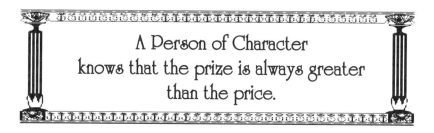

Λ Person of Character
knows that the prize is always greater
than the price.

If we want to move up higher in our spiritual walk and take our God-ordained position in the Body of Christ, we have to be willing to destroy every trace of rebellion in our lives and begin to obey the Word without grumbling, murmuring, complaining, or fault-finding. This just isn't an option, for God will not allow recalcitrant, rebellious, insubordinate sons and daughters to run His Kingdom.

How do I know that? Because God is eternal; He will never die. Therefore, He doesn't need to give a position of responsibility in His Kingdom to someone who is unqualified. He can outlast that person.

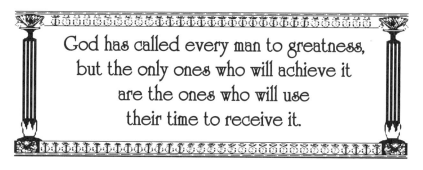

God has called every man to greatness,
but the only ones who will achieve it
are the ones who will use
their time to receive it.

God will not promote us to the next grade in the school of life until He knows we can handle it. He knows we're not ready for grade ten when we haven't even passed our kindergarten test yet!

God is waiting for qualification. If someone takes too long to become qualified, He says, "I had hopes for you, but now you have run out of time. I cannot give you that promotion." Then God moves on to look for someone else to promote who was willing to pay the price of qualification.

Does that mean God doesn't love us if we are unqualified? No, of course not. He loves us very much. In fact, He loves us enough to prevent us from becoming failures in the lives of those around us!

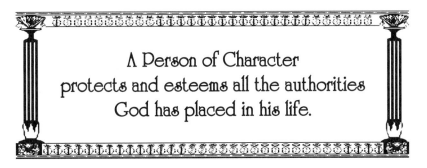

A Person of Character
protects and esteems all the authorities
God has placed in his life.

One of the most damaging things we can ever do to ourselves is disregard a person in authority over us. When we do that, we are actually showing a disregard for *God's* authority in our lives. We are forgetting that every one of our thoughts, words, and actions is a seed we are planting in the field God gave to us.

A person of disobedience is someone who continually disregards the instructions that are required of him. He might even be a nice person; however, when you ask him to do something, he just doesn't seem to find the time to get around to doing it.

Here's a small example of what I'm talking about. Suppose I ask my wife to pick up the dry cleaning the next day. Tomorrow comes, and I ask her if she picked up the dry cleaning. She says, "Oh, I forgot."

I reply, "Well, I'll go get it myself then."

She says, "No, I'll get it tomorrow."

On my way out the door the next day, I say, "Honey, remember the dry cleaning." But when she comes home that evening, my wife says, "Oh, I forgot again." At that point, she has left the realm of forgetfulness and entered the realm of disregard, which is actually passive rebellion.

We can't operate like that in the Kingdom of God if we expect to be used by Him. With God, everything is very precise. Does He forgive us? Yes. Does He love us? Absolutely! Does He think we are wonderful? We're the tops in His eyes! But are we going to be used by Him? No! Why not? Because as Proverbs 25:19 (*NLT*) says, **"Putting confidence in an unreliable person is like chewing with a toothache or walking on a broken foot."**

I'll tell you one thing you can conclude from this verse: Relying on an unreliable person *hurts*! When you put confidence in an unfaithful person to do what you have asked him to do, it's like chewing steak with an abscessed tooth in your mouth. That is something you do not want to do when you have an abscessed tooth. Your jaw is just pulsating with pain, and you don't even want to look at soup!

And have you ever put your weight on a broken foot and then tried to walk? Now, *that* is a horrible sensation you don't want to put yourself through! In the same way, God will not put His confidence in an unreliable person, because He doesn't want to put Himself through that kind of pain!

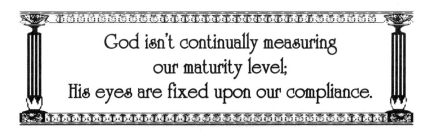

God isn't continually measuring
our maturity level;
His eyes are fixed upon our compliance.

Before I was ever in the ministry, I conducted a growing Bible study that was quite successful. One evening an individual was present at the Bible study who went back to the pastor and reported that I had taught something that was wrong.

That Sunday, the pastor's secretary told me, "Pastor wants to see you in his office tonight before the service."

When the pastor walked into the office that evening, he said to me, "I bet you wonder why I called you here today."

I replied, "No, Sir. I'm convinced the reason you called me here is that you want to give me some type of promotion. I know there couldn't be any other reason you'd want to see me."

The pastor replied, "Wrong. Actually, I have a mind to bench you and make sure you never preach again."

I stopped him there and said, "Excuse me, Sir. Please forgive me for interrupting, but if you tell me right now to never preach the Gospel again for the rest of my life, I will never stand up in front of a group of people and preach the Gospel."

At that, the pastor became silent. He couldn't think of an answer, so the conversation ended. But for years afterward, he tried to do everything he could possibly do to discredit me.

I asked him, "What are you going to do with the Bible study I gave you?"

He said, "You can take it."

I replied, "I'm not taking anything. Taking isn't even a consideration here, because I turned the Bible study over to you. Now, if you'd like to give it to me, that is another thing. But the Bible study is no longer mine to take."

Then the pastor said, "Oh, go ahead and take it. I don't care what happens to it. It can die for all I care."

In my own heart, I had no choice but to keep teaching that Bible study. I didn't want to do it. After all, the very one from whom I needed affirmation was the one who was competing with me!

I remember the time this same pastor said to me, "You know what? You're just more mature than I am." But the truth is, it doesn't matter how mature we are — it matters whether or not we will obey what God tells us to do.

At that moment, I had a choice: Either I led that Bible study, or it was going to die. So I determined not to let God's children die for lack of spiritual sustenance, and out of that Bible study grew the largest Charismatic church the city of Chicago had ever seen up to that time.

All the glory for what has taken place goes directly to the Lord, for all I have ever wanted to do is please my Father. But the fact remains: There is absolutely no substitute for a compliant and submitted heart.

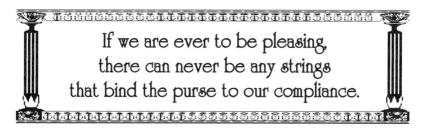

If we are ever to be pleasing,
there can never be any strings
that bind the purse to our compliance.

Let's talk a little more about that word "submission." For many in the Church today, that is almost a four-letter Christian swear word. But I have found it tremendously valuable to break down that word into two parts — *sub-mission* — so I could better understand its meaning.

When we submit, we stop considering ourselves to be "mission number one" in our lives. Instead of being the major mission we are pursuing, we allow our own mission to become a *sub*-mission as we turn our will over to the will of another based on God's delegated authority structure.

In true submission, you start with a good attitude and then add to that a desire to become pleasing to the person to whom you are submitting. In order to fulfill that desire, however, you can never put any type of strings on your compliance.

Remember, when you submit, you are submitting *to* God *through* another person. You are actually demonstrating to that person your willingness to submit to God. As a result, that person becomes the beneficiary of your relationship with God.

Many people have a difficult time succeeding in their walk with God because they will only submit to God partially. In certain areas of their lives, they remain disobedient. But if a person doesn't obey all the way, he isn't obeying at all.

Some people say, "I know I did that wrong, but why don't you talk to me about the things I did right?"

No, we're supposed to do what is right. We shouldn't expect any praise for doing what is expected of us. This was Jesus message in Luke 17:7-10 (*NLT*):

> **"When a servant comes in from plowing or taking care of sheep, he doesn't just sit down and eat.**
>
> **He must first prepare his master's meal and serve him his supper before eating his own.**
>
> **And the servant is not even thanked, because he is merely doing what he is supposed to do.**
>
> **In the same way, when you obey me you should say, 'We are not worthy of praise. We are servants who have simply done our duty.'"**

Some Christians have the attitude, "God, I've given You my life, so what am I going to get out of it?" I don't understand that attitude because I don't kid myself. I know I'd either be dead already or finding some way to end my life early if it weren't for Jesus. Since I know that to be true, what right do I have to remind God of what I've given Him? No, I'm just going to stay very thankful that Jesus chose to give me *His* life. The least He can expect from me is my obedience!

This is how you live life on a highway of blessing, for obedience is the paramount characteristic of the person whom God blesses. The moment you become willing to put your life on the altar, then God can have His way. You have laid the cornerstone — now you can build a successful life in Him on the bedrock of obedience!

PRINCIPLES FOR
OBEDIENCE: THE CORNERSTONE
TO GODLY CHARACTER

✰ The refusal to conquer negativity will ensure that it ultimately becomes our master.

✰ In the realm of obedience, there is no middle ground.

✰ A Person of Character continually expresses gratitude, which flows from a thankful heart.

✰ A Person of Character pursues the opportunity to give honor to whom honor is due.

✰ A Person of Character frequently checks his foundations in life to ensure that his ethics always exceed the temptations of compromise.

✰ A disciplined lifestyle is not something that is done *to* us; it is something that is done *for* us.

✰ A Person of Character will always place Heaven's requests before his own desires.

✰ The Person of Character proves the Lordship of Christ through compliance to His divine commands.

✰ A Person of Character bases his life on his all-encompassing love for God.

✰ Accuracy must become a pursuit in order to protect God's Word in our lives.

✰ The Person of Character understands that obedience is not just *desired*; it is *required*.

★ Obedience is the only proof that you have faith in God.

★ The Person of Character makes sure that his every word and deed reflects God's will for his life.

★ A Person of Character knows that the prize is always greater than the price.

★ God has called every man to greatness, but the only ones who will achieve it are the ones who will use their time to receive it.

★ A Person of Character protects and esteems all the authorities God has placed in his life.

★ God isn't continually measuring our maturity level; His eyes are fixed upon our compliance.

★ If we are ever to be pleasing, there can never be any strings that bind the purse to our compliance.

NOTES:

_____

_____

_____

_____

_____

_____

NOTES:

_____

_____

_____

_____

_____

_____

_____

_____

_____

_____

_____

_____

_____

_____

_____

_____

_____

_____

_____

_____

_____

_____

_____

_____

_____

CHAPTER EIGHT

GOD'S WAY OF RELATING TO AUTHORITY

Once you lay the cornerstone of obedience in your life, you will immediately be confronted with the issue of submission. How will you respond to those in authority over you — especially in situations when you don't want to do what you have been asked to do?

That's why we need to take this subject of obedience and submission further and discuss what God says about relating to authority. We simply cannot ignore this subject, for until we set this foundational cornerstone firmly in place, everything else we try to build in our lives will be vulnerable to the devil's attacks. The moment we start getting somewhere — just about the time when promotion is right around the corner — the enemy will find a way to knock down what we have worked so hard to build and take us back to square one.

In the arena of developing godly character, the issue of relating to authority is perhaps the most difficult to comprehend and apply to our lives. This is especially true in our modern-day society.

Today's generation of young people is growing up even more individualistic-minded and rebellious than the generation that grew up before them. Young people are advancing toward adulthood as single units rather than as members of a team. More and more they sit in front of their computer screens and relate electronically to other people rather than in face-to-face encounters. Many don't even look for opportunities to develop relationships within a team setting where they can learn from and share experiences with a variety of people. As a result, an entire generation is being raised up with an extremely self-centered mindset that disdains authority — presenting a tremendous challenge for us as a society in the days to come.

Many adults, including Christians, have also gotten sucked into this self-centered, rebellious mindset that is so prevalent in society today. They don't have any trouble believing that if they drive 95 miles an hour in a 55-mile-an-hour speed zone, they will probably get a ticket. But somehow they have the idea that God doesn't rule in every area of their lives. They assume they can escape the consequences of violating spiritual laws because the spiritual realm can't be seen with their natural eyes.

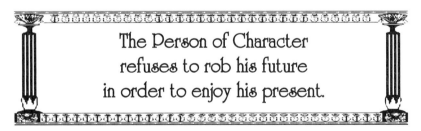

The Person of Character
refuses to rob his future
in order to enjoy his present.

Here is what these Christians fail to understand: *Everything in God's realm is prolonged.* There is a prolonged season of sowing seed, and there is a prolonged season of reaping the harvest. However, because it *is* a prolonged harvest, a person often won't notice the cause-

and-effect connection between the seed he sowed years ago and the negative consequences he is currently reaping. He doesn't realize he is experiencing a harvest from his own past seeds of rebellion. The reaping has been so long in coming that he doesn't put the two together.

This is why it is so important to trust that what God has said to us in His Word is the truth. If He says we will reap what we sow, then sooner or later, that is exactly what we will do.

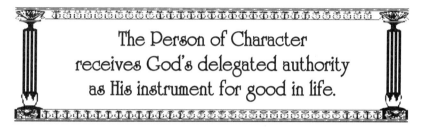

The Person of Character
receives God's delegated authority
as His instrument for good in life.

The trump card often used by willful and headstrong people is the word "control." When they don't want to do what the person God has placed over them has suggested that they do, they lash out with the accusation, "You're just trying to control me!"

But when a person in a leadership position asks someone under him to do something that is line with the Word of God, is that leader controlling the other person? No, for it is the Holy Spirit who wants to lead that person to do right. The leader is only operating in his God-given position. He is God's instrument in helping that person become all God has called him to be.

Notice that word "lead." When we lead an animal, we put a leash around its neck so we can cause the animal to go where it does not want to go. Yet many times, we assume that when the Holy Spirit leads *us*, it is always where we want to go. However, this just doesn't make sense. If we were already headed in the correct direction, the Holy Spirit wouldn't have to lead us, since our original intention would be to do the right thing!

Romans 13:1-5 (*NIV*) confirms that it is God who established a specific authority structure on this earth:

> **Everyone must submit himself to the governing authorities, for there is no authority except that which God has established. The authorities that exist have been established by God.**
>
> **Consequently, he who rebels against the authority is rebelling against what God has instituted, and those who do so will bring judgment on themselves.**
>
> **For rulers hold no terror for those who do right, but for those who do wrong. Do you want to be free from fear of the one in authority? Then do what is right and he will commend you.**
>
> **For he is God's servant to do you good. But if you do wrong, be afraid, for he does not bear the sword for nothing. He is God's servant, an agent of wrath to bring punishment on the wrongdoer.**
>
> **Therefore, it is necessary to submit to the authorities, not only because of possible punishment but also because of conscience.**

Christians can apply these verses to every area of their lives: the workplace, their marriage, their children, their church family. Why are there so many breakdowns in relationship? Because people rebel against the authority structure that God has instituted!

Notice verse 4, where it says that a God-delegated authority "...is **God's servant to do you good**...."

Authorities are divine instruments on this earth because God is a God of order. And when operating according to the Word, those whom God has placed over us don't take away our freedom; rather, they help us stay out of bondage as we learn to walk in compliance with the Word as God intends.

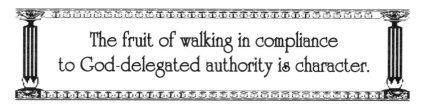

The fruit of walking in compliance to God-delegated authority is character.

People who use the "control" trump card are those who suffer from the "I" syndrome — a spiritual malady that finds its roots in pride and self-centeredness. When someone in authority gives these people instruction, they respond, "Well, that's not what God told *me*. He told *me* something different. God gave me a different vision, so I'm not going to do what you're telling me to do."

We can see the destruction to which this rebellious attitude leads in the written Word of God:

> **Don't be naive. There are difficult times ahead.**
>
> **As the end approaches, people are going to be self-absorbed, money-hungry, self-promoting, stuck-up, profane, contemptuous of parents, crude, coarse,**
>
> **dog-eat-dog, unbending, slanderers, impulsively wild, savage, cynical,**
>
> **treacherous, ruthless, bloated windbags, addicted to lust, and allergic to God.**

They'll make a show of religion, but behind the scenes they're animals. Stay clear of these people.

2 Timothy 3:1-5[6]

Verse 7 (*KJV*) tells us what happens to someone who does *not* stay clear of such people: That person enters a state of **"ever learning, and never able to come to the knowledge of the truth."**

What gets a person started in this destructive direction of pride and rebellion? *His attempt to bypass the authority structure that God has set up.* A person who fits this description has an unjustifiable sense of the importance of his own opinion. Everything he says is full of egotism, centered around "I" or "me." He has the attitude: "I can handle my own consequences. Nothing bad is going to happen to me because I can hear from God *myself.*"

If you can get a handle on this area of your character, you will win every time. If you can learn how to give up your rights to another according to God's ordained authority structure in your life, you'll become a person who always and inevitably comes out on top.

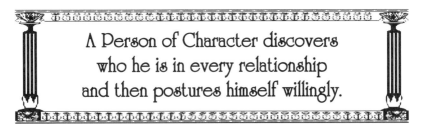

A Person of Character discovers
who he is in every relationship
and then postures himself willingly.

---

[6] Eugene H. Peterson, *The Message* (Colorado Springs: NavPress Publishing Group, 1993), pp. 527-528.

God has given us a posture to assume in every relationship in our lives. That posture is our link to God's favor through any given relationship. Therefore, when entering a new relationship, we have to understand who we are in that relationship and how to relate to the other person. Then we must posture ourselves in the relationship according to the responsibility God has given us in it.

For instance, I cannot act with the same authority before Peter Daniels that I do when I stand before my own congregation. I assume two different postures because these are two different types of relationships. I go before my congregation making statements, but I walk before Peter Daniels asking questions. Why? Because he is over me in the Lord.

This is the posture Romans 13:1 (*KJV*) tells us to take in regard to our superiors: **"Let every soul be subject unto the higher powers...."**. We are to be *subject* to those whom God has placed over us. That word "subject" means we are *to bow our own desires to their desires.*

The correct posture becomes much easier to assume in a relationship when we determine to stay faithful to our relationship with God as it pertains to that individual. For instance, I may get upset with a person with whom I have relationship, but I don't have the right to spout off in the flesh at him. I must relate to that person according to my relationship with God, and First Corinthians 4:2 tells me what God expects of me: **"Moreover it is required in stewards that one be found faithful."**

Paul didn't say that one had to be found eloquent, innovative, or possessing great leadership skills. He just said, "It is required among stewards that one be found *faithful.*" So that is my goal. My goal isn't to be the slickest person on the block or the sharpest pencil in the box. I just want to be found faithful. That is all I'm interested in.

When you look at this issue of relating to authority, relationship becomes very simple. *Whatever position you hold determines the posture you are to take.* And never forget this truth: It is equally as important to know who you are *not* as it is to know who you *are* in each and every relationship. As you come to understand and posture yourself according to your position in each of your relationships, God can then promote you to the next level in His plan for your life.

This principle is especially important in the marriage relationship. In marriages where no one is the boss or the wrong person has assumed the position of leader, utter chaos and dysfunction often prevails.

Many women have husbands who are poor leaders. These husbands may be carnal; they may not make very good decisions — and the list could go on and on. The wives often feel like they have to take the lead in the family because their husbands won't.

Nevertheless, it is the husband whom God has called to lead in the home. And since Romans 13:4 can be applied to every arena of authority, the Bible even tells the wife that her husband is God's minister to do her good as she submits to his leadership in her life.

God is the One who has placed the husband and wife in their respective positions in the marriage relationship. Thus, those positions do not change depending on how well each individual fulfills his or her God-ordained role.

For instance, if Linda didn't have to fulfill her role as a wife to me, she would still have to do it for someone else. Her life doesn't change because I am here. God has still called her to take the position of a wife in the marriage relationship. In the same way, if Linda wasn't in my life and I was married to someone else, I would still be called to fulfill my role as a husband. My role doesn't change just because I am relating to a different person.

This same principle is true in every realm of life. The posture we are to assume in our relationships with our superiors doesn't change depending on how well they exercise their authority in our lives. Whether they are easy or very difficult to submit to, they still occupy that leadership position and we are still called to relate to them according to God's principle of obedience and submission.

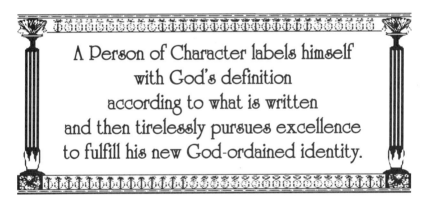

A Person of Character labels himself
with God's definition
according to what is written
and then tirelessly pursues excellence
to fulfill his new God-ordained identity.

Whether you are a husband or wife, father or mother, son or daughter, employer or employee, you will find a definition of who you are in the Scriptures. This is why you need to define who you are in every one of your relationships and then posture yourself accordingly. You will never find success in your pursuit of excellent character until you have taken this step.

Proverbs 29:18 (*NIV*) says, **"Where there is no revelation, the people cast off restraint...."** When we have no revelation of how God wants us to posture ourselves in our relationships, we begin to cast off restraint, disrespecting and trespassing boundaries in those relationships. Therefore, we must search the Scriptures and allow the Word of God to reveal to us the specific role we are to fulfill in each relationship.

Only a very small percentage of Christians even attempt to fulfill the role God has given them in their relationships. But life becomes very simple when people come to understand the parameters of their lives and stop looking over the fence, wishing they were something they are not.

Everything becomes easier in our lives when we understand our boundaries and operate accordingly. For instance, I have boundaries as a husband. I make a great husband, but I don't make a great wife — and I certainly don't make a great God!

Because I understand the importance of defining one's parameters in life, I don't try to mold the people around me into what I want them to be. Instead, I try to encourage people to be who God has called them to be as defined by the written Word of God.

To be who God has called you to be — that should be your constant aim as well. You should be continually searching the Word as you ask this question in your heart: *God, what is it that You have said about me?*

In Hebrews 10:7, these words of Jesus are recorded:

"Then I said, 'Behold, I have come — in the volume of the book it is written of Me — to do Your will, O God.'"

Jesus was able to define who He was by discovering what was written in the Book concerning Him. Similarly, it is written in the Book concerning you as well. You don't have to go through a big identity crisis as you try to "find yourself." God tells you who you are, and He gives you the desire and the opportunity to become who He has made you to be.

The stakes are extremely high regarding this issue, for the outcome of your life will be based on how much you embrace of what God says about you. Certainly that includes fulfilling your God-ordained role in every relationship of life.

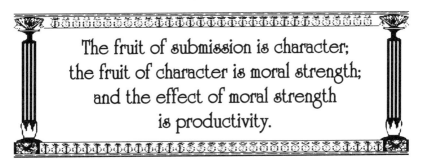

The fruit of submission is character;
the fruit of character is moral strength;
and the effect of moral strength
is productivity.

Whenever you willingly submit to the authorities God has placed over you, character is the harvest that will come forth in your life. Why? Because those over you will often ask you to do things you don't want to do, and character is only developed as you willingly fulfill those undesired assignments.

Character is *not* developed by doing whatever *you* want to do — unless, of course, you have previously fulfilled your present assignments. It is only when you have left no assignments undone that you can ever experience the satisfaction of completion and the joy of being pleasing.

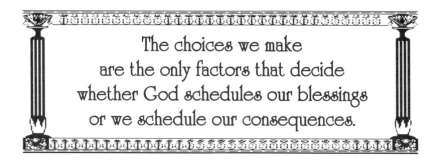

The choices we make
are the only factors that decide
whether God schedules our blessings
or we schedule our consequences.

But what if we *don't* fulfill our role in relationship with those whom God has placed in charge in every area of our lives? Make no mistake — there *are* consequences to the way we act toward them. If we don't live up to God's standard of submission and obedience, a day will come when we will not be allowed to remain in the presence of our superiors any longer.

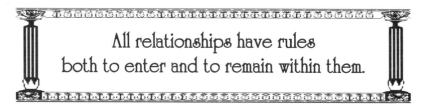

All relationships have rules
both to enter and to remain within them.

One way people disqualify themselves is by continually challenging their superiors. That is a manifestation of that "spirit of Absalom" we talked about earlier. When a person challenges his superior, he may cause the authority to back off for a while. But whenever an authority is backed into a corner like that, a day will come when he responds. And when he does, the person he is responding to will definitely *not* enjoy the outcome!

Remember, God says that those whom He has placed within our lives to lead us do not bear the sword in vain. That means God has not scheduled our destruction, but He *has* scheduled the consequences of our choices. If our superiors have to use the "sword" on us, we will know that we did not qualify for God's rewards.

God has scheduled the benefits I will enjoy if I love my wife as Christ loves the Church. He has also scheduled the negative consequences of my failure to love her. God tells me, "This is the consequence if you fail to love your wife: You will have trouble in this life." That is why I'm not interested in what Linda does or does not do in her role as wife. Her performance is not my responsibility. My job is to make certain that I fulfill *my* role as husband so I can enjoy the benefits of my obedience to God!

God cannot change the consequences of our choices, for consequences are dictated by the universal law of sowing and reaping. If we choose to be disobedient and unsubmissive to authority, our rebellion has an emotional hand grenade tied to it that will eventually explode and bring destruction into our lives and possibly the lives of those around us.

I realize that every day I am having an effect in the lives of those who are close to me. If that effect isn't a positive one in a given relationship, then I don't qualify for that relationship. Knowing this to be true, my prayer is that my friends and my superiors will confront me and tell me what I need to do to change — and I better be willing to make the needed changes.

This is the attitude God requires all of us to maintain in our relationships. For instance, look at these two scriptures:

Open rebuke is better than love carefully concealed.

Faithful are the wounds of a friend, but the kisses of an enemy are deceitful.

Proverbs 27:5,6

Let the righteous strike me; it shall be a kindness. And let him rebuke me; it shall be as excellent oil; let my head not refuse it.

Psalm 141:5

Remember, the Bible says, **"If you are willing and obedient, you shall eat the good of the land"** (Isa. 1:19). Christians want to eat the good of the land. However, most of them are not eating well at all, and I can tell you why: *They are not willing to submit to authority.* The minute a superior has a conversation with them about needed change, they consider it a lecture and get offended.

The Person of Character responds to authority as those appointed by God Himself.

Let's look again at Romans 13 so we can find out how God wants us to view those whom He has placed over us in life. First, verse 1 tells us that all legitimate authority in this world comes from God:

Let every soul be subject to the governing authorities. For there is no authority except from God, and the authorities that exist are appointed by God.

Every authority in every arena of life comes from the Lord. Psalm 115:16 backs up this truth: **"The heaven,** even the heavens, are the Lord's; but the earth He has given to the children of men."

This doesn't necessarily mean that every individual is God's choice for the leadership positions He has established. For instance, in the realm of government, He creates the office because He is a God of government and of order. Then it is our responsibility to make the right choice regarding who fills that position so we can live in peace and our children can live in safety.

As a side note, you would do well to remember this particular aspect of God's nature in your own pursuit toward excellent character. Because He is a God of order, any movement toward order in your personal life will bring productivity and cause you to grow spiritually. Even the simplest step toward order can make an enormous difference. For instance, the moment you refuse to leave your bedroom in the morning without first making your bed, you have taken a step toward a life that is defined by order.

So God creates the governmental office, but He does not vote in the person who will fill that office. People do that. This is very important for us to understand; otherwise, we might be tempted to suggest that God is the One who put into office an unjust ruler. But God doesn't schedule pain in our lives; we do it to ourselves through our own wrong choices.

In the realm of government, we determine who will fill a particular office of authority when we participate — or fail to participate — in the voting process. And we should never complain about what we permit!

Romans 13:1 does not just apply to governmental authorities. *Every* leadership position that exists on this earth is appointed by God. Without this understanding of God's established authority structure on this earth, you and I will never go any further in the development of our character. We must accept that this is the way God put His plan into play and that He did it for an important purpose.

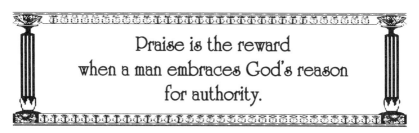

Praise is the reward
when a man embraces God's reason
for authority.

We find God's purpose for authority in First Peter 2:13,14:

> **Therefore submit yourselves to every ordinance of man for the Lord's sake, whether to the king as supreme,**
> **or to governors, as to those who are sent by him for the punishment of evildoers and for the praise of those who do good.**

Notice the reason God places people in positions of leadership: "**...for the punishment of evildoers and for the praise of those who do good.**" Ecclesiastes 8:11 gives us more insight into the divine purpose for authority:

> **Because the sentence against an evil work is not executed speedily, therefore the heart of the sons of men is fully set in them to do evil.**

Unless the punishment for wrongdoing is carried out quickly, the hearts of men will turn completely to evil schemes. They will start thinking about how to do things wrong. This is exactly the reason why there is so much chaos and destruction at this present time in man's history: There is often no retribution for wrongdoing. And when people actually do suffer legitimate consequences for their wrong choices, they act like victims instead of perpetrators.

"How dare they say I can't write graffiti on that wall! My rights are being violated!"

But a person's poor response to governmental authority does not change the fact that he is liable to receive punishment for his wrong deed. That is why Paul tells believers, **"Therefore submit yourselves to every ordinance of man for the Lord's sake...."** People need to see that believers are willingly submitting to the legitimate "higher powers" — *not* adopting a worse attitude toward those who are over them than people out in the world!

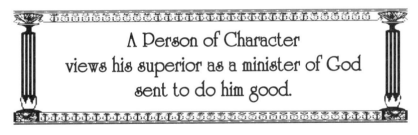

A Person of Character
views his superior as a minister of God
sent to do him good.

Three separate times in Romans 13:4-6, authorities are called *ministers of God*. This principle is true in every arena: Authority is a minister of God in our lives to reward us when we are compliant and to get us back on track when we go astray.

Why is it so important to understand this? Because if we don't adjust our thinking in this area, our thinking will be off-base in other areas of our lives as well. But if we start relating to our authorities as God's ministers for our good, God will then help us when we make errors in judgment. He will get us out of the messes we make for ourselves just because we have obedient hearts.

On the other hand, we cannot remain rebellious and disobedient to authority and then expect God to move on our behalf to deliver us from our self-imposed difficulties. After all, disobedience was the source of our problem in the first place!

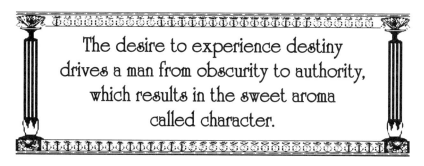

The desire to experience destiny drives a man from obscurity to authority, which results in the sweet aroma called character.

From the very beginning, God has delegated authority. Genesis 2:15-18 is the first instance we see of this:

> **Then the Lord God took the man and put him in the garden of Eden to tend and keep it.**
>
> **And the Lord God commanded the man, saying, "Of every tree of the garden you may freely eat;**
>
> **but of the tree of the knowledge of good and evil you shall not eat, for in the day that you eat of it you shall surely die."**
>
> **And the Lord God said, "It is not good that man should be alone; I will make him a helper comparable to him."**

The Lord God formed man and put him in the midst of the Garden for a purpose: to delegate His authority over the earth to the man and to command him to dress and keep it. From that moment on, Adam was responsible for the earth and could do with it what he wanted.

So why didn't God step in and intervene when Adam chose to give the earth away to the devil? Because He had put man in charge, and He wasn't going to violate the order of authority He had established on the earth.

God has continued to delegate His authority ever since by putting people in charge of what He initiates. He also still refuses to intervene in a situation where He has delegated His authority to man.

"But if the Lord wanted to change things in my life, He'd just change them."

No, He put *you* in charge. If an area of your life needs to be changed, *you* have to change it because you're in charge. God isn't going to do it for you.

Many husbands would love it if God talked to their wives instead of to them about the changes that need to take place in their homes. But God is not going to do that because He has already given His delegated authority to the husband.

I remember one time when Linda and I were having a difficult time in our marriage. Suffice it to say that our marriage was not a well-oiled machine at that time! It was as if I was speaking a foreign language that Linda didn't understand.

One day during a particularly dynamic conversation between the two of us, I decided to go AWOL from the front lines of battle by taking a shower.

I'm warning you — don't go into the shower stall if you don't want God to speak to you. I found out that He is in the shower too! We simply cannot get away from God when He wants to talk to us.

I remember well what God spoke to my heart as I stood in the shower that day. He said, "I want you to go and tell Linda that she is having a problem with you at this moment because she is having a problem with *Me*."

With as much respect as I could muster, I asked, "Lord, why don't *You* tell her?" At that moment, I did *not* want to say anything that might add fuel to the fire!

The Lord replied, "Because you're in charge."

"Can't You put someone else in charge right now?"

There was no answer. So I got out of the shower, got dressed, and gingerly made my way to the top of the staircase. Linda stood at the bottom of the stairs, looking up at me. I mentally made a note of nearby rooms to which I could make a quick getaway and lock the door if needed. Then I said to my wife, "Sweetheart, the Lord just spoke to me and told me the reason you are having trouble with me at this moment is that you're having trouble with *Him*."

Much to my surprise, Linda began to cry. Then she said, "That's true. I've known it all along."

Linda may have known it all along, but until I assumed my place of authority, the problem in our marriage could not get fixed.

The same principle holds true in every area of our lives. The problems we face can't be fixed until we take the place of authority God has delegated to us and become who God has called us to be. As long as we fail to do that, the devil will accommodate us by taking the place of authority in our lives that we have left vacant.

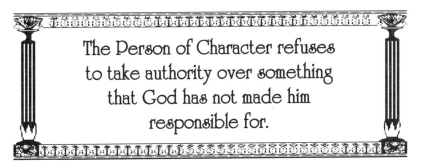

The Person of Character refuses to take authority over something that God has not made him responsible for.

Every authority appointed by God has a jurisdiction. "Jurisdiction" can be defined as *authority and power based on right*. In other words, jurisdiction refers to *authorized power and responsibility*. It also refers to those areas and spheres over which such authority can be exercised — boundaries defined in His Word that are not to be violated. That means there are people God has placed in our lives who have jurisdiction in one area but none in other areas.

Upon close examination, we will find that the majority of strife and conflict in the Church and in the world comes as a direct result of jurisdictional principles and boundaries being violated in some way. What are these principles of jurisdictional authority that God has placed in effect?

First, the leader of any jurisdiction:

1. Has final authority over his jurisdiction.

2. Has the authority to delegate and designate subordinate jurisdictions, if need be.

3. Has the responsibility to effectively communicate God's Word, wisdom, and direction to those within his jurisdiction.

4. Will be ultimately accountable to God for how he exercises his authority and oversees his jurisdiction.

Second, all those who function within any given jurisdiction have the responsibility to:

1. Honor and respect their leader(s).

2. Have a submissive heart toward their leader(s).

3. Obey and follow their leader, imitating him in both word and deed, as long as what he speaks and does is not contrary to the Word of God.

God Himself follows these jurisdictional principles.

1. As Creator of the universe, He has all authority and jurisdiction over all things (Gen. 1:1-3).

2. All things are upheld (held together and remain intact) by Him and in Him (Col. 1:16,17 *AMP*; Heb. 1:3 *AMP*).

3. God the Father has chosen to give all authority to Jesus (Matt. 28:18).

It is apparent that Jesus was a Man under authority who followed jurisdictional principles. Look at what He said in John 12:49,50 (*AMP*):

...I have never spoken on My own authority or of My own accord or as self-appointed, but the Father Who sent Me has Himself given Me orders [concerning] what to say and what to tell.

And I know that His commandment is (means) eternal life. So whatever I speak, I am saying [exactly] what My Father has told Me to say and in accordance with His instructions.

It is imperative that you remember two key principles when dealing with matters of jurisdiction:

1. Be diligent to discover, understand, and fulfill all your responsibilities within your given jurisdiction(s).

2. Never infringe upon or transgress jurisdictional boundaries. In other words:

   • Do not attempt to take charge or control in an area where responsibility has not been authorized to you.

   • Do not attempt to pass off to an unauthorized and unequipped person a duty or responsibility that is yours to fulfill.

   • If a responsibility is to be delegated, delegate it to someone within the same jurisdiction. It is not wise to cross jurisdictional boundaries and delegate that responsibility to another jurisdiction (e.g., the government declaring a "state religion," or children (under family jurisdiction) being raised or taught by the state (governmental jurisdiction).

God does not want jurisdictional boundaries to be transgressed. That is why I don't let myself get dragged into the family matters of my church members. Unless one of the spouses is violating the Word of God, I do not have jurisdiction in their personal family matters, and I refuse to extend my jurisdiction where I do not have the authority to do so.

It is important for you to understand this so you can know what to do when you face conflicting commands from different authorities in a particular situation. The first question to ask yourself in such a situation is this: *Does this person have the jurisdiction to give me this command?* Once you know the answer to that question, it becomes much easier to answer the next: *Should I submit to this person's authority in this situation?*

In Acts 4:18-20, Peter and John were commanded by Jewish leaders not to preach anymore in the Name of the Lord. At that moment, the two apostles had to decide who had jurisdictional authority over them in that situation. Look at their response:

> **And when they [the Jewish leaders] had summoned them, they commanded them not to speak or teach at all in the name of Jesus.**
> **But Peter and John answered and said to them, "Whether it is right in the sight of God to give heed to you rather than to God, you be the judge;**
> **for we cannot stop speaking what we have seen and heard."**
> **Acts 4:18-20 *NAS***

In essence, Peter and John were saying to the Jewish leaders, "Even though you have governmental authority, we have determined that we must submit to an even higher authority — God. Because you have crossed jurisdictional boundaries, we must obey God above all. Therefore, we will continue to obey what Jesus told us to do."

God only gives me the right to speak about what He has made me responsible for. He never gives me the right to speak about someone else's area of responsibility.

Whenever we attempt to exercise authority in a situation where God has not given us responsibility, we will not succeed. If we are not responsible for something, we need to keep ourselves clear of it.

People who have no stake in a situation are often the ones with the greatest amount of advice to give. That is why my advice almost has to be dragged out of me at times. I realize that what I think matters to someone else; therefore, I always make certain that what I am saying is in line with the Word and that God has given me the authority to speak into that situation.

Let's talk about the primary jurisdictions of authority that God has established in our lives. First, there is *parental authority*. Parents are entrusted by God to do what is right and to raise their children in the nurture and the admonition of the Lord (Eph. 6:4).

Our parents are in our lives to train us to serve the Lord and to promote us to a place where we can be used by God. Although the greatest thing we could ever have in our lives is a set of mature Christian parents, many of us do not have parents who fulfilled their God-ordained role in our lives. Yet even if our natural parents acquiesced their responsibility to raise us in the reverence of God, He is faithful to send a new set of spiritual parents into our lives to help us develop our character and to bring us to maturity. Our natural parents may not have taken their place of authority, but we are never forgotten or disqualified. God gives us a fresh start to "obey our parents in the Lord" (Eph. 6:1).

Second, there is *governmental jurisdiction*. God has actually ordained governmental authorities to act as His ministers to carry out justice on the earth. Let's look at Romans 13:3,4 once again:

> For rulers are not a terror to good works, but to evil. Do you want to be unafraid of the authority? Do what is good, and you will have praise from the same.
> For he is God's minister to you for good. But if you do evil, be afraid; for he does not bear the sword in vain; for he is God's minister, an avenger to execute wrath on him who practices evil.

At times someone will come to me and say, "Will you pray with me that God would help me get out of this lawsuit? I know what I did was wrong, but now I'm believing for Him to deliver me."

"But if you did what was wrong, you need to make restitution and pay up!"

"Oh, no, I'm believing that I won't have to pay anything. God is going to deliver me."

No, the Bible says God delivers the righteous who fear the Lord (Ps. 34:7,17) — not those who blatantly violate the law of the land and then expect to get away with it!

However, even though government officials are ministers of God for good and not for evil, there are times when man's laws are unjust according to the laws of God set down in Scripture. When that happens, God wants His people to appeal for an overturn of those unjust laws. You see, God never said He established man's system of laws; He said that He established the *positions* of authority.

Third, there is *church jurisdiction.* In this arena, heads of households voluntarily submit to the leadership of the church elders. However, God does not call the church elders to overstep their bounds by instructing someone who is under someone else's authority.

For instance, the elders are not to go beyond their jurisdiction by instructing wives or children to disregard the guidance and the wishes of the husband and father, as long as his instruction is consistent with Scripture. When the husband's instruction *is* inconsistent with Scripture, the church leaders should tell him what the Word says. But other than that, church leaders are not to circumvent the divine order of parental jurisdiction by taking a place of authority God did not give to them.

Finally, there is *vocational jurisdiction.* God tells employees to obey their employers with wholehearted service:

> **Servants (slaves), be obedient to those who are your physical masters, having respect for them and eager concern to please them, in singleness of motive and with all your heart, as [service] to Christ [Himself] —**
> **Not in the way of eye-service [as if they were watching you] and only to please men, but as servants (slaves) of Christ, doing the will of God heartily and with your whole soul;**
> **Rendering service readily with goodwill, as to the Lord and not to men,**

Knowing that for whatever good anyone does, he will receive his reward from the Lord, whether he is slave or free.

Ephesians 6:5-8 *AMP*

But what if the employer requires the employee to do something that is against the commandments of God or the biblical convictions of the employee? The same principles apply to any situation in which we are asked by an authority figure to violate the Word of God.

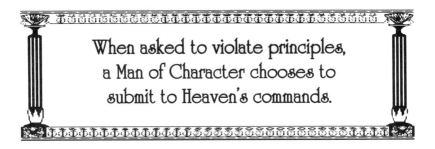

When asked to violate principles, a Man of Character chooses to submit to Heaven's commands.

As we saw in Acts 4, Peter and John chose to submit to a higher Power, God Himself, when a lower authority commanded them to disobey God's command to preach the Gospel. We must follow the same principle if we are ever told to do something that violates God's Word.

Colossians 3:23,24 provides the principle:

And whatever you do, do it heartily, AS TO THE LORD AND NOT TO MEN,
knowing that from the Lord you will receive the reward of the inheritance; for you serve the Lord Christ.

What are the steps we should take if someone over us asks us to do something contrary to the Word of God?

(1) Number one, *we must discipline our own poor attitude.* You see, as soon as we're asked to do something out of the will of God, that request immediately elicits a response from us. If our response is also contrary to the will of God, we suddenly become as guilty as the person who instructed us to do something wrong.

For instance, we might respond negatively, saying, "I don't agree with that person, so I'm not going to submit to him!" But remember, God never told us to submit *to* anyone. He told us to submit *to* Him *through* someone else. This is where we often make a grand mistake.

The truth is, ever since we were born to a certain set of parents, we couldn't choose the ones whom we wanted to obey. But we *can* choose whether or not we obey our authorities. Parentage is God's responsibility; obedience is ours. Regardless of what anyone else does, God still expects *us* to obey Philippians 2:12, which says, **"Work out your own salvation with fear and trembling; for it is God who works in you both to will and to do for His good pleasure."**

(2) Number two, *we must bring the matter before God and ask Him to intervene.*

"Yes, but what happens if God doesn't immediately change my situation?"

Jesus is our Example of how to respond when an authority figure steps across the line and betrays his or her position of authority in our lives. First Peter 2:23 tells us what Jesus did when He was faced with an extreme version of that situation:

Who, when He was reviled, did not revile in return; when He suffered, He did not threaten,

but committed Himself to Him who judges righteously.

As we discipline our attitudes and submit ourselves to the Father who judges righteously, He will be faithful to lead us to the other side of every difficult situation with our character unviolated and intact.

Number three, *we must appeal to authority through Scripture.* Second Timothy 3:16 tells us that **"all Scripture is given by inspiration of God, and is profitable for doctrine, for reproof, for correction, for instruction in righteousness."**

I really appreciate it when a person appeals to me with the Word of God. People who appeal to me with their opinions and their attitudes never get anywhere with me. But if both of us will submit ourselves to the Book, we'll arrive at a peaceable solution in every situation.

I'm very simple that way. I have trained myself so that if a person can show me the point he's trying to make in the Book, I'll immediately make the necessary adjustment. On the other hand, if that person is contending for a truth that isn't in God's Word — if he is doing nothing but sparring over opinions with me — that person has lost his opportunity to convince me of anything.

But when is it appropriate to appeal to those whom God has placed over us through Scripture?

First, we appeal to our authorities through the Scriptures if they fail to do their duty.

If a person has been placed in a leadership position, the responsibilities of that position are his to fulfill. He is never to leave ranks and acquiesce the position God has given him. If he attempts to do so, those who are under his authority should make an appeal according to the Word of God.

Second, we appeal to our authorities through the Scriptures if they go beyond their duty.

A leader goes beyond his duty as he begins to operate according to his own opinions rather than according to what God says in His Word. In that case, the leader will begin to tell those under him what *he* wants from them for his own personal benefit rather than what God's Word describes. When an authority steps out of his position in this way, he is in danger of promoting personality worship. At this point, he has gone beyond his duty, and an appeal made through Scripture is in order.

Lastly, we appeal to our authorities through the Scriptures if they ask us to compromise God's Holy Word.

When this happens in the workplace, the employee should make an appeal. If his appeal is denied and his convictions are continually violated, he should resign.

The employee might say, "Yes, but I need a job!"

No, that employee needs to trust God. God won't have any problem helping him find a better job. Jobs aren't the problem; people's unbelief is the problem. Many individuals continually violate their conscience at their place of employment because they are afraid they won't have enough money to live on if they resign.

That is a choice we all must make if we find ourselves in this kind of situation. Are we going to be obedient to God, trusting Him to provide another job, or are we going to live in fear that we won't have enough money?

Whichever choice we make is the one that will have power over our lives.

The bottom line is this: If a superior commands us to do things contrary to the Word of God or to the laws of man, he is operating outside his jurisdiction and has thus acquiesced his responsibility as our authority. God will therefore put us under another set of rules as we yield to a higher Power.

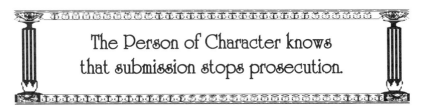

The Person of Character knows
that submission stops prosecution.

Now let's talk about those in leadership positions who require obedience from us in line with the Word of God. When we disobey God-given authority, we should expect the law of reaping to overtake us.

First Peter 1:17 (*NAS*) tells us that there is no favoritism with God. We will be judged on what we do in the body, whether good or bad, for God is no respecter of persons:

> **And if you address as Father the One who impartially judges according to each man's work, conduct yourselves in fear during the time of your stay upon earth.**

We make a mistake if we think that once we are saved, we don't have to be concerned any longer about what we do because we are already forgiven. In reality, God wants us to prove we belong to Him by the way we act — to live our lives from the inside and not according to the outside world. As we do that, we won't have to be told what is right or wrong. Instead, we will be self-correctors, discerning right from wrong and choosing to obey, even in the most challenging situations.

But what happens when we choose to disobey? Let's go back to Romans 13:2 and notice what Paul says about this:

Therefore whoever resists the authority resists the ordinance of God, and those who resist will bring judgment on themselves.

No one can submit for us; it is up to each of us to make that decision for ourselves. But God tells us in no uncertain terms what will happen if we resist authority: *We will inevitably bring judgment upon ourselves.*

I understood this principle even when I was a new Christian working at a delivery company. I can't tell you how many times my supervisors said to me, "I'm going to bury you, Thompson. Do you understand? You'll never make it."

I'd reply, "Sir, whatever your heart desires is exactly why I'm here today. I'm here to get you a promotion. That's the reason I exist this day — to make you better than you were before I walked in here."

A supervisor would say, "I'm going to get you."

"That's fine, Sir," I would answer. "Whatever you think about me is all right with me. I have nothing to say. But whatever it is you'd like for me to do, that's the reason I'm here."

Then the supervisor would ask another worker: "Have you delivered everything you were scheduled to deliver today?"

"Most of it, Sir."

"Well, you can just stop and go on home, because I'm giving Thompson the rest of your work."

I'd just say, "That's fine, Sir. Whatever you want me to do is just fine with me."

You might ask, "But how could you respond that way to those supervisors? They were being unjust!"

I understood even then that all authority comes from God. Therefore, whether or not my supervisors were just or unjust didn't matter to me. I was just interested in pleasing God, and I knew that when it comes to my walk with Him, He doesn't care how my superior relates to *me*; He cares about how *I* relate to my superior.

Many people speak disrespectfully of their superiors, saying things like, "My boss doesn't know anything. Why should I listen to him?" But I realized early on that if my superior didn't know anything, he wouldn't have been placed in a position over me. Someone must have believed he had what it took to be placed in that position of authority.

Therefore, how my supervisor behaved toward me didn't really matter to me. That was none of my business. It was my responsibility to study to be quiet and to do right as God had commanded me to do. God didn't tell me, "If the person over you ever acts unjustly toward you, you're allowed to disobey him." No, He told me to entrust myself to the Father who judges righteously as I willingly *obeyed*.

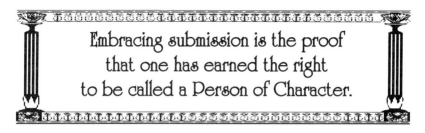

**Embracing submission is the proof
that one has earned the right
to be called a Person of Character.**

Our authorities in life have been appointed by God, but in one sense they are also chosen by us. We must choose those to whom we will give our hearts and willingly obey. Because our choice is involved, that means we can never say to God, "My superior is wrong in this situation, so I don't want to submit to him anymore!" It was our choice to submit to that authority to begin with, so we immediately condemn ourselves when we point our finger at the person who is over us.

Romans 2:1 warns us that God is very unhappy when we judge others in the Body of Christ. Since this is true in our relationships with our fellow believers, it is especially true in our relationships with our superiors!

> **Therefore you are inexcusable, O man, whoever you are who judge, for in whatever you judge another you condemn yourself; for you who judge practice the same things.**

Romans 14:4 says something similar:

> **Who are you to judge another's servant? To his own master he stands or falls. Indeed, he will be made to stand, for God is able to make him stand.**

I am *not* going to criticize those above me, because I know that God can make them stand. They are on a different level with Him than I am, so I yield to their wisdom. If they call to talk to me, I don't consider whether or not I want to listen to what they have to say. I am immediately available to talk to them. I refuse to show contempt in those relationships by making my superiors' presence in my life seem inconsequential.

We already looked at Romans 13:2 to find the consequences of resisting our God-ordained authorities. But notice the first part of this verse: "...Whoever resists the authority resists the ordinance of God...." Paul doesn't say we resist *God* when we resist those who are over us. He says we resist the *ordinance* (or *the order*) of God. God establishes the ordinance of willing submission to His authority structure; then we choose whether or not we obey or resist that divine command.

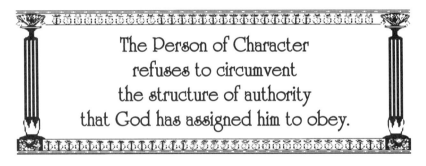

The Person of Character
refuses to circumvent
the structure of authority
that God has assigned him to obey.

I never want to cause God any pain or embarrassment. I want to make Him proud of me every day. I also don't want to force Him to send someone into my life to correct me. I would much rather correct myself.

However, in order for me to qualify to correct myself, I must deal with the problem before anyone else ever sees it and before someone else has been sent by God to deal with me.

Let's look again at First Peter 2:13,14 to see the reason God institutes authority into our lives:

> Therefore submit yourselves to every ordinance of man for the Lord's sake, whether to the king as supreme,
>
> or to governors, as to those who are sent by him for THE PUNISHMENT OF EVILDOERS and for THE PRAISE OF THOSE WHO DO GOOD.

Verse 14 tells us that God delegates to man the ability to give both demotions and promotions to those who are under his authority. Acts 13:1-4 (*NIV*) illustrates this principle within the jurisdiction of the church:

> In the church at Antioch there were prophets and teachers: Barnabas, Simeon called Niger, Lucius of Cyrene, Manaen (who had been brought up with Herod the tetrarch) and Saul.
>
> While they were worshiping the Lord and fasting, the Holy Spirit said, "Set apart for me Barnabas and Saul for the work to which I have called them."
>
> So after they had fasted and prayed, they placed their hands on them and sent them off.
>
> The two of them, sent on their way by the Holy Spirit, went down to Seleucia and sailed from there to Cyprus.

Notice that the Holy Ghost didn't send out Barnabas and Saul to fulfill their call to the ministry until the church elders had first sent them out.

When a person goes out into ministry before hands are laid on him, he circumvents the authority God has sent into his life either for punishment or for praise. This same principle applies to every other arena of life as well.

Now, we may wish it didn't work this way in God's Kingdom, but that doesn't change anything. This principle holds true no matter how many Christians float in and out of commitments and relationships saying, "Well, this is the way the Lord is leading me." That faulty way of thinking is still a lie, no matter how many people believe it.

Some Christians focus so much on the priesthood of the believer that they reject any concept of authority in their lives. However, I am personally convinced of the fact that the counterfeit side to the teaching on the priesthood of the believer is nothing more than the humanistic teaching of the supremacy of man. The establishment of an authority structure was *God's* idea. He is the One who injected authority into the equation. Nevertheless, ever since the Fall, man has been rebelling against the structures of authority in his life.

We can see this in modern society. Take Deon Sanders as an example. Deon was once the idol of many in the world of professional football. His picture was plastered everywhere. At the height of his rebellion, people adored the man. But then he got born again, and suddenly no one heard much about him anymore. Why? Because the world rejects God's authority to rule its affairs. Therefore, it does *not* want one of its heroes to be a man who has publicly surrendered his life to the Lord of lords!

I don't know if you think about these kinds of things, but I do. Why? Because I want to see how the principles in God's Word are demonstrated in everyday life on this earth.

The truth is, many times life will show us the truth of God's principles much more quickly than Christians will.

Christians often try to hide the consequences of their poor choices behind a façade of doing everything right. But life won't deceive us; it will show us the consequences of man's unregenerate nature right up front!

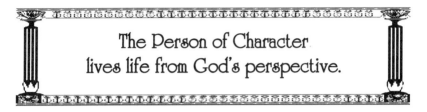

The Person of Character lives life from God's perspective.

In order to relate to the authorities in your life the way God expects you to, you can't ever live your life from your own perspective. Living your life from anything except *God's* perspective will lead to more pain than you ever want to deal with!

I know what I'm talking about, because I have lived through some of that pain. When Linda and I first began to date, I wasn't a very nice person. I saw life entirely from my own perspective and didn't really care what anyone else thought. My attitude was, "Listen, Sweetheart, if you don't see the train going the same direction I do, you need to transfer to another train!"

I did everything I could think of to make Linda reject me. But there was something really wonderful about this woman. She was everything I had ever needed or wanted and more.

Before we got married, Linda used to come to my house at six o'clock every morning to make me breakfast. She didn't have a car at that time, but she would ride her bike three and a half miles to where I worked every day to bring me a hot lunch. I decided, *I may have been born at night, but I wasn't born LAST night! I need to marry this woman so she doesn't get away!*

Then I got saved about a year and a half after Linda and I were married, and Linda was born again a month later. Suddenly I entered into an entirely new love for Linda that I couldn't explain. God put such a deep love for her in my heart that I would have done anything for her. I was head over heels in love with that lady, and I started showing my love to her in every way I could think of.

Things went fine for about a year. Then I began to notice that the woman who had always been so loving, so forgiving, and so understanding to me had suddenly acquired a "wicked witch of the west" broom, and she knew how to use it!

The truth of the matter is, Linda became a very difficult individual to live with at that time. Finally, I couldn't stand it any longer. I said to her, "Honey, please help me here. I need to ask you a question. While I was a stupid and uncaring person who treated you terribly, you loved me. You tolerated my behavior. You made me think there wasn't anyone in the world like you. I kept trying to get rid of you, and you kept bouncing back. You did everything for me that I could have possibly desired.

"Now I've changed. I can't imagine not having you in my life. I'm doing all I can to love you and take care of you. But all of a sudden, it seems like someone else has come to live in your body! What in the world happened to you? Why did you suddenly get rebellious when everything was going so great between us?"

Linda replied, *"Because now I know you're not going to leave me."*

What did my wife mean by that? She had been motivated to treat me well before I got saved because she was afraid I would leave her. But once she was convinced I had truly changed, she started feeling safe enough to let out all that hurt I had dispensed on her in the past.

Now, I'm not at all proud of the way I treated Linda before I got saved, nor am I proud of the effect my terrible behavior had on *her* behavior for a period of time. But there is an interesting point we need to understand here in order to get *God's* perspective on the situation. Even though I treated Linda the way I just described to you, she still didn't have the right to rebel against me as her husband. She disobeyed God the moment she did it.

That's why the Lord told me to relay a message to Linda that day I was standing in the shower. He said, "Tell her that she has a problem with *Me*, not with you." God had already told my wife in His Word what to do concerning her relationship with me as her husband: she was to submit, subject, and adapt herself to me as a service to the Lord. But she wanted to deal with me as a person rather than to live her relationship with me from God's point of view.

We can only pursue God's highest in life as we do everything from a divine perspective. That's how we avoid stumbling over offense every time we turn around, because we stop taking personally what others do or say. We know that God is the ultimate Authority and that His words do not change. Therefore, if our feelings get hurt, we just assume that those feelings were sitting in a place they shouldn't have been!

This is a crucial key to pursuing excellence in God. God has formed and created you to be an individual. You can choose to obey Him, no matter what other people do and say or how they treat you. You don't have to go down the tubes just because others may want to take you down with them. All you have to do is live every moment from God's perspective and walk in godly character. As you do, He *will* make a way for you to fulfill His plan in your life!

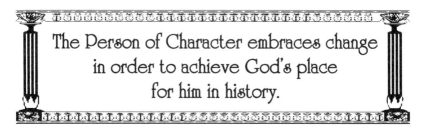

The Person of Character embraces change
in order to achieve God's place
for him in history.

We have talked about the importance of relating to authority according to the Word. But what if we are called to stand in a position of authority ourselves? What are God's character qualifications for leadership that we need to pursue?

In First Timothy 3:1-7, Paul provides a list of divine qualifications for authority:

> **This is a faithful saying: If a man desires the position of a bishop, he desires a good work.**
> **A bishop then must be blameless, the husband of one wife, temperate, sober-minded, of good behavior, hospitable, able to teach;**
> **not given to wine, not violent, not greedy for money, but gentle, not quarrelsome, not covetous;**
> **one who rules his own house well, having his children in submission with all reverence**
> **(for if a man does not know how to rule his own house, how will he take care of the church of God?);**
> **not a novice, lest being puffed up with pride he fall into the same condemnation as the devil.**

Moreover he must have a good testimony among those who are outside, lest he fall into reproach and the snare of the devil.

The word "bishop" in verse 1 is the word *episkope* and refers to *the ability to oversee.* Verse 1 goes on to say that if a person desires to be an overseer, he desires something good.

However, although it is good to aspire to the position of authority God has called you to fill, you need to understand this: The higher you go, the more your life means to people. The higher you go, the greater number of people will be affected by whether you succeed or fail. Consequently, the higher you go, the less vices God expects you to tolerate in your own life.

Personally, I am determined that those who look to me as an authority will never see me fall into sin. That is why I live my life in front of people, not behind them. That is why I'm not hiding anything behind closed doors.

This is what you must do as well in order to be a leader who walks in the character of God. You have to be willing to be transparent — to tell on yourself when necessary.

Every once in a while, I'll look in the mirror, point my finger at my image, and say, "I'm telling on you. You've been bad." Now, other people may not think that what I did was bad. But I know when I have compromised the principles I live by, and I'm not willing to fall short in my walk with God. I am well aware of the people I could adversely affect if I allowed myself any slack in my pursuit of excellent character.

The Apostle Paul taught this principle in Romans 14. He sums it up well in verse 13 (*NIV*):

Therefore let us stop passing judgment on one another. Instead, make up your mind not to put any stumbling block or obstacle in your brother's way.

Paul was saying in effect, "What I do matters to other people. Therefore, if something I do offends my brother, I will never do it again."

Too many Christians don't really care what others think about what they do. They're going to do what they do because they are "free in Jesus." They don't care if their freedom is another man's bondage.

But as I said, the more a person moves into leadership, the less freedom he has with God. I'm telling you, the path he walks gets *very* narrow! Why? Because God holds those whom He has called to lead His people to a greater accountability. When a person leads God's people, that person doesn't lead with the freedom to do anything he wants. He is bound to his divine call to live a life of discipline and love. God expects him to continually consider other people in the way he lives his life, for he no longer lives for himself, but for others.

Let's look at some of the specific characteristics that define a godly leader. First, First Timothy 3:2 says, **"A bishop then must be blameless, the husband of one wife...."** This last phrase has been taught incorrectly in the past — namely, that someone who has been divorced and then remarried cannot be a leader. But that isn't what this phrase means. It means that at this present time, this man is married to one woman and not committing adultery with someone else.

Verse 2 goes on to say that a godly leader must be **"...temperate, sober-minded, of good behavior...."** That word "sober" means he is of a *sound* mind. In other words, this leader doesn't go off on little tangents — the little sidetrack doctrines that periodically come along in the Body of Christ. Instead, he stays continually on the straight path of the Word. He sticks to that which is written and he never changes, for he is of a sound and sober mind.

Verse 3 goes on to say that a godly leader is **"not given to wine...."** Let me explain something to you about this subject of drinking alcoholic beverages, because there are so many different opinions regarding this issue in the Church today.

When a person becomes an apostle, evangelist, prophet, pastor, or teacher, he finds himself in a position of much greater influence than was previously the case. What he does in his life matters to more people than ever before, for he now has a position of authority in their lives.

Take this subject of drinking alcohol as an example. The Bible says that a person in a leadership position is not to drink — period. When God places that person in one of those five ministry offices, from that day forward he is never again to touch an alcoholic beverage.

This principle is actually found in Bathsheba's words to her son Solomon as he prepared to assume his role as king of Israel:

> **It is not for kings, O Lemuel, it is not for kings to drink wine, nor for princes intoxicating drink;**
> **Lest they drink and forget the law, and pervert the justice of all the afflicted.**
> **Proverbs 31:4,5**

In other words, this verse is saying, "If you want to be king, remember that you're in training. If you drink, you won't be able to perform the duties of the position to which God has promoted you."

Hosea 4:11 (*AMP*) tells us why this is true: **"Harlotry and wine and new wine take away the heart and the mind and the spiritual understanding."** In other words, drunkenness clouds one's judgment.

You see, Jesus never said that you couldn't have a drink or that having a drink is a sin. The Bible defines sin as not believing the Word. But His Word also says that alcohol clouds your judgment. Do you want clouded judgment? Or do you want to be fully trained for whatever role God is preparing you to take in His plans for the coming days?

Ephesians 5:18 (*KJV*) also has something to say about drinking alcohol: **"And be not drunk with wine, wherein is excess; but be filled with the Spirit."** Now, you might say, "All right, I won't be drunk with wine. But if I sit down and have a glass of wine with dinner, that's just fine. I have faith for it."

Let's go back to Romans 14 for a moment. Paul tells us that we have certain rights and liberties as believers. But Romans 14:20,21 (*NIV*) tells us that if our liberty causes our brother to stumble, we are to put away our liberty out of hearts motivated by love:

> **Do not destroy the work of God for the sake of food. All food is clean, but it is wrong for a man to eat anything that causes someone else to stumble.**

It is better not to eat meat or drink wine or to do anything else that will cause your brother to fall.

If what I do causes my brother to stumble, I don't count that as liberty any longer; I count it as bondage to the person I am offending. Therefore, by an act of my own will, I choose to put away my liberty to do anything that causes my brother to stumble in Christ. The day I entered the ministry was the last day I ever drank an alcoholic beverage, and I'll never drink one again in my entire life.

I hold to that standard because I know that many people who look to me as their spiritual leader come from an alcoholic background. Therefore, they cannot have leaders whose example might encourage them to return to their old habits.

There is a tremendous amount of freedom involved in my choice not to drink another alcoholic beverage. I'm so free that if I have to put away something like drinking alcohol forever, I'll just put it away forever.

That's how free we all need to be. If we're free to do something, we're also free *not* to do it. And when it comes to drinking alcohol, it's just better for us to stay away from it altogether rather than risk seeing a brother or sister in the Lord stumble due to our "freedom."

Verse 3 also says that one who aspires to be a godly leader should not be "greedy of money." In other words, everything doesn't revolve around his ability to receive monetary gain from other people. This person is in the ministry to help others and to minister for the Lord, *not* to satisfy his own selfish greed.

I can tell you from personal experience that there are *many* easier ways to make money than to be in the ministry! Money isn't the issue in ministry; *people's lives* are the issue. That is the way it must be for anyone who wants to qualify for a leadership position in the Body of Christ.

Let's look at one more characteristic that qualifies a godly leader:

> **One that ruleth his own house well, having his children in subjection with all gravity**
>
> **(for if a man does not know how to rule his own house, how will he take care of the church of God?).**
>
> 1 Timothy 3:4,5 *KJV*

Verse 4 says a person must be **"one that ruleth his own house well...."** The word "rule" is the Greek word *proistemi*, which means one who *governs, manages,* or *presides* over his house well. Paul goes on to say that a leader must keep **"...his children in subjection with all gravity."** The alternate word for the word "gravity" is the word "respect."

It unnerves me to see how many children in this modern age don't show respect toward others. But our children cannot fit that description if we ever aspire to be leaders or to enter the ministry. We must ensure that our children live lives of dignity and respect, never seeing themselves as being better than anyone else. In fact, that word "gravity" actually implies that our children must treat others as if they were royalty! And if they choose not to live in this manner as they grow toward adulthood, it will become increasingly difficult for them to remain in the God-centered home of their parents.

These are just some of the qualities that define a leader who walks in the character of God. Therefore, these are the qualities that must be developed in *us* whenever we are called to represent Jesus in the authority structure God has established on this earth.

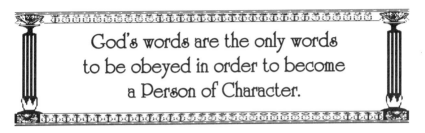

God's words are the only words
to be obeyed in order to become
a Person of Character.

Let me stress one more time: Satan is dedicated to causing you to slip up. He knows if he can get you stuck in the mire of rebellion against authority, you might sink so far in the muck that you never get out of it.

There is only one way to extricate yourself from the mire of disobedience and rebellion: You must rise above it by listening to God's truth rather than your own perspective. You have to realize that there is a difference between reality and truth. Truth never changes. No matter what argument you might have against the Word of God or against an authority who comes to you with the Word of God, the Word is still the truth. That is why you have to determine not to listen to any perspective that causes you to respond subjectively to your situation.

Subjectivity is the number-one attribute of immaturity, for it speaks of a person who is only interested in what matters to him as an individual. On the other hand, the number-one attribute of maturity is objectivity — the unselfish perspective of interdependence. In the case of relating to authority, the subjective person asks the question, "What do I get out of obeying my superior when I don't want to?" By contrast, the objective person asks the question, "How would my disobedience affect those around me?"

It is our choice. We must choose for ourselves whether or not we are going to obey. But if we will make the right choice and willingly submit to our authorities as God sets forth in His Word, we will begin to see a dramatic transformation take place in our lives. We will get rid of fear; we will feel safer than ever before; and joy will return to our lives in abundant measure. In other words, we will eat the best of the land!

PRINCIPLES REGARDING GOD'S WAY OF RELATING TO AUTHORITY

✯ **The Person of Character refuses to rob his future in order to enjoy his present.**

✯ **The Person of Character receives God's delegated authority as His instrument for good in life.**

✯ **The fruit of walking in compliance to God-delegated authority is character.**

✯ **A Person of Character discovers who he is in every relationship and then postures himself willingly.**

✯ **A Person of Character labels himself with God's definition according to what is written and then tirelessly pursues excellence to fulfill his new God-ordained identity.**

★ The fruit of submission is character; the fruit of character is moral strength; and the effect of moral strength is productivity.

★ The choices we make are the only factors that decide whether God schedules our blessings or we schedule our consequences.

★ All relationships have rules both to enter and to remain within them.

★ The Person of Character responds to authority as those appointed by God Himself.

★ Praise is the reward when a man embraces God's reason for authority.

★ A Person of Character views his superior as a minister of God sent to do him good.

★ The desire to experience destiny drives a man from obscurity to authority, which results in the sweet aroma called character.

★ The Person of Character refuses to take authority over something that God has not made him responsible for.

★ When asked to violate principles, a Man of Character chooses to submit to Heaven's commands.

★ The Person of Character knows that submission stops prosecution.

✫ Embracing submission is the proof that one has earned the right to be called a Person of Character.

✫ The Person of Character refuses to circumvent the structure of authority that God has assigned him to obey.

✫ The Person of Character lives life from God's perspective.

✫ The Person of Character embraces change in order to achieve God's place for him in history.

✫ God's words are the only words to be obeyed in order to become a Person of Character.

NOTES:

_____

_____

_____

_____

_____

_____

_____

_____

_____

_____

NOTES:

CHAPTER NINE

THE PILLAR OF TRUTHFULNESS

In our modern society where ethical relativism runs rampant, truthfulness remains one of the foundational pillars of life. It is simply not possible to walk in character without a lifelong commitment to speak and to live by the truth.

David understood this well, saying to the Lord in Psalm 51:6, **"Behold, You desire truth in the inward parts...."** Sadly, David learned this principle the hard way after choosing deception over truth in order to attain what his flesh had craved.

David's Psalm 51 prayer of repentance came after he had acknowledged his sin concerning Bathsheba — a sin committed at a time when he wasn't doing what he was supposed to do. The incident occurred in the spring, a time when kings normally went out to battle (2 Sam. 11:1). Nevertheless, David decided to stay at home — and while standing on the roof of his palace, he observed Bathsheba bathing.

This didn't happen just once or twice; in fact, we can't be sure how many times David was up on the roof watching Bathsheba bathe. But we do know this: A person can avoid a temptation after seeing it once; he can even avoid yielding to it after seeing it twice. But there comes a point after that person sees the same temptation a third time that he starts looking for it. He can say that he didn't mean to yield to it; he can say it was all a mistake. But in reality, he allowed his flesh to take him to a place he didn't really want to go.

This is what David did when he committed the sin of adultery with Bathsheba (*see* 2 Samuel 11). He watched her and lusted for her, knowing all the while that she was a faithful man's wife. Finally, he called for her to come to him at the king's palace. It wasn't long afterward that he learned Bathsheba was pregnant.

At that point, David could have chosen to acknowledge his wrongdoing and face the consequences of his sin in truth. But instead, he tried to use deception to cover up his sin. First, he brought Bathsheba's husband, Uriah, home from the battlefield in an attempt to get him to sleep with his wife. But Uriah, a man of honor, refused to enjoy the pleasures of marriage while his men were still out on the field fighting. So David looked for another way of deception to get himself out of his self-made mess: He secretly ordered his commander Joab to have Uriah the Hittite killed in battle.

This order must have infuriated the troops, for they were ordered to make a mistake on purpose that only inferior armies would make. Joab commanded them to pull back from fighting at a crucial moment in the battle, leaving a valiant man exposed to the onslaught of enemy forces.

Uriah had gone to the battlefield in the truth of his own heart. He didn't know the king he served had just betrayed him. But within moments of Joab's order for the troops to pull back, Uriah was slain in battle. It looked like David was off the hook.

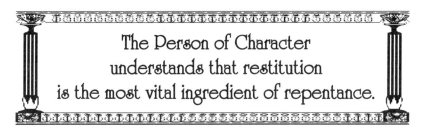

The Person of Character understands that restitution is the most vital ingredient of repentance.

But that isn't the way guilt leaves. Guilt doesn't leave when the people we have sinned against have left our lives. Guilt remains, for there is no true repentance until there is a wholehearted attempt at restitution.

Repentance doesn't mean we finally become willing to say, "I'm sorry" or even "Please forgive me." No, repentance without restitution is nothing at all but a Christian game.

There has to be some type of restorative process to show the person we have wronged that godly sorrow for our sin has struck us so deeply within that we are willing to make changes forever. This is what Paul is referring to in Second Corinthians 7:10 when he says, "...**Godly sorrow produces repentance leading to salvation, not to be regretted; but the sorrow of the world produces death.**"

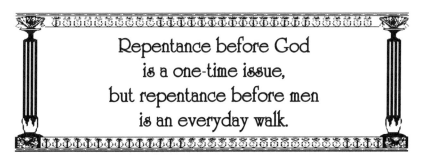

Repentance before God is a one-time issue, but repentance before men is an everyday walk.

We might try to squirm our way out of the responsibility of restitution by saying, "But I repented for what I did. That person just hasn't forgiven me." But if we have truly repented for what we did — if we are truly different now — it should be absolutely no problem whatsoever for us to go to the person we have wronged every day if necessary to let him know how much we need his love and acceptance.

David could have chosen the way of repentance and restitution after committing the sin of adultery with Bathsheba, but he chose instead to continue to deceive. As a result, his guilt increased immeasurably as he added the sin of murder to his account.

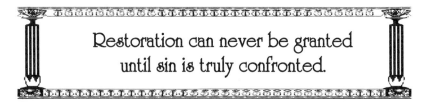

Restoration can never be granted
until sin is truly confronted.

David continued to cover up his sin for almost a year. Throughout that time, he lived outside of fellowship with God — an unfamiliar place to him before that time.

David didn't know what to do. Fear set in as he struggled inwardly with his dark secret. Yet as long as David remained in deception, refusing to confront his sin, he was incapable of receiving restoration from the Lord.

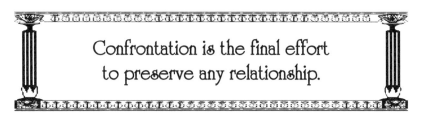

Confrontation is the final effort
to preserve any relationship.

Finally, God sent the prophet Nathan to confront the king with his thievery of another man's wife. The prophet began by telling David a story of a rich man who stole a poor man's beloved lamb.

After hearing Nathan's story about the rich man, David said, "**...The man who has done this shall surely die!**" (2 Sam. 12:5).

But Nathan immediately exclaimed, "*You* are the man!" (v. 6).

It was at this point that David finally stepped back into truth. Accepting without argument the accuracy of Nathan's words, David said, "**...I have sinned against the Lord**" (v. 13).

Nathan replied, "Because you have acknowledged your sin, you shall not die."

This was the moment when restoration could begin in David's life. There would still be consequences to endure for the sins he had committed. But his decision to acknowledge his sin opened the way for David's fellowship with God to be restored.

This, then, was the context in which David wrote Psalm 51:

> **Behold, You desire truth in the inward parts, and in the hidden part You will make me to know wisdom.**
> **Purge me with hyssop, and I shall be clean; wash me, and I shall be whiter than snow.**
> **Make me hear joy and gladness, that the bones You have broken may rejoice.**

> Hide Your face from my sins, and blot out all my iniquities.
>
> Create in me a clean heart, O God, and renew a steadfast spirit within me.
>
> **Psalm 51:6-10**

God desires for us to embrace truth in our innermost being. But before we can do that, we must first understand what truth *is*.

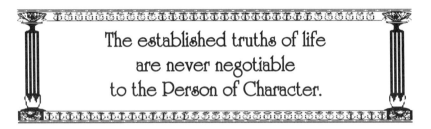

The established truths of life are never negotiable to the Person of Character.

The word "truth" comes from the Hebrew word *emeth*, which means *stability; certainty; right and sure.* It is derived from another word called *aman*, which means *to build up or support; to foster as a parent or nurse; to be firm and faithful;* or *to be permanent, steadfast, and verifiable.*

The dictionary says that truth includes the qualities of *loyalty, trustworthiness, sincerity, genuineness,* and *honesty.* Honesty is *the quality of being in accordance with the facts or with reality* or *the possession of an agreement with a standard.*

Setting a standard of truth in our lives is extremely important if we are to walk in the character of God. This implies that we must maintain a habitual adherence to accuracy in every situation.

In John 18:38, Pilate mockingly asked Jesus, "What is truth?" Jesus stayed silent as He stood before the

Roman governor. However, He had already answered that very question as He spoke to His disciples the night before: "...I am the way, the truth, and the life. No one comes to the Father except through Me" (John 14:6).

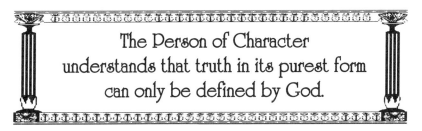

The Person of Character understands that truth in its purest form can only be defined by God.

Jesus is the very embodiment of truth. This means that truth isn't according to the way you or I see it. Truth is according to the way *God* sees it. We have to be willing to admit that someone else acted on the truth, even when we are embarrassed about our lack of doing the same. We must also be willing to admit when we have disagreed with someone who has spoken the truth just because we want to cover up our own weaknesses.

In Christendom, we play a game with each other — we all silently agree not to discuss the real issues. Our secret hope is that as long as no one discusses the real issues, those real issues do not exist as far as we are concerned.

But it doesn't work that way. The real issues exist whether we want to talk about them or not. Our short-comings and weaknesses exist whether we want to avoid them, discount them, or pretend they're not there. Regardless of what we do with truth, it remains an unchanging standard that continues throughout time. And it is only by truth that we can know God, for God *is* truth in His very essence. His principles don't slide up and down a scale of man's changing opinions and perspectives.

That is why I'm not interested in the standards of the Body of Christ. I want to examine everything Christians believe to be orthodox and sound in light of the Word of Truth. If I find out something isn't true, I will challenge it because I'm interested in *true* honesty, not in what the democracy of Christianity calls "honest."

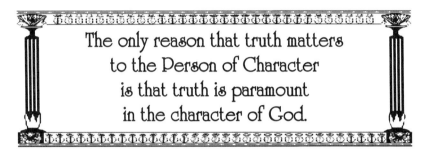

The only reason that truth matters
to the Person of Character
is that truth is paramount
in the character of God.

Why am I so adamant about this issue of truth? Because truth matters very much to God. Ananias and Sapphira were two people who found this out too late.

Ananias and Sapphira were members of the Early Church who watched as a man named Joseph was honored for his sacrificial giving to the Church. The apostles changed Joseph's name to Barnabas, meaning "son of consolation."

Ananias and Sapphira liked the idea of having their name changed, so they followed Barnabas' example. After selling a piece of land they owned, Ananias brought the proceeds to the apostle Peter and laid the money at his feet. There was one problem, however: The couple had privately agreed together to leave out a portion of the money for themselves, even though they told the apostles they were giving it all.

Now, Ananias and Sapphira didn't have to sell their land. And once they did sell it, they didn't have to tell the apostles they were giving the entire amount to the

Church. But they chose to deceive, making it seem like they were giving it all so they could look better than they really were.

I believe this last statement reflects one of the greatest problems the modern Church faces today. Christians spend all their time trying to look better than they really are rather than simply walking in transparency and truth!

So Ananias laid the money at Peter's feet under the assumption that the amount being given was the total price of the property sold. But Peter wasn't fooled.

> **But Peter said, "Ananias, why has Satan filled your heart to lie to the Holy Spirit and keep back part of the price of the land for yourself?**
> **"While it remained, was it not your own? And after it was sold, was it not in your own control? Why have you conceived this thing in your heart? You have not lied to men but to God."**
>
> **Acts 5:3,4**

Upon hearing Peter's words, Ananias fell to the ground dead. A few hours later, the same thing happened to Sapphira after she came in and agreed with her husband's lie.

You can see why truth needs to be as important to *us* as it is to *God*!

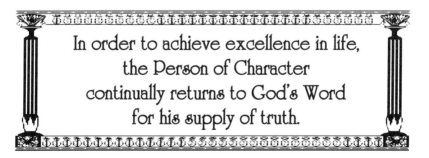

In order to achieve excellence in life, the Person of Character continually returns to God's Word for his supply of truth.

How do we accelerate our own personal pursuit of truth? By focusing our search on the sources of truth.

Number one, *God is truth.* Truth starts with God, for without Him, there exists no firm, absolute reference point, no unchanging truth.

Who [God] made heaven and earth, the sea, and all that is in them; who keeps truth forever.

Psalm 146:6

For the word of the Lord is right, and all His work is done in truth.

Psalm 33:4

He is the Rock, His work is perfect; for all His ways are justice, a God of truth and without injustice; righteous and upright is He.

Deuteronomy 32:4

God doesn't have integrity — He *is* integrity. The Bible says that it is *impossible* for Him to lie (Heb. 6:18; Titus 1:2):

"God is not a man, that He should lie, nor a son of man, that He should repent. Has He said, and will He not do? Or has He spoken, and will He not make it good?"

Numbers 23:19

We may try to walk in truth and integrity apart from God, but in reality, these qualities cannot exist apart from Him. Ultimately, if we try to base "truth" on a faulty or an incomplete belief system, we will not withstand the intense pressure of the ungodly culture that surrounds us.

Number two, *Jesus the Son of God is truth.* The apostle John declared this truth in John 1:14:

And the Word became flesh and dwelt among us, and we beheld His glory, the glory as of the only begotten of the Father, full of grace and truth.

As we already saw in John 14:6, Jesus Himself confirmed that He is the Source of truth:

"...I am the way, the truth, and the life. No one comes to the Father except through Me."

People may contend that there are other ways to gain access to God. But Jesus said, "You don't get to God without going through Me."

That is the unchanging truth, no matter what anyone else says. If a person doesn't have Jesus, who *is* the Way, the Truth, and the Life, that person doesn't have God. The world may try to crucify us for declaring this truth, but it is the truth nonetheless.

The Pharisees' words to Jesus in Matthew 22:16, although used in an attempt to trick Him, still reveal that the multitudes perceived Jesus' utter truthfulness:

And they sent to Him their disciples with the Herodians, saying, "Teacher, we know that You are true, and teach the way of God in truth...."

First Peter 2:22 (*KJV*) gives us further insight into Jesus' truthfulness: **"Who did no sin, neither was guile found in his mouth."** Jesus was completely void of all guile and deception. When He opened His mouth to speak, He spoke only words of truth.

Once again, we see this word "guile" used as the very antithesis of truth. I want to explain further what this word means, for guile is more than a lie. Even if a person tells a lie, he still may not fit the description of a person of guile.

A person of guile is someone who has systemically set up a framework of lies in his mind. That framework has become so established that it now defines the way he portrays himself in real life. He has told these lies to himself so much that he now believes they are the truth. He truly believes that his little framework of lies is the way things really are.

Thus, guile refers to the way a person lives his life. This is a person who has begun to believe his own press releases. He sees things only from his own perspective. In fact, he has set himself up as the truth. That presents a big problem for this person, for he now occupies a place in his heart reserved only for *the* Truth, Jesus Christ!

Number three, *the Holy Spirit is truth*. First John 5:6 specifically says, **"...It is the Spirit who bears witness, because THE SPIRIT IS TRUTH."** Then in John 16:13, the apostle John tells us that the Holy Spirit is our Guide out of deception into truth:

> **Howbeit when he, the Spirit of truth, is come, he will guide you into all truth: for he shall not speak of himself; but whatsoever he shall hear, that shall he speak: and he will shew you things to come.**

Number four, *God's Word is the truth*. Jesus confirmed this as He prayed to the Father in John 17:17 (*AMP*):

Sanctify them [purify, consecrate, separate them for Yourself, make them holy] by the Truth; Your Word is Truth.

The book of Psalms refers in several places to the absolute veracity of God's Word:

The law of the Lord is perfect, restoring the soul; the testimony of the Lord is sure, making wise the simple.

The precepts of the Lord are right, rejoicing the heart; the commandment of the Lord is pure, enlightening the eyes.

Psalm 19:7,8 *NAS*

Your righteousness is an everlasting righteousness, and Your law is truth.

Psalm 119:142

You are near, O Lord, and all Your commandments are truth.

Psalm 119:151

Number five, *the Gospel is the truth,* according to Colossians 1:5,6:

Because of the hope which is laid up for you in heaven, of which you heard before in the word of the truth of the gospel,

which has come to you, as it has also in all the world, and is bringing forth fruit, as it is also among you since the day you heard and knew the grace of God in truth.

When a person is lost in a desert, he looks for a source of pure water so he can quench his thirst and keep moving on to find a safe destination. The same principle applies to us as Christians. We are called to seek the Source of all truth, for only then can we quench our spiritual thirst in our hot pursuit for more of Him.

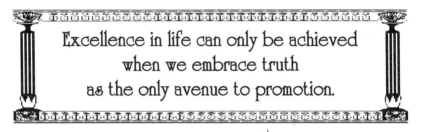

Excellence in life can only be achieved
when we embrace truth
as the only avenue to promotion.

There is great power in truth, for truth is Heaven's road to true promotion. It will never let us down. When we live in truth, we never have to remember what we lied about. We won't have to back up to the throne of God for our reward at the end of time. We will never have to use grace as our cover-up for doing wrong, as so many must do. Grace can then be used in our lives the way God originally intended — to provide us with the divine ability to fulfill His will on this earth while granting us the knowledge that our flawed humanity has been destroyed, covered, and made righteous.

I know how important it is to grab hold of truth, for I come from a long line of liars. I had family members who would tell any kind of lie they needed to tell in order to get what they wanted. Their attitude was, "It doesn't matter — just tell me what you want to hear, and I'll say it!"

That's the reason I stay so principle-oriented. I can't ease off God's principles for one second; I have to stay on my flesh all the time. Why? Because what my outer man learned when he was little is *not* the way I want him to act now that he is big!

Every one of us must keep our flesh in check. We cannot afford to step out of truth even for a second, for the older we get, the more our deceptions mean to other people. The more influential we become, the more our influence will trickle down to future generations. *What we say matters.* One lie is too many! One omission of truth is too much.

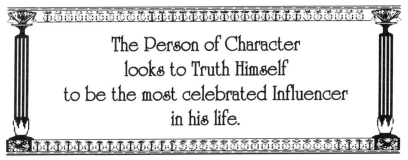

The Person of Character
looks to Truth Himself
to be the most celebrated Influencer
in his life.

Yes, there is power in truth — but what exactly does truth do for us in this life?

1. *Truth is what introduced us to our relationship with God.*

> **Of His own will He brought us forth by the word of truth, that we might be a kind of first-fruits of His creatures.**
>
> **James 1:18**

2. *Truth forces us into the light.*

> **But he who does the truth comes to the light, that his deeds may be clearly seen, that they have been done in God.**
>
> **John 3:21**

3. *Truth leads us to purify our soul.*

> **Since you have purified your souls in obeying the truth through the Spirit in sincere love of**

the brethren, love one another fervently with a pure heart.

1 Peter 1:22

4. *Truth demands our freedom in the courtroom of eternity.*

And you shall know the truth, and the truth shall make you free.

John 8:32

You can see whether or not a person is walking in truth. If he is bound up by a stronghold or a poor attitude, you can know that he lacks truth in his life.

5. *Truth is the interior light that guides our actions.*

Thy word is a lamp unto my feet, and a light unto my path.

Psalm 119:105 *KJV*

Oh, send out Your light and Your truth! Let them lead me....

Psalm 43:3

However, when He, the Spirit of truth, has come, He will guide you into all truth; for He will not speak on His own authority, but whatever He hears He will speak; and He will tell you things to come.

John 16:13

6. *Truth is the agent that cleanses us of iniquity.*

By mercy and truth iniquity is purged: and by the fear of the Lord men depart from evil.

Proverbs 16:6 *KJV*

7. *Truth causes us to be pursued by God.*

"But the hour is coming, and now is, when the true worshipers will worship the Father in spirit and truth; for the Father is seeking such to worship Him.

God is Spirit, and those who worship Him must worship in spirit and truth."

John 4:23,24

Too often people spend hours singing and worshiping God without ever getting anywhere near Heaven. What is their problem? They haven't allowed themselves to come to the point of truth before God.

If we want to truly worship God, we have to first get ourselves in a position of truth. In other words, we must be willing to unladen ourselves of anything that separates us from Him every time we come into His Presence.

8. *Truth preserves leaders.*

Mercy and truth preserve the king, and by lovingkindness he upholds his throne.

Proverbs 20:28

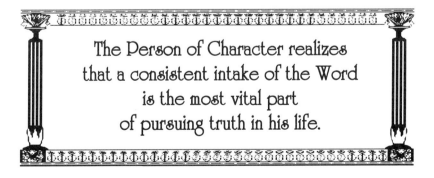

The Person of Character realizes
that a consistent intake of the Word
is the most vital part
of pursuing truth in his life.

How can you learn the truth? First, you have to understand this about yourself: *Your body and your mind are not you.* You need to get a handle on that fact, because your body and your mind have a tendency or a draw toward what is wrong.

You and I have a flaw within us that was given to us at the Fall — *a propensity toward deception.* Our natural tendency is to accept false ideas. In fact, according to Proverbs 14:12, the ways of death actually appeal to our human reasoning: **"There is a way that seems right to a man, but its end is the way of death."**

The bottom line is that we are easily deceived by the father of lies (John 8:44). That's why the intake of Bible doctrine is the most important habit we need to make in our pursuit of excellent character. Consistent intake of the Word of God every day, every day, *every day* is the only thing that will bring us to a point of truth in our lives.

We must therefore continually seek to learn truth by first *filling our souls with truth.*

Third John 2 says, **"Beloved, I pray that you may prosper in all things and be in health, just as your soul prospers."** Any growth or increase that happens in your life occurs only through soul prosperity. When your soul prospers in an area, that prosperity will then permeate your life from the inside out. From the abundance of your heart, your mouth will speak. Those words of faith will then push God's life out of your spirit and into the circumstances that surround you, causing the situation to line up with God's will.

Many Christians have tried to do it the opposite way. They think that just because they say what they desire, that means they have it. But James 1:21 tells us the way it really works in God's Kingdom:

Therefore lay aside all filthiness and overflow of wickedness, and receive with meekness the implanted word, which is able to save your souls.

In regard to any area of life, a person has to continually take nourishment from the Word into his soul. As his soul becomes filled with faith and the life of God, it will then force everything that is opposite to God's truth out of that area of his life.

Second Corinthians 10:4,5 gives us further insight on how to go about filling our souls with the Word:

For the weapons of our warfare are not carnal but mighty in God for pulling down strongholds,

casting down arguments and every high thing that exalts itself against the knowledge of God, bringing every thought into captivity to the obedience of Christ.

We have to commit ourselves to casting down natural reasonings and every imagination that exalts itself against the knowledge of God. Every moment of every day, we must determine to bring every thought into captivity, making it wholly obedient to Christ.

That is why we cannot focus on our outward circumstances; rather, we must continually look within. The life of God residing within us is the barometer of what will happen on the outside as long as we keep filling our souls with the Word and refuse to give up and quit.

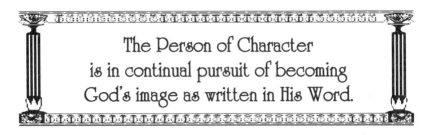

The Person of Character
is in continual pursuit of becoming
God's image as written in His Word.

Second, we grow in our knowledge of truth *by studying the truth.*

Study to shew thyself approved unto God, a workman that needeth not to be ashamed, rightly dividing the word of truth.

2 Timothy 2:15

Why is it so important to study the Word? Because others will see in our lives what we read in the Book. That's how the world is to identify us as Christians — by the profile of the new man described in the Word of God.

Peter calls this new man "the hidden man of the heart" (1 Peter 3:2). Paul calls him the "new creature" (2 Cor. 5:17). Regardless of what the new man is called, however, his entire profile is contained inside the Book. And as we diligently study that information, taking it deeply into our souls, we will eventually be transformed into what we read.

This is the way God designed for us to grow in the truth. We won't get anywhere in our walk with God if we pursue Him as if He were only an escape from the consequences of our own poor decision-making. We have to get serious about finding out who we are in Christ instead of continually talking about who we are *not.*

Some don't want to hear that. They say, "Yes, but you just don't know what's going on in my life!"

This is how I respond to people like that: "You have told me everything about who you used to be, but you haven't told me anything about who you are *now*. That's the information you need if you are ever going to walk in victory in your life. But you will only discover those truths by rightly dividing the Word of Truth and studying to show yourself approved unto God."

This, then, is the goal of pursuing truth in our lives: First Samuel 12:24 confirms this:

> **Only fear the Lord, and serve Him in truth with all your heart; for consider what great things He has done for you.**

Psalm 145:18 (*KJV*) tells us the rest of the story regarding the goal of pursuing truth:

> **The Lord is nigh unto all them that call upon him, to all that call upon him in truth.**

We pursue truth in order to draw near to God. If we truly love Him, that is all we need to know in order to make truth our lifelong pursuit.

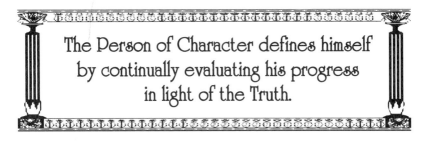

The Person of Character defines himself by continually evaluating his progress in light of the Truth.

I want to share with you a personal checklist I have developed to determine the level of my own commitment to walk in truth. You can use this same checklist to locate where *you* are right now in the pursuit of truth:

1. *Do I trust anyone enough to allow that person to point out my blind spots?*

In Genesis 18, we read about the time the Lord and two angels visited Abraham's home. During the visit, the Lord told Abraham, "Next year at this time Sarah will hold a son."

Sarah was standing unseen behind the door of a nearby tent when the Lord spoke those words, and when she heard what He said, she laughed silently to herself. When the Lord wanted to know why Sarah laughed, she protested, saying that she *didn't* laugh. But the Lord replied, "Yes, you *did* laugh."

I believe that Sarah didn't realize she had laughed. I certainly know there are things I do in my own life that I don't realize I do.

We all have blind spots in different areas of our lives that we have no idea about. That is why we have to be willing to trust someone enough to tell us that we "laughed." We need to come to the place of trust that says, "If you say I have a blind spot that I'm not recognizing, then it must be true because I know that you wouldn't lie to me. I'm going to take responsibility for it. I'm not going to deny it anymore."

We see that Sarah didn't live in denial forever. She came to trust the Lord's words so much that she was able conceive her son by faith:

> **By faith Sarah herself also received strength to conceive seed, and she bore a child when she was past the age, because she judged Him faithful who had promised.**
>
> **Hebrews 11:11**

We have to be willing to "judge Him faithful who has promised" as well — even when He points out our blind spots through another human being!

2. *Am I willing to confront my blind spots with the Word of God?*

Remember, we can never conquer what we are unwilling to confront. Every day we all must face our own Goliaths, whether the giant is our past, a habit, or a particular weakness we struggle with. Every day we have to deal with those issues because when we are weak, we are strong in Christ.

I face my own personal Goliaths every day on a regular basis. I am determined that they will not control me at the end of any day. Those giants will not steal even one hour from me, because I have made a quality decision to walk in truth in my life!

3. *Am I deceiving myself into believing that I am perfect and have no fault?*

It is the easiest thing in the world to start looking for someone else to blame for the negative things that happen in our lives. But God wants us to point the finger of accusation back at ourselves and allow Him to show us where *we* need to change.

4. *Do I think of myself more highly than I should think?*

Knowing who you are is only half of what it takes to walk in truth. You also have to know who you are *not* so you don't fall into the trap of pride and arrogance.

5. *Do I exaggerate my own abilities because I am embarrassed about my lack of the same?*

We are to strive to be all that God has created us to be — no less and no more. We don't have to lie to prove our worth, for God has already given us great value in His eyes.

6. *Do I tell only part of the truth so I can escape the consequences, avoid hurting someone, or protect myself?*

Truth is only truth when it is *all* the truth. We shouldn't deceive ourselves into thinking that an omission of the truth is any less than what it is — a lie.

7. *Do I flatter people to gain their approval?*

It is right for us to seek to please every person who is in authority over us in life. If we are not actively solving our authority's problems and making him feel good about his day, we are actually being a problem to him, for at any given moment, we are either problem-solvers or problem-creators. Until we understand this particular principle of relating to authority, we will never walk in truth.

So what is the difference between flattery and a compliment? The difference is so slight that you won't hear it; you will only see it. The difference is this: Someone who flatters does it because he wants something from the other person. Someone who compliments has no desire to take anything from the other person; he is just looking to *give*. Both people use exactly the same words, but their motives are different.

8. *Am I misrepresenting the Lord by harboring inconsistent or negative attitudes?*

When you rule your attitudes, you rule your own heart. That is extremely significant, because the Bible says a person who can rule his own spirit is greater than he who can take a city (Prov. 16:32). Think of it — if you learn how to rule your attitudes, you become greater in

God's eyes than a four-star general with an army at his command who is able to take an entire city by force!

9. *Do I give damaging reports about others in order to make myself look good?*

All these questions must be answered honestly if we are to erect the pillar of truthfulness in our lives. Like David, we must come to the place where we willingly say, "I have done wrong."

Each of us must go to the Word and prayerfully determine within ourselves whether we have been walking in truth or believing the enemy's lies. For instance, if we have been dealing with anger or resentment toward someone in authority over us, we need to recognize the problem for what it is: The spirit of Absalom has been operating in our lives, and it needs to be crucified.

But *wherever* we find deception dominating us in our lives, we must be willing to humble ourselves and make a change once and for all. It's time to come face-to-face with our old man and declare, "That person is *not* going to live here anymore. I will walk in truth in every area of my life!"

PRINCIPLES REGARDING THE PILLAR OF TRUTHFULNESS

✯ **The Person of Character understands that restitution is the most vital ingredient of repentance.**

✯ **Repentance before God is a one-time issue, but repentance before men is an everyday walk.**

✯ **Restoration can never be granted until sin is truly confronted.**

✯ Confrontation is the final effort to preserve any relationship.

✯ The established truths of life are never negotiable to the Person of Character.

✯ The Person of Character understands that truth in its purest form can only be defined by God.

✯ The only reason that truth matters to the Person of Character is that truth is paramount in the character of God.

✯ In order to achieve excellence in life, the Person of Character continually returns to God's Word for his supply of truth.

✯ Excellence in life can only be achieved when we embrace truth as the only avenue to promotion.

✯ The Person of Character looks to Truth Himself to be the most celebrated Influencer in his life.

✯ The Person of Character realizes that a consistent intake of the Word is the most vital part of pursuing truth in his life.

✯ The Person of Character is in continual pursuit of becoming God's image as written in His Word.

✯ The Person of Character defines himself by continually evaluating his progress in light of the Truth.

NOTES:

_____

_____

_____

_____

_____

_____

_____

_____

_____

_____

_____

_____

_____

_____

_____

_____

_____

_____

_____

NOTES:

CHAPTER TEN

BEING HONEST WITH YOURSELF

Don't expect your face-to-face encounter with the old man to be a simple "walk in the park." It is a good possibility that the person who is deceived more than anyone else about that old man is *you.*

How do I know that? Because a toxic "blameshifting victimitis" permeates the very air we breathe in this modern age. Humans are inventing new ways to spin and twist a lie in almost every area of life. They do this because they don't believe they can bear the pain or pay the price for being honest. Worst of all, they do this because they won't even tell *themselves* the truth.

A simple definition of honesty is this: It is *behavior in words and actions that aims to convey the truth.* As we discussed in the last chapter, it is an essential quality required of all those whom God calls His people.

Conversely, dishonesty is *a way of speaking or acting that causes people to be misled or deluded.* This deception continues until they are cheated out of something that belongs to them in the relationship.

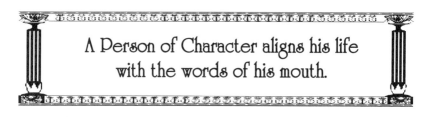

A Person of Character aligns his life
with the words of his mouth.

A person who doesn't tell himself the truth is not a person who acts according to truth. He may speak words that seem very kind. But in reality, he is more interested in convincing people that he is kind than he is in eliminating the lies that he perpetually tells himself.

So if you want to find out what a person's value is, don't just read his resume — watch what he *does*. Always listen with your *eyes*, not with your *ears*, for your eyes will tell you more than your ears will ever know.

The apostle Paul understood this principle:

> **Brethren, join in following my example, and observe those who walk according to the pattern you have in us.**
>
> **Philippians 3:18 *NAS***

A person who plays both sides of the fence at the same time is a dishonest person — self-preserving on one side while pretending to buy into everything you're saying on the other side. Watch out for a person like this, because this kind of behavior is only the beginning.

Next, this person will begin to cheat you out of the benefit of the Word you have sown in him as he fails to produce a harvest from the seed you have planted in his life. Suddenly you will notice that he has begun to cover up the truth of his situation not only from other people, but from himself as well.

That is exactly what happened with Adam and the first woman. They began to cover up and hide from each other. They no longer told each other the truth. In fact, the woman couldn't even tell the devil the truth! Instead, she added to the truth that Adam had previously told her.

What are you to do when you recognize a person who fits this description? Understand that he needs to return to the last level at which he was successful. That is where he should remain until he is ready to honestly face himself and allow God to bring about the necessary change for promotion.

You might say, "Yes, but I don't really like to do it that way. I like to promote everyone as soon as possible."

But it is unfair to try to force a person to grow who doesn't want to grow. On the other hand, it is also unfair to expect a person who wants to move on in life to pull someone else along who is undermining the vision for the first person's future!

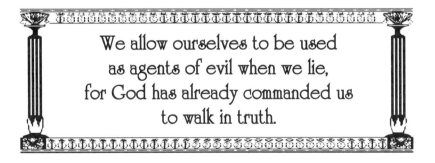

We allow ourselves to be used as agents of evil when we lie, for God has already commanded us to walk in truth.

I want you to understand that lying isn't just demonic — it is *satanic*. Jesus' words in John 8:44 confirm this:

You are of your father the devil, and the desires of your father you want to do. He was a

murderer from the beginning, and does not stand in the truth, because there is no truth in him. When he speaks a lie, he speaks from his own resources, for he is a liar and the father of it.

We might try to wiggle out of this sobering principle by saying, "Well, you know, I don't really lie. I just tell half-truths."

But people can actually be destroyed by half-truths. We see an example of this in Genesis 20, when Abraham got himself and his wife in potentially *big* trouble with one half-truth.

> And Abraham journeyed from there to the South, and dwelt between Kadesh and Shur, and stayed in Gerar.
>
> Now Abraham said of Sarah his wife, "She is my sister." And Abimelech king of Gerar sent and took Sarah.
>
> But God came to Abimelech in a dream by night, and said to him, "Indeed you are a dead man because of the woman whom you have taken, for she is a man's wife."
>
> But Abimelech had not come near her; and he said, "Lord, will You slay a righteous nation also?
>
> Did he not say to me, 'She is my sister'? And she, even she herself said, 'He is my brother.' In the integrity of my heart and innocence of my hands I have done this."
>
> And God said to him in a dream, "Yes, I know that you did this in the integrity of your heart. For I also withheld you from sinning against Me; therefore I did not let you touch her.

Now therefore, restore the man's wife; for he is a prophet, and he will pray for you and you shall live. But if you do not restore her, know that you shall surely die, you and all who are yours."

So Abimelech rose early in the morning, called all his servants, and told all these things in their hearing; and the men were very much afraid.

And Abimelech called Abraham and said to him, "What have you done to us? How have I offended you, that you have brought on me and on my kingdom a great sin? You have done deeds to me that ought not to be done."

Genesis 20:1-10

Abraham's response to Abimelech's question was in effect a casual "Sorry about that." Then Abraham went on to explain that he had told a partial truth — that Sarah was his sister — in an attempt to save himself in a foreign land from those who might desire his beautiful wife. But although Sarah *was* Abraham's half-sister, she was also his wife, and God was *not* happy with the results of Abraham's half-truth!

Personally, I would have been much sterner with Abraham if I had been in Abimelech's position. After all, Abraham almost got Abimelech killed as a result of that half-truth!

Have you ever noticed how nonchalant a person of half-truths can be? He doesn't really believe that he lies. He thinks that if he tells half the truth, he hasn't told half a lie. However, there is a big problem with that way of thinking, for it will keep that person from ever walking fully in the truth.

Abraham was quite nonchalant about *his* half-truth; yet that one lie almost destroyed a nation! God told Abimelech, "If you touch her, you're dead, and so is everyone around you!"

As a whole, Christians are far too nonchalant about telling half-truths. In fact, it often seems like many Christians believe the Bible has "Ten Suggestions" instead of Ten Commandments! Their lives demonstrate the attitude, "Well, this is the way God wants us to live if we have the time and it's convenient for us."

Here is a common excuse I often hear: "God knows my heart." Yes, God does know our hearts. But He also wrote Jeremiah 17:9 by the inspiration of the Holy Spirit:

"The heart is deceitful above all things, and desperately wicked; who can know it?"

If we really want to know what is in our hearts, we just need to listen to our mouths. We don't really know our own hearts until we start speaking.

We may say, "I believe I'm healed." But if that is true, why do we keep talking about being sick?

Or we may say, "I believe I'm prosperous." Then why do we always talk about what we don't have?

I'll tell you why — too often we just don't tell ourselves the truth. We fail to do this for one of three reasons:

1. *We don't tell ourselves the truth because of pride — an OVERinflated idea about ourselves.*

This is the characteristic that causes us to think more highly of ourselves than we ought to think (Rom. 12:3).

2. *We don't tell ourselves the truth because of pride — an UNDERinflated opinion of ourselves.*

This is more commonly known in our circles as low self-esteem.

One form of pride makes us believe that we are better than we are; the other form makes us believe that we are not good enough for anything. Both of these are lies from the enemy that keep us from being honest with ourselves.

Now, I don't think any of us want to lie because we already realize that liars have their place in the lake of fire (Rev. 21:8). However, sometimes we get into pride without realizing it. For instance, we might hold an overinflated opinion of ourselves when we think, *How dare that person think that he's a better Christian than I am! Just look at the way he's acting!* Or we may yield to feelings of low self-esteem that cause us to fall apart the moment someone approaches us about needed change in our lives.

3. *We don't tell ourselves the truth because of ignorance.*

In Hosea 4:6, God says, **"My people are destroyed for lack of knowledge."** A lack of knowledge, or ignorance, actually has two sides. First, a person is ignorant of an issue when he doesn't know about it or isn't aware of it.

More and more I have come to the conclusion that Christians are not always as lacking in knowledge as they pretend to be. The great majority of them fit in the second category of ignorance: *those who know the truth but ignore it.*

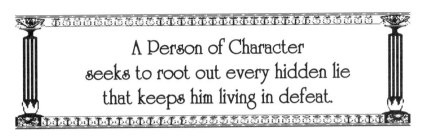

A Person of Character
seeks to root out every hidden lie
that keeps him living in defeat.

Peter is an example of someone who lived inside a lie of his own making. Let's begin by looking at what Jesus said to Peter at the Passover meal He shared with His disciples on the night He was arrested.

> "Little children, I shall be with you a little while longer. You will seek Me; and as I said to the Jews, 'Where I am going, you cannot come,' so now I say to you....
>
> Simon Peter said to Him, "Lord, where are You going?" Jesus answered him, "Where I am going you cannot follow Me now, but you shall follow Me afterward."
>
> Peter said to Him, "Lord, why can I not follow You now? I will lay down my life for Your sake."
>
> Jesus answered him, "Will you lay down your life for My sake? Most assuredly, I say to you, the rooster shall not crow till you have denied Me three times."
>
> **John 13:33,36-38**

If Jesus had said that to me, I think I know how *I* would have handled it. I would have gone home, taken several sleeping pills, put tape on my mouth, and gone to bed for the night until the cock crowed the next morning!

Consider Peter's position in this situation. He had watched Jesus perform miracles for three and a half years. He had observed the way Jesus told only the truth in every circumstance. Now Jesus says to him, "Listen, Peter, tomorrow morning isn't coming without your denial of Me — not once, not twice, but three times."

So this is my question: After Peter's first denial of Jesus, why didn't he think back to what Jesus had said to him and get out of that situation? It seems like that first denial would have been an effective wakeup call! Then Peter denied Jesus a second time. That was another good opportunity for Peter to conclude, *Uh, oh! I'm getting real close to that third denial! I better go home!*

Since we are on the outside of this situation looking in, we might find it very difficult to understand why Peter didn't do *something* to prevent himself from fulfilling Jesus' somber prediction. But there was something going on inside Peter that kept him from telling himself the truth.

Matthew 26:58 gives us further insight into Peter's behavior:

> **But Peter followed Him at a distance to the high priest's courtyard. And he went in and sat with the servants to see the end.**

Peter was with Jesus in the Garden of Gethsemane when a great multitude came with swords and clubs to lay hands on Jesus and take Him to the place where the high priest and elders were assembled. This verse tells us what was going on inside Peter at that difficult time: *He was waiting to see the end.*

A few hours earlier, Peter had declared to Jesus, "I will *never* deny You!" But just a little while later, he was in the courtyard of the high priest, waiting for the end!

That was the lie that lived in Peter. On the outside, he could act very positive and strong in his commitment to Jesus. But on the inside lived a weak and negative side that he didn't admit even to himself.

Many people are like Peter in this regard. They don't tell themselves the truth, and therefore they live inside a lie. I see this quality in some people who try to be bubbly on the outside but who are not at all bubbly on the inside. When these people lose their bubbles, everyone around them better watch out. After all, there is nothing pleasing about the taste of a flat carbonated beverage!

So we see what was going on inside Peter on the night of Jesus' arrest: He was waiting for the end. Let's read further in Matthew 26 to find out what Peter did next.

> **Now Peter sat outside in the courtyard. And a servant girl came to him, saying, "You also were with Jesus of Galilee."**
>
> **But he denied it before them all, saying, "I do not know what you are saying."**
>
> **And when he had gone out to the gateway, another girl saw him and said to those who were there, "This fellow also was with Jesus of Nazareth."**
>
> **But again he denied with an oath, "I do not know the Man!"**
>
> **And a little later those who stood by came up and said to Peter, "Surely you also are one of them, for your speech betrays you."**
>
> **Then he began to curse and swear, saying, "I do not know the Man!"**
>
> **Immediately a rooster crowed.**

And Peter remembered the word of Jesus who had said to him, "Before the rooster crows, you will deny Me three times." So he went out and wept bitterly.

Matthew 26:69-75

First, someone said, "You were with Jesus!" and Peter denied it by exclaiming, "I don't know what you're saying!" Then later, someone else said, "This fellow *was* with Jesus!" This time Peter denied it with an oath, declaring, "I do not know the Man!"

As I said, that would have been a good time for Peter to decide to go home! But he stayed in the courtyard, still waiting for the end. Later the third accusation came when someone said, "You even sound like one of Jesus' disciples!" This time Peter began to curse and swear to make his denial more emphatic: *"I do not know this Man!"* Things were getting tough for Peter at this point!

That's the way it is when a person lives inside a lie. That lie becomes the "mother lie" that suddenly begins to breed new lie after new lie. Why? Because the person has to keep telling another lie to make the last lie seem believable!

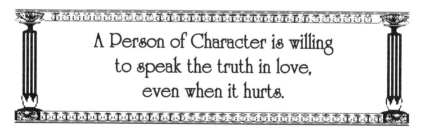

A Person of Character is willing to speak the truth in love, even when it hurts.

It is up to each of us to make sure we don't live inside our own self-made house of lies. To that end, we need to take the time to honestly evaluate whether or not we are telling ourselves the truth in every area of our lives. For instance, are we unapproachable about certain issues?

Have we failed to allow the seriousness of our need for change to touch our hearts?

God also requires us to be honest with others when confrontation is needed. He may lead us to talk to someone who just doesn't seem to understand the severity of his own situation. If that person doesn't recognize the potential consequences of his wrong behavior, we may come to the point where we realize we cannot let the lie go on any longer — we have to confront that person with the truth.

But what happens if that person won't listen? People have the idea that friendship means we have to stick with a person even if he persists in his sin. But Romans 16:17 says we are to mark those who cause divisions within the Body and to separate from them so they might be shamed to the point of repentance. The Bible does *not* say, "Don't ever turn your back on anyone for any reason."

Proverbs 27:6 tells us what to do when someone close to us needs correction: **"Faithful are the wounds of a friend...."** Ephesians 4:15 (*NAS*) confirms this, telling us that **"...speaking the truth in love, we are to grow up in all aspects into Him, who is the head, even Christ."**

"But my friend just doesn't want to talk about the areas he needs to change."

Well, then, that person isn't your friend.

"Yes, but I don't have many friends, so I really want to work with this person."

No, if that person insists on pursuing his lack of character, he does not qualify to be your friend. You would have to lower your idea of friendship in order to keep that particular "friend."

How important is it to speak the truth at *all* times, even when it is painful? To answer that question, we will consider a hypothetical situation.

Let's say that someone was standing behind your front door with a gun. Then let's suppose that you had already told 999 correct facts that day.

A friend walks into the room and asks you the question: "Is there anyone in here with a gun?"

You reply, "No."

The next thing you know, the man behind the door steps out and shoots your friend, who falls down dead.

You had already told 999 truths that day, but then you told one lie. What, then, was the key factor that got your friend killed? Was he blessed because you told 999 true facts earlier in the day, or did he lose his life over your one lie?

Christians don't understand how important this principle is. They want to spend all their time telling a person how great he is instead of loving him enough to tell him the truth he needs to hear, even if it hurts. But remember — faithful are the *wounds* of a friend.

The Bible never says a person is faithful when he talks only about how wonderful his friend is. It says that person is faithful when he confronts his friend with the truth about shortcomings that will keep him from becoming all God has created him to be.

That is why I want the people in my life to come to me when I have failed in some way in my relationship with them. In fact, I ask this question on a regular basis: "What have I not done in fulfilling what God wants me to do in this relationship?"

After all, the Bible says, "If your brother offends you, go to him" (Matt. 18:15). Don't talk about him. Don't storm out of his life. *Speak the truth in love.*

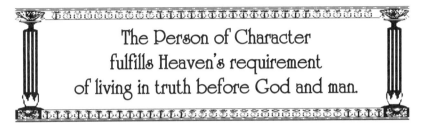

The Person of Character
fulfills Heaven's requirement
of living in truth before God and man.

Many Christians wonder why their prayers are not being answered. They just can't figure out why things aren't going the way they need to go in their lives. But there is often one primary reason that explains why people are having a difficult time in their lives — they are not telling the truth to themselves or to others.

Honesty is demanded of us as believers, for we are called to **"...provide things honest in the sight of all men"** (Rom. 12:17 *KJV*). Notice we are to provide that which is honest in the sight of *people*, not just in the sight of *God*. The truth is, we are never going to get anywhere in God if we are not willing to first confront ourselves with the truth and then make those around us aware that we have lied.

I know a simple way we can convince our flesh to quit lying very quickly. All we have to do is stop protecting our flesh and start telling on ourselves when we lie! Instead of trying to get out of it by saying, "Well, I didn't really mean it that way," we just need to say, "There is no excuse — I lied!" That would stop our flesh from lying in a split second!

Colossians 3:9 says, **"Do not lie to one another, since you have put off the old man with his deeds."** In order to "put off the old man," we have to tell our flesh to be quiet instead of indulging it when it wants to cover up its sin. We will never be happy until we do that. After all, if we don't have control of our lives, the enemy does.

Paul goes on to say that we are to **"...put on the new man who is renewed in knowledge according to the image of Him who created him"** (v. 10). Paul is saying in essence, "As you lose your identity of who you were before you received Jesus, you won't have to lie anymore. Instead, you can focus on being renewed in the knowledge of the One who recreated you."

We just need to know more about who we are in Christ and less about who we used to be as a result of our momma and daddy. No matter how wonderful our parents were, they still had weaknesses and shortcomings for which Jesus had to go to the Cross. But we don't have to live our lives according to the fleshly weaknesses handed down through our family tree. As new creatures in Christ we can act like Jesus, for **"...as He is, so are we in this world"** (1 John 4:17)!

The more you spend time meditating on who you are in Christ instead of on who you *were*, the more your new man gains strength. Romans 10:17 tells you why: **"So then faith comes by hearing, and hearing by the word of God."**

Faith doesn't come by *what you heard* or by *what you know*. Faith comes by *what you are listening to right now*. What are you listening to? What is on your mind? Is the new creation on your mind, or are your thoughts focused on the way your momma and daddy raised you or what their genes passed on to you?

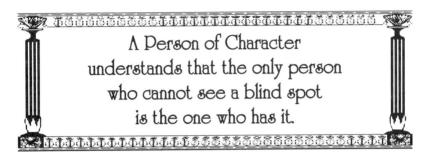

A Person of Character
understands that the only person
who cannot see a blind spot
is the one who has it.

It is Heaven's requirement that we provide things honest before all men, including ourselves. Therefore, we cannot afford to deceive ourselves even for a moment that everything is all right in our lives when, in fact, everything is *not* all right.

This is why God sends people into our lives to help us recognize those needed areas of change that we cannot or *will* not see on our own. We must welcome people who fill that role into our lives; otherwise, we will hit impasses where we can go no further in our walk with God.

We talked earlier about the blind spots we all deal with in our lives. Let's go back to Genesis 18 — the time when the Lord and two angels visited Abraham and Sarah — and discuss this principle a little further.

> **Then they said to him, "Where is Sarah your wife?" So he said, "Here, in the tent."**
> **And He said, "I will certainly return to you according to the time of life, and behold, Sarah your wife shall have a son." (Sarah was listening in the tent door which was behind him.)**

Now Abraham and Sarah were old, well advanced in age; and Sarah had passed the age of childbearing.

Therefore Sarah laughed within herself, saying, "After I have grown old, shall I have pleasure, my lord being old also?"

And the Lord said to Abraham, "Why did Sarah laugh, saying, 'Shall I surely bear a child, since I am old?'

"Is anything too hard for the Lord? At the appointed time I will return to you, according to the time of life, and Sarah shall have a son."

But Sarah denied it, saying, "I did not laugh," for she was afraid.

And He said, "No, but you did laugh!"

Genesis 18:9-15

The Lord said to Abraham, "About this time next year I will return, and at that time, your wife Sarah shall bear a son."

Sarah was listening to this conversation from the nearby tent. Since she and Abraham were both very old and she was long past child-bearing age, Sarah chuckled to herself, thinking, *How can this old babe have a new one?* But the Lord looked at Abraham and asked, "Why did she laugh?"

Sarah stuck out her head from behind the door of the tent and protested, "I didn't laugh!"

Let's give Sarah the benefit of the doubt and say that she really didn't realize she had laughed. If that is true, she had to come to the place where she trusted someone enough to listen when he said to her, "You did this" and to respond by saying, "I believe I did it because You said

I did. I trust You because I know that You wouldn't lie to me."

Do you have a person in your life that you trust to that extent? Do you trust *yourself* to that extent? If you are like most people, you may be the one who lies to yourself more than anyone else in the world does!

I have certain people in my life whom I esteem so highly that if they tell me something, I don't even ask a question. If they said I did something, I just accept the fact that I did it.

I have found that we immediately disarm a person the moment we agree with him. The Bible talks about this as well:

> **Agree with your adversary quickly, while you are on the way with him, lest your adversary deliver you to the judge, the judge hand you over to the officer, and you be thrown into prison.**
> **Matthew 5:25**

How does this scripture apply to our lives? For one thing, it is a warning about how *not* to respond when someone tells us about something we did wrong. The more we deny that we did it, the more we descend into strife, unforgiveness, and bitterness. At that point, we are in prison lawfully, because we have allowed ourselves to get angry. And in order to get out of prison, we may have to ask for forgiveness regarding something we didn't even do!

In Galatians 4:16, the apostle Paul asked the Galatian church, **"Have I therefore become your enemy because I tell you the truth?"** Why did Paul ask the Galatians that question? Because they always seemed prepared to believe other people's lies while at the same time resisting the truth that Paul offered them.

It is amazing how far some people will go in resisting the truth. Some of the conversations I have had with people who do this have almost seemed as ridiculous as this one:

"If you jump out of the plane without a parachute, you're going to die."

"Oh, no. I won't die."

"Yes, if you jump out of a plane, you're going to die."

"No. I won't die. I know I won't die."

"How do you know that you won't die?"

"Well, I know I won't die because I believe I won't die."

"Wait a minute. You are thousands of feet above the ground. If you jump out of the plane, you're going to come down. And the further up you go, the faster you will come down. Besides, if you have never jumped out of a plane without a parachute before, how do you know you won't die? You *don't* know!"

This particular principle boils down to one thing: being willing to *trust*. We have to trust that what God has said is the truth. We have to trust that there are people in our lives who will speak the truth to us when we need it the most.

Biblical Examples of Honesty

What are some examples of honesty in the Bible? First, let's look back at Abimelech for a moment in

Genesis 20. This king had just discovered that the beautiful woman he had taken with the intention of marrying her was not only Abraham's sister, but also Abraham's *wife*. Abraham had put Abimelech in a precarious position by telling him a half-truth born out of fear.

Nevertheless, Abimelech's response to the situation revealed that he was an honest man of character:

> **Then Abimelech took sheep, oxen, and male and female servants, and gave them to Abraham; and he restored Sarah his wife to him.**
>
> **And Abimelech said, "See, my land is before you; dwell where it pleases you."**
>
> **Then to Sarah he said, "Behold, I have given your brother a thousand pieces of silver; indeed this vindicates you before all who are with you and before everybody...."**
>
> **Genesis 20:14-16**

Abimelech didn't ever want to be seen as one who would do anything contrary to good character. Therefore, he made it right with the one who had wronged *him*.

The prophet Samuel is another example of honesty in the Word. Samuel was so honest and upright in his dealings with people that he was able to make the following claim regarding his godly character that no person in Israel could refute:

> **"...I am old and grayheaded, and look, my sons are with you. I have walked before you from my childhood to this day.**
>
> **"Here I am. Witness against me before the Lord and before His anointed: Whose ox have I taken, or whose donkey have I taken, or whom**

★ 276 ★

have I cheated? Whom have I oppressed, or from whose hand have I received any bribe with which to blind my eyes? I will restore it to you."

And they said, "You have not cheated us or oppressed us, nor have you taken anything from any man's hand."

Then he said to them, "The Lord is witness against you, and His anointed is witness this day, that you have not found anything in my hand." And they answered, "He is witness."

1 Samuel 12:2-5

Daniel is another excellent example of honesty. Daniel's strength of character was so evident that his enemies couldn't even find anything about which to criticize him!

Daniel soon proved himself more capable than all the other administrators and princes. Because of his great ability, the king made plans to place him over the entire empire.

Then the other administrators and princes began searching for some fault in the way Daniel was handling his affairs, but they couldn't find anything to criticize. He was faithful and honest and always responsible.

Daniel 6:3,4 *NLT*

Daniel was faithful, honest, and always responsible. His enemies were so unsuccessful at finding any character flaws with which they could accuse Daniel that they had to resort to other methods. They began to pick on Daniel's relationship with God in order to find a way to discredit and destroy him. Ultimately, Daniel's excellent character before God saved him from the worst that his enemies could throw at him, and he walked away unharmed from the lions' den.

God also viewed David as a man of truth. Years after repenting of his sin with Bathsheba, David dedicated the material he and his people had gathered for the building of God's temple. In his prayer before the people, David called himself an honest man:

> "I know, my God, that you test the heart and are pleased with integrity. All these things have I given willingly and with honest intent. And now I have seen with joy how willingly your people who are here have given to you."
>
> **1 Chronicles 29:17** *NIV*

Having dealt with his own sin, David was well-qualified to write these words in Psalm 32:1,2 (*NLT*):

> Oh, what joy for those whose rebellion is forgiven, whose sin is put out of sight!
>
> Yes, what joy for those whose record the Lord has cleared of sin, whose lives are lived in complete honesty!

When you talk to an honest person about honesty, it doesn't bother him; in fact, it makes him happy to know that he fits the Bible's description of an upright, honest person. Only a dishonest person gets upset when the subject of honesty comes up.

But this subject of honesty must be taught, for we are not going anywhere in our walk with God as long as we remain dishonest with ourselves and with others. Without honesty, everything God has given us will fall through the gaping crack we have created with our own lack of truth.

This is true for all of us. We all have to come to a place in our lives where we say, "I refuse to let deception rule my life any longer!"

I remember how excited I was the day I decided to stop hiding and was set free from myself. I finally quit trying to make other people think that I was somebody I wasn't. Only then did I find out that I really *was* somebody!

Jesus said in Matthew 10:26, "**...There is nothing covered that will not be revealed, and hidden that will not be known.**" Just give it enough time, and the lies that live inside a person *will* eventually come out. If he is a person of truth, that will also be revealed:

> "**But he who does the truth comes to the light, that his deeds may be clearly seen, that they have been done in God.**"
>
> **John 3:21**

People are able to recognize the person who walks in honesty and integrity. It is also evident when the conviction of the Holy Spirit weighs heavy on someone who has not been honest about his sin. In Psalm 32, David describes what that is like from his own personal experience:

> **When I kept silent, my bones grew old through my groaning all the day long.**
> **For day and night Your hand was heavy upon me; my vitality was turned into the drought of summer.**
>
> **Psalm 32:3,4**

Whenever we feel God's heavy hand of conviction on us, we might run, but we will never be able to hide from

Him. That loving divine hand will remain on us until we finally submit to *truth*:

> I acknowledged my sin to You, and my iniquity I have not hidden. I said, "I will confess my transgressions to the Lord," and You forgave the iniquity of my sin.
>
> Psalm 32:5

Think about all that God has provided for us to help us walk in truth. We have the Word of truth to teach us and the Spirit of Truth to guide us. We have the examples of great men and women of God who lived in truth before us. We therefore have no excuse for living in deception for even one second of our lives on this earth. It's time to live in honesty in every aspect of our lives — before God, before man, and most certainly before ourselves!

PRINCIPLES FOR BEING HONEST WITH YOURSELF

⋆ A Person of Character aligns his life with the words of his mouth.

⋆ We allow ourselves to be used as agents of evil when we lie, for God has already commanded us to walk in truth.

⋆ A Person of Character seeks to root out every hidden lie that keeps him living in defeat.

⋆ A Person of Character is willing to speak the truth in love, even when it hurts.

★ The Person of Character fulfills Heaven's requirement of living in truth before God and man.

★ A Person of Character understands that the only person who cannot see a blind spot is the one who has it.

NOTES:

_____

_____

_____

_____

_____

_____

_____

_____

_____

_____

_____

_____

_____

_____

NOTES:

CHAPTER ELEVEN

DEMONSTRATING DIVINE COMPASSION

Compassion is an absolutely vital quality for us to cultivate in our lives if we want to walk in the character of God. Again and again, the Bible proclaims that the God we serve is a God of compassion.

> **Blessed be the God and Father of our Lord Jesus Christ, the Father of mercies and God of all comfort.**
>
> **2 Corinthians 1:3**

> **But You, O Lord, are a God full of compassion, and gracious, longsuffering and abundant in mercy and truth.**
>
> **Psalm 86:15**

> **The Lord is merciful and gracious, slow to anger, and abounding in mercy.**
>
> **Psalm 103:8**

> **Your compassion is great, O Lord; preserve my life according to your laws.**
>
> **Psalm 119:156 *NIV***

Too often Christians think that God is a God of *indifference* rather than a God of compassion. They assume that it doesn't matter to Him how they live their lives or the way they treat others. Others feel like God has abandoned them or that He doesn't understand what they're going through.

But God *is* a God of compassion. We just have to understand that He has no compassion for sin. We are recipients of His compassion as we walk in His light, not as we participate with the world in the deeds of darkness.

This was even true in regard to God's own Son. Why did the Father accept Jesus? Hebrew 1:9 tells us why:

"You have loved righteousness and hated lawlessness; therefore God, Your God, has anointed You with the oil of gladness more than Your companions."

Jesus enjoyed a never-ending supply of His Father's compassion and power for one primary reason: because Jesus loved what the Father loved and hated what the Father hated.

So what does it mean to be a compassionate person? Compassion is *an attitude of care and concern grounded in pity and sympathy toward others.* It refers to *the ability to commiserate with another individual who is going through difficult times in life.* Other ingredients of this mighty spiritual force include *pity, sympathy, mercy, kindness, tenderness, clemency, empathy, solicitousness, caring,* and *consideration.*

The dictionary says that compassion also includes the meaning of *suffering with another person* or *painful sympathy.* Compassion actually combines both love and sorrow, for a person of compassion is willing to share in the pain that someone else is going through. Thus, compassion also refers to *a sensation of sorrow that is activated by the distress or the misfortunes of another.* At times a person of compassion will even feel anger in response to the pain that the other person has to endure.

For instance, a well-known pastor once shared with me about a painful situation he was going through involving some other people. I knew the pain he was describing; I had felt that pain myself at different times in my life. As I put myself in his shoes and commiserated with him, I could feel the anger rise up in me because of the emotional pain that my friend was feeling.

That righteous anger was actually a manifestation of God's compassion coming through me to my friend. In sharing his pain, I helped lift his burden that day — a common result when divine compassion starts to flow.

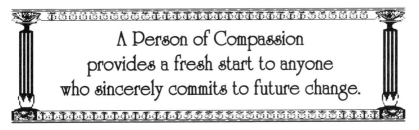

A Person of Compassion
provides a fresh start to anyone
who sincerely commits to future change.

Some people have the idea that compassion is not a very important quality to pursue. However, they would think differently if they stood in a position of authority, for compassion is a *very* important attribute when one is dealing with other people.

Many times a person just needs a fresh start. He sees what he did wrong, and he wants the opportunity to make it right again. Only someone in authority can provide the person with that fresh start. But in most cases, once a person has failed, those who are over him are not interested in giving him another opportunity to prove he can do it right.

Personally, I am interested in giving people a fresh start. However, I am only interested in helping those who are sincere about it. These are the people who are willing to admit they did wrong and who now embrace the Word of God as their standard for getting it right the second time around.

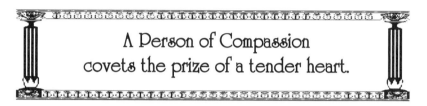

A Person of Compassion
covets the prize of a tender heart.

Compassion is the character quality that Paul is describing in Ephesians 4:32:

And be kind to one another, tenderhearted, forgiving one another, even as God in Christ forgave you.

Compassion and tenderheartedness are integrally connected; in fact, we cannot have one quality without the other. We should therefore ask God to give us tender hearts.

I actually don't know a lot of people who have tender hearts. I'm talking about the rare person who responds to the promptings of the Holy Spirit as soon as his heart is touched. If you can just get past that person's natural reasoning and penetrate his heart with the truth, he will do what is right every time.

Parents can often see the difference between a tender heart and a stubborn heart by looking at their children.

Many times one set of parents will have children who fit in both categories. One child might be strong-willed and stubborn, whereas another child might be soft-hearted and pliable.

A child who fits the latter description is like putty in God's hands. As the tenderhearted child grows, God will be able to form him into the person He created him to be.

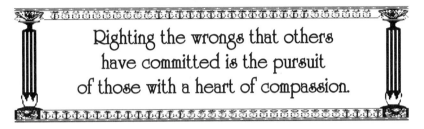

Righting the wrongs that others have committed is the pursuit of those with a heart of compassion.

People don't mind receiving compassion from others, but they often hold back from giving compassion because they think it is a sign of weakness. But compassion is not weakness; it is actually a rare demonstration of *strength*, for compassion requires an unrelenting pursuit of desiring what is right.

A compassionate person wants to right every wrong he sees. He yearns to silence the roar of years of disappointment in the life of another. He wants to answer questions that others are unwilling to even acknowledge. He willingly takes the responsibility of becoming the shock absorber for other people's lives — even when he doesn't feel like doing it, even when those individuals don't deserve it. His heart desire is to help remove the obstacles from people's lives so they can get in a position to start winning.

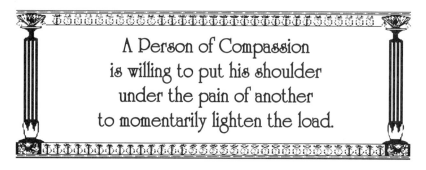

A Person of Compassion
is willing to put his shoulder
under the pain of another
to momentarily lighten the load.

One antonym for compassion is *indifference*. The attitude of an indifferent person says, "I don't care what you're going through because I'm not the one who has to deal with it. You deal with your own pain, and I'll deal with mine."

But that is the attitude of the world — not of a believer who is walking in the character of God. In Galatians 6:1, Paul tells us what God expects of us when a fellow believer is going through a difficult time:

> **Brethren, if a man is overtaken in any trespass, you who are spiritual restore such a one in a spirit of gentleness, considering yourself lest you also be tempted.**

What is Paul talking about in this verse? In verse 2 he explains, giving us a mental picture that aptly describes the spiritual force of compassion: **"Bear one another's burdens, and so fulfill the law of Christ."**

The word "bear" means that a believer has positioned himself underneath the pain or the weight that another person has been carrying alone and lifted that burden off the person's shoulders. This enables that person to stand upright and gain enough strength to eventually be able to carry his own burden of responsibility, as Paul says in verse 5: **"For each one shall bear his own load."**

Momentarily, however, the person of compassion relieves the pain of another. He erases the shame. He lifts off the weight. He shares the heavy burden that someone else has been enduring alone.

You can see, then, why another antonym for compassion is *self-centeredness.* This means that as we pursue compassion in our lives, we will set ourselves free from the self-centeredness that has plagued us from our earliest memories.

I don't want to live my life centered on *my* needs and interests — not for a moment! I want to live my life through another's eyes, not through my own.

You, too, can develop a heart desire to live a life of uncompromised principle for one primary purpose — to show others how to walk out of their own personal prisons of pain. How do you do it? By pursuing the compassion of God until it flows freely through you to the people whose lives you touch every day.

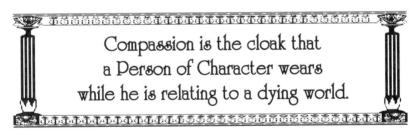

Compassion is the cloak that
a Person of Character wears
while he is relating to a dying world.

Colossians 3:12 *(NIV)* presents a mental picture that should help us learn how to make compassion an integral part of our character:

Therefore, as God's chosen people, holy and dearly loved, clothe yourselves with compassion, kindness, humility, gentleness and patience.

Paul tells us to clothe ourselves with compassion, kindness, humility, gentleness, and patience. If we can clothe ourselves with these character qualities, that means we can learn to continually manifest them in our lives. It doesn't matter if we didn't learn how to be tenderhearted and compassionate while we were growing up. We can learn how to put off the negative attributes that have ruled our lives until now and begin to put on compassion, kindness, and mercy every morning of every day, just as we would put on a coat.

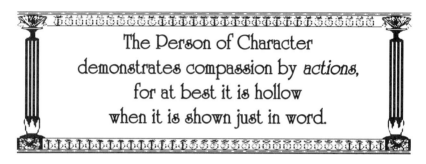

The Person of Character demonstrates compassion by *actions*, for at best it is hollow when it is shown just in word.

Compassion is a verb, not a noun. It must be shown in our *actions*.

This is the apostle John's message in First John 3:17 (*AMP*):

> **But if anyone has this world's goods (resources for sustaining life) and sees his brother and fellow believer in need, yet closes his heart of compassion against him, how can the love of God live and remain in him?**

John asks a very good question: If we see someone struggling with problems, yet we are not willing to help that person overcome those problems, how does God's love dwell in us?

Of course, it is important to stay alert for spiritual "con artists." These people are usually Christians who realize we are called to help those who are needy. But these Christians take advantage of that fact by playing on our emotions with their frequent requests for help.

We might even be included at times among those who receive compassionate help. But *we* are helped because we helped *someone else* first, not because we looked for someone to help us. The law of sowing and reaping will always operate for our benefit as we demonstrate God's compassion to those around us.

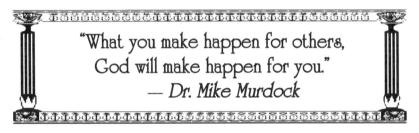

"What you make happen for others, God will make happen for you."
— Dr. Mike Murdock

We make something happen for someone else, and God makes things happen for us. Why? Because many times our harvest is not destined to come from the people in whose lives we have sowed our seed.

The principle that compassion is demonstrated through action is not just a New Testament concept. God establishes its truth under the Old Covenant as well:

> **"Is this not the fast that I have chosen: to loose the bonds of wickedness, to undo the heavy burdens, to let the oppressed go free, and that you break every yoke?**
>
> **Is it not to share your bread with the hungry, and that you bring to your house the poor who are cast out; when you see the naked, that you**

cover him, and not hide yourself from your own flesh?

Isaiah 58:6,7

Notice what we are called to do as people of God. We are to:

1. loosen the bands of wickedness that keep people bound;

2. undo the heavy burdens that people are struggling with;

3. help the oppressed go free;

4. break every yoke;

5. share our bread with the hungry;

6. provide hospitality to the poor and to the outcasts of society; and

7. cover those who lack the necessary clothing.

In short, we are to express God's compassion through *actions*.

So determine to become a person of action instead of just a person of words. Your Christian life is what you *do*, not what you *say*. You may think you believe what the Bible says, but until your life is tried and you see how you respond to the tests that come your way, you will never truly know what kind of person you are.

Christians often think they are doing better spiritually than they really are. They need to look carefully at their lives and evaluate what they have actually done, not what they *think* they have done.

All you need to do is stop listening to a person's mouth and start watching what he *does*. Watch how he responds to stressful situations. Check to see if he bounces checks or charges the limit on his credit card. Ask his wife how he treats her behind closed doors. That is how you can know who a person truly is.

"I'm a man of integrity," someone might say. Yet the same person who makes such a claim is often the person who owes money to all sorts of creditors and never gets around to paying them back!

We are not people of integrity because we say we are; we are people of integrity because *others* say we are. Life becomes very simple when we understand this principle.

Let's go back to Isaiah 58:8 for a moment and see what happens after we have shown our compassion through our actions:

Then your light shall break forth like the morning, your healing shall spring forth speedily, and your righteousness shall go before you; the glory of the Lord shall be your rear guard.

Why doesn't our light break forth like the morning *before* we are obedient to show compassion to others? Because prior to our compassionate actions, our faith is only expressed with *words*, not with *deeds*. As soon as action follows what we say we believe, that is the moment our light — our own personal deliverance — breaks forth in our lives, just as immediately and faithfully as the sun comes up over the eastern horizon every morning at sunrise!

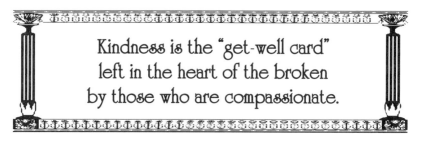

Kindness is the "get-well card"
left in the heart of the broken
by those who are compassionate.

The Bible gives us many examples of compassionate behavior toward the oppressed and the needy.

In Job 29:12-16, Job talks about his deeds of compassion to the poor and needy before calamity hit his own life:

> Because I delivered the poor who cried out, the fatherless and the one who had no helper.
> The blessing of a perishing man came upon me, and I caused the widow's heart to sing for joy.
> I put on righteousness, and it clothed me; my justice was like a robe and a turban.
> I was eyes to the blind, and I was feet to the lame.
> I was a father to the poor, and I searched out the case that I did not know.

In Proverbs 31:8,9 (*NIV*), Bathsheba exhorts her son Solomon to show compassion to the poor and the needy as king of Israel:

> "Speak up for those who cannot speak for themselves, for the rights of all who are destitute.
> "Speak up and judge fairly; defend the rights of the poor and needy."

Ruth 2 talks about Boaz's example of compassion shown toward Ruth. Boaz knew that Ruth was a virtuous Moabitess woman who was now without a husband. He had also heard how Ruth had traveled from her native land to care for her elderly mother-in-law, who had also lost her husband. So Boaz had compassion on Ruth, allowing her to glean extra grain from his field before the reapers came.

Exodus 2:5-9 gives us an example of compassion shown toward children. In an effort to save her infant son from the Pharaoh's edict to kill all Hebrew male babies, Moses' mother placed him in a little ark covered with pitch and set the ark in the river. When Pharaoh's daughter came down to the river to bathe, she saw the little ark.

> **And when she opened it, she saw the child, and behold, the baby wept. So she had compassion on him, and said, "This is one of the Hebrews' children."**
>
> **Exodus 2:6**

The princess's compassion for the infant moved her to take Moses in and hire a nursemaid for him until he was old enough for her to raise him as her own.

In Isaiah 49:15, God compares His compassion for His people to a mother's compassion for her children:

> **"Can a woman forget her nursing child, and not have compassion on the son of her womb? Surely they may forget, yet I will not forget you."**

Acts 16:33 provides an example of compassionate behavior shown toward prisoners. The prison guard had compassion on Paul and Silas, setting them free from their chains and washing their wounds.

**And he took them the same hour of the night
and washed their stripes. And immediately he
and all his family were baptized.**

Hebrews 13:3 exhorts us to show compassion toward
prisoners, commiserating with those who are in bonds as
if we were in those very bonds ourselves.

**Remember the prisoners as if chained with
them — those who are mistreated — since you
yourselves are in the body also.**

We are also to have compassion on those who have
been forgiven for straying from the Lord:

**Brethren, if a man is overtaken in any tres-
pass, you who are spiritual restore such a one in
a spirit of gentleness, considering yourself lest
you also be tempted.**

Galatians 6:1

That word "restore" gives us a picture of an physician
expertly mending a person's broken bone. Similarly, we
are to mend our fellow believers' spiritual broken bones —
those "crooked" areas in their lives that only God can
straighten out and make whole.

Notice that last phrase: **"....considering yourself, lest
you also be tempted."** We should never trust ourselves
so much that we would say, "Oh, I would never do that."
Many men and women of God have fallen into sin after
saying the same thing. The person who keeps standing is
the one who says, "I'm going to hold fast to the Lord
because I don't trust me."

The Bible also gives us examples of people showing
compassion toward the sick. For instance, when Job was
dealing with great loss and with boils all over his body,

three friends visited him to show compassion for his suffering.

> Now when Job's three friends heard of all this evil that was come upon him, they came every one from his own place; Eliphaz the Temanite, and Bildad the Shuhite, and Zophar the Naamathite: for they had made an appointment together to come to mourn with him and to comfort him.
>
> Job 2:11 *KJV*

In Psalm 35:13 and 14, David wrote about having compassion on those who are sick. (By the way, compassion on the sick would include *not* asking them, "Where is your faith?" or judging them for what they're going through!)

> But as for me, when they were sick, my clothing was sackcloth; I humbled myself with fasting; and my prayer would return to my own heart.
>
> I paced about as though he were my friend or brother; I bowed down heavily, as one who mourns for his mother.

Interestingly, David was talking about his enemies here! He actually felt his enemies' physical pain and made himself one with their sickness as he prayed and fasted for them. Then he said, "...**My prayer would return to my own heart.**"

In other words, David was saying, "I wasn't out for revenge against my enemies. I wasn't praying, 'God, get them for their wickedness against me!' Instead, when my enemies were sick, I dealt with the situation as if I were the one going through the pain, and I received credit with God for the compassion I showed toward them."

James 1:27 tells us about another group of people on whom we are to have compassion:

Pure and undefiled religion before God and the Father is this: to visit orphans and widows in their trouble, and to keep oneself unspotted from the world.

James 1:27

We are to visit the fatherless and the widows, showing compassion toward them and looking for ways to help meet their needs. This would include those who come from broken homes and the elderly who live alone.

When people grow older, we sometimes forget that they have a need for conversation and fellowship with other people, just as we all do. It is therefore important that we find time to visit the elderly and look for ways to show God's love toward them.

As for the elderly, the widows, or the fatherless who don't have family members with whom to share the holidays, we need to remember to reach out to them during those special times of the year. We can probably all find someone who doesn't have anywhere to go and invite that person to share in our holiday festivities.

How does God view our showing compassion to the needy? Proverbs 14:31 says that we actually honor Him when we demonstrate His loving nature to others in need:

He who oppresses the poor reproaches his Maker, but he who honors Him has mercy on the needy.

Compassion is a rare find on this earth. Many people show sympathy toward other people at times; many others crusade for all kinds of humanitarian causes. However, there are very few people of true compassion.

We need to realize that there is a counterfeit to every truth God's Word reveals and that it is up to us to seek for that which is true. Regarding the subject at hand, we will know we are demonstrating true compassion when we want to feel the pain that others feel and to help free them from every yoke of bondage that keeps them struggling in defeat.

That is the reason it is so important to consistently remind those we are endeavoring to help of our own past deliverance from bondage and defeat. People need to realize that they can come out of their present difficulties victoriously, just as we came out of our past trials in victory. God came through for us, and He will do the same for them!

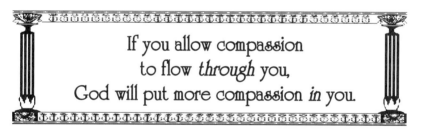

If you allow compassion
to flow *through* you,
God will put more compassion *in* you.

God is the author of human compassion. Daniel 1:9 confirms this truth:

Now God had brought Daniel into the favor and goodwill of the chief of the eunuchs.

If someone demonstrates compassion toward you, you can know that it is God showing you favor through that person. Psalm 106:46 (*NAS*) also presents this same principle:

He [God] **also made them** [His people] **objects of compassion in the presence of all their captors.**

This verse is referring to the time God delivered the children of Israel from Egypt. Before they left, He caused the Egyptians to give His people great quantities of silver and gold: **"Then He brought them out with silver and gold; and among His tribes there was not one who stumbled"** (Ps. 105:37 *NAS*).

That is a good example of how God's people can prosper from the flow of divine compassion into their lives through others!

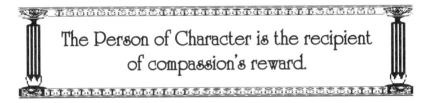

The Person of Character is the recipient of compassion's reward.

I want to feel what people go through, but I still will not compromise. I want to understand their plight and be moved by compassion to help them, but that does not mean I am willing to change my stance on principle.

We must always prize integrity above relationship. That is why we can't be persuaded to compromise — because God's principles means more to us than people do. If we will stick with principle, we will still be on the road to success many years after those who thought they were going somewhere have fallen by the wayside. And if we determine to walk that road with God's compassion continually flowing out of us to others, we will enjoy a life of rich and abundant reward.

Psalm 112 is the greatest exposition on prosperity in all of the Scriptures. It talks about what happens to a righteous man and his children when he lives a lifestyle that reflects the principles and the compassionate nature of God.

Blessed is the man who fears the Lord, who delights greatly in His commandments.
His descendants will be mighty on earth; the generation of the upright will be blessed.
Wealth and riches will be in his house, and his righteousness endures forever.

Psalm 112:1-3

Blessed is the man who fears God, because he delights greatly in what God has to say. He doesn't have his own opinions. He is not a legalistic religious man. He just delights greatly in what God tells him about how to live his life.

Verses 4-6 go on to describe the character of God, which is then reflected in the character of the righteous man:

Unto the upright there arises light in the darkness; He is gracious, and full of compassion, and righteous.
A good man deals graciously and lends; He will guide his affairs with discretion.
Surely he will never be shaken....

Verse 4 promises that as you seek to walk uprightly in all your ways, "...there arises light in the darkness...." The psalmist is saying that your darkest hour will be as bright as the noonday. When you are facing the greatest trials of your life, you will still be walking in the light, knowing which way to go, for you are in the generation of the upright.

Notice in verse 5 the way that the Word describes this righteous man: He is *gracious.* He is *full of compassion.* He *shows favor and lends.* He *guides his affairs with discretion.*

In other words, the foundation the righteous man builds consists of *godly character*, which is expressed in part through gracious compassion to others.

That word "gracious" doesn't necessarily mean that you agree with the way a person is living his life. *Gracious* means that you are overlooking what you disagree with as you communicate with him. You are being kind to someone who actually deserves judgment. *That* is graciousness.

Because this man builds his family upon these character principles and not upon personality, God promises that his children will be mighty (v. 2). Verse 2 goes on to say that **"...the generation of the upright shall be blessed."**

The psalmist also stresses a material side to the righteous man's reward: **"Wealth and riches will be in his house..."** (v. 3). Most individuals never come to the point where they experience this particular blessing in their lives. Why not? Because the cares of this world, the deceitfulness of riches, and the lust for other things enter in and choke the Word, and they become unfruitful (Mark 4:18,19).

The greatest test we ever face in our lives is not cancer or heart trouble; it is the test of *money.* If God blesses us financially, will we still stay humble? Will we still lay on our faces before the Lord and worship Him? Will we still pray? Or will we allow the financial increase we receive from God to become more important to us than He is?

God always gives His people a choice; He will give them what they want. For instance, Psalm 106:15 says that God gave Israel what they wanted when they asked for meat in the wilderness. However, He also sent unto them leanness of soul. Why? Because they wanted their natural desire more than they wanted God.

So make certain that you focus on your desire for God rather than on the blessings that will come as a result of pursuing Him. As Jesus promised in Matthew 6:33, if you will seek first the Kingdom of God and His righteousness, everything else will be added to you. You don't have to worry about it.

However, there is another side to this issue. Some Christians walk around with holes in their pants, thinking that living in perpetual lack is God's will for them. Because these people believe they are already in the will of God, they are not continually pressing toward a higher level of abundant life in Him.

But we need to press toward a higher level of excellence, no matter where we are in our Christian walk. We might earn the biggest salaries in our circle of friends. We might be the ones who push the hardest. But even if we have pushed the hardest today, it will still be time to push again tomorrow. It *won't* be time for us to say, "Well, everyone who is trying to keep up with me is behind me. So, praise the Lord, I can just take a break!"

You see, we're not competing with other people; we are competing with our own *flesh*. That is why we must trust fully in God's grace as we build our lives upon the foundation of fearing Him and delighting greatly in His doctrines.

That foundation will then become the platform from which our children can launch out to enjoy all the blessings described in Psalm 112. Our greatest joy will be in witnessing the harvest of divine favor bestowed on our children as they rise up and declare, "I delighted greatly in God's commandments and His doctrines; I meditated in them day and night. And now I enjoy the rewards of the righteous that He promised to me!"

The generation of the upright *shall* be blessed — that is the Lord's eternal promise to us!

The reward of compassion is yours to claim, friend. Just keep on building a strong, solid foundation of character in your life. Be gracious and full of compassion, always ready to help bear the burden of pain that others are facing. As you do, you will find that God is a present help at every juncture in your life. Because you have borne the pain of others, the God of all comfort will demonstrate His compassion toward you as He meets you in your time of need and fulfills the deepest desires of your heart.

Principles for Demonstrating Divine Compassion

✯ A Person of Compassion provides a fresh start to anyone who sincerely commits to future change.

✯ A Person of Compassion covets the prize of a tender heart.

✯ Righting the wrongs that others have committed is the pursuit of those with a heart of compassion.

✯ A Person of Compassion is willing to put his shoulder under the pain of another to momentarily lighten the load.

✯ Compassion is the cloak that a Person of Character wears while he is relating to a dying world.

✯ The Person of Character demonstrates compassion by *actions*, for at best it is hollow when it is shown just in word.

✯ "What you make happen for others, God will make happen for you." — *Dr. Mike Murdock*

✯ Kindness is the "get-well card" left in the heart of the broken by those who are compassionate.

✯ If you allow compassion to flow *through* you, God will put more compassion *in* you.

✯ The Person of Character is the recipient of compassion's reward.

NOTES:

_____

_____

_____

_____

_____

NOTES:

CHAPTER TWELVE

ATTENTIVENESS: YOUR ONE-WAY TICKET TO PROMOTION

Awhile back I sat in the office of a very successful businessman late at night. The man's desk was surrounded by people who worked for him, including his administrator, his business manager, and his accountant. All these people were trying get their boss's attention so they could find out what he wanted them to do.

But I noticed that some type of miscommunication was occurring between the employer and the employees in that office. After several minutes of increasing frustration, the businessman suddenly turned to me and asked, *"Why can't I get what I want?"*

I felt sorry for the rest of the people in the room who had heard that comment. But later as I pondered the matter, I came to understand what this man meant. I realized that the character quality of attentiveness is the factor that determines the outcome in many situations of life. In fact, attentiveness determines how far a person will go in any endeavor he undertakes.

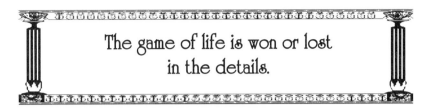

The game of life is won or lost
in the details.

Just what *is* attentiveness? The word "attentive" or "attention" actually comes from the French word *attendere*, meaning *to wait; to stay; to hold;* and *to expect.* The Latin word *attentio* carries a slightly different meaning. It gives us the picture of a horse twitching its ears as it gives its attention to something. Thus, attentiveness means *showing the worth of a person, an object, or an idea by giving it one's undivided concentration.*

So why is this character trait so significant? Because the outcome of our lives is not usually determined by the big things we think are important. Details — the small particulars of life that most people don't pay attention to — will cause us to either win or lose in our pursuit of all that God has planned for us in life.

I remember the time I was invited for dinner over at a couple's home. As we sat eating dinner, the wife got up from the dining room table to get her husband another serving of the main dish. As she left for the kitchen, she exclaimed to me, "Oh, he just loves this dish!"

But as soon as his wife was out of earshot, the husband said to me, "I've always hated this stuff. But she keeps making it and then expects me to eat it."

"Have you ever told her that you don't like this dish?" I asked.

"Well, yes, I've told her, but it's as if she doesn't hear. I don't ever want to eat this food again, but I can't say anything about it. If I do, she's going to think I hate everything else she does!"

This type of situation happens in every area of life, not just in the home. It happens on the job. It happens between friends. It happens in our relationship with the Lord. People are not attentive to detail and thus fail to be what someone else actually wants or needs.

Saul and Joseph: A Contrast in Attentiveness

Saul and Joseph are two biblical characters who provide a sharp contrast in this character trait of attentiveness. Let's start with Saul. In First Samuel, we read that Israel cried out to God for a king, even though they already had God as their King and the prophet Samuel to lead them. Finally, God granted their request, and Samuel anointed a young man named Saul as the king of Israel.

Years after becoming king, Saul faced a crucial test of his character before God. Samuel went to Saul and told him, "The Lord says to go forth into battle and destroy the Amalekites — every man, every woman, every child, every beast, every bit of livestock. God wants you to destroy them utterly because they have come against His people" (1 Sam. 15:2,3).

So Saul and his army prevailed against the Amalekites in battle, destroying all the people and livestock — all, that is, except for the Amalekite king and the best of the livestock.

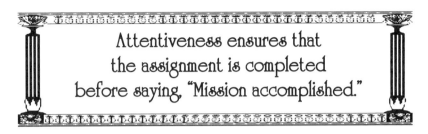

Attentiveness ensures that
the assignment is completed
before saying, "Mission accomplished."

Afterward, Samuel came to Saul, and Saul said to him, "Blessed are you of the Lord! I have performed the commandment of the Lord."

But Samuel said, "What then is this bleating of the sheep in my ears, and the lowing of the oxen which I hear?"

And Saul said, "They have brought them from the Amalekites; for the people spared the best of the sheep and the oxen, to sacrifice to the Lord your God; and the rest we have utterly destroyed."

1 Samuel 15:14,15

Saul told Samuel, "I did everything the Lord wanted me to do," but the prophet didn't let him get by with that lie. Instead, Samuel immediately asked Saul, "If you did everything God wanted you to do, what is the bleating of animals that I hear?"

Saul replied that he had saved the best of the live-stock for a great sacrifice to the Lord. In other words, Saul wanted a grandiose way to show the whole world that he had done what God had told him to do!

But God doesn't want us to do just *part* of our divine assignment. That isn't obedience. What if we underwent internal surgery, and the doctor put only some of our body parts back in place? Or what if we rebuilt the engine on our car and, after putting the engine back together again, had a couple of parts to spare? "Mission almost accomplished" doesn't work well in this natural realm, and it certainly doesn't work well in God's Kingdom!

When Samuel asked him about those animal noises he heard, Saul probably thought, *Samuel, why are you jumping my case? All I wanted to do was sacrifice to the Lord. Give me a break!*

But God doesn't see situations the way the flesh sees them. To Him, it was a simple matter of obedience or disobedience, so He simply said to Saul, "That isn't what I asked you to do."

What was the result of Saul's lack of attentiveness to every detail of God's instruction? Saul lost his kingdom and eventually his life, never fulfilling what he had been anointed to do as king of Israel.

Now let's contrast Saul with Joseph. We discussed Joseph earlier in a different context, but let's look again at his life as it pertains to this quality of attentiveness (*see* Genesis chapters 37 through 46).

When Joseph was seventeen years old, he possessed one primary trait that gave him more favor than his brothers: *He was attentive to his father, the authority in the family.*

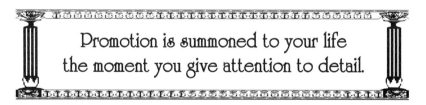

Promotion is summoned to your life the moment you give attention to detail.

Joseph continued to follow this principle of attentiveness to authority throughout his life, no matter what kind of circumstances he found himself in. As a result, his diligent attention to detail was the primary quality that brought him promotion in every situation, no matter how dark it seemed.

Joseph's life teaches us a simple fact: We will never receive a promotion through rebellion. We will never be chosen by our passive resistance. We will never obtain the prize by countering our authority's instruction with a defiant "But this is what *I* want to do."

There is another aspect to attentiveness that Joseph understood. When you give someone a gift, you are not to give him something *you* want to give. Give him something he actually wants, because that is the gift that person will keep in front of him all the time.

But how can you know what a person actually wants? By being attentive to him.

This is what distinguished Joseph from his ten older brothers: He was attentive to his father and thus received greater favor from his father than did any of his brothers.

Jacob's preference of Joseph made Joseph's older brothers *very* upset. (Of course, it doesn't matter if everyone in the world is upset when your dad is the boss!) They became even more upset when Joseph told them about the two dreams he'd had in which his brothers bowed down in homage to him.

The brothers became so embittered toward Joseph that one day they conspired together to destroy him. After first throwing him into a pit to die, they then decided to sell him into slavery.

An onlooker might have said, "Oh, look! Now God can't do anything with Joseph. He's been sold as a slave!"

But God's purposes are not restrained by the plans of man. Those two dreams were still alive in Joseph even as he was taken by the slave traders into Egypt and sold to a man named Potiphar.

This man Potiphar was not only the steward of Pharaoh but also Pharaoh's chief executioner. That means Joseph had death looming in front of him all day long every day!

But the Bible says that while Joseph was in Potiphar's service, God made everything Joseph put his hand to prosper. Potiphar even put Joseph in charge of his entire household. No matter where Joseph was, he became a prosperous man!

How does a person become prosperous? In America today, people assume that prosperity is linked to money. But I know many people who have a great deal of money and yet are actually very poor.

Joseph chose to be attentive and faithful in whatever situation he found himself in. Therefore, Joseph's prosperity was *God's* prosperity. And when a person is living in God's prosperity, it doesn't matter what anyone thinks or whether that person has a dime in the bank — *he's going to win.*

Then one day the wife of Joseph's boss tried to seduce him, and Joseph had to decide what to do. It is in his response to Potiphar's wife that we find the reason he was so attentive to Potiphar. Potiphar's wife said, "Lie with me," and Joseph replied, "**...How then can I do this great wickedness, and sin against God?**" (Gen. 39:9).

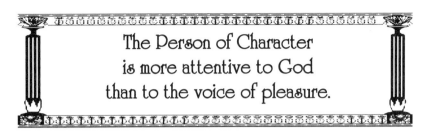

The Person of Character
is more attentive to God
than to the voice of pleasure.

That is a perfect description of Joseph. *He was more attentive to God than he was to the voice of personal pleasure.* In the end, Joseph fled from the woman's presence, leaving his robe behind — which was all the "proof" she needed to accuse Joseph of violating her while her husband was away.

Nevertheless, those dreams were still alive in Joseph, even after he was thrown in prison on false charges. Joseph just kept on staying attentive and obedient to God, believing that the dreams God had given him would one day come to pass.

Years passed. Then one day Pharaoh's butler and baker showed up in prison. Something in the character and demeanor of Joseph caused both men to go to him when they woke up from mysterious dreams that needed an interpretation. Joseph interpreted the dreams exactly as the Lord gave him the wisdom to do it: The cupbearer would soon be released from prison, and the baker would soon be put to death.

When you know that God's will is going to work out in your life no matter what, you don't have to be anything but honest. All you have to do is be attentive to God and refuse to move off your stance of faith.

Joseph didn't think, *Maybe I should tell the baker that everything is going to be cool. He looks tough, and he might react badly to the news that he's going to die soon!*

Maybe I should "soft-pedal" the interpretation of his dream to make sure everything works out all right for me.

No, Joseph didn't do that, even though that baker could have killed him right then and there. After all, this wasn't an inconsequential person. This was the chief baker of Egypt! But Joseph simply entrusted himself to God and then spoke the truth to the baker: "Listen, here's the interpretation to your dream. In three days, your head is going to be taken off your shoulders."

Joseph's words came to pass in both men's lives. The baker was put to death, and the other man was restored to his position as Pharaoh's cupbearer. However, more years of prison were to follow for Joseph as he waited for the cup-bearer to remember to plead his case before Pharaoh.

But then one day Pharaoh had a dream that couldn't be interpreted by his wise men. Finally, the cupbearer remembered what Joseph had done for him years earlier, and Pharaoh commanded that Joseph be brought before him.

Joseph effortlessly interpreted Pharaoh's dream and then gave him wisdom regarding what he should do about it. Joseph said, "You're going to have seven years of plenty and then seven years of famine. Therefore, you need to find someone who is very wise to help you store seven years of food during the years of plenty so your people can survive through the seven years of famine."

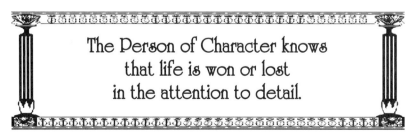

The Person of Character knows
that life is won or lost
in the attention to detail.

To Pharaoh, it was obvious that the search for that wise administrator began and ended with Joseph. "You are the governor of Egypt now!" Pharaoh declared.

No matter how many people tried to destroy Joseph, he continually rose back to the top. Why? Because a person who possesses the quality of attentiveness cannot be denied.

We live in a country where missed responsibility is a continual occurrence. But a person can only hide or cover up his neglected responsibility for only so long. Without the quality of attentiveness, he may fill a slot, but he will never be called upon for promotion. To become valuable, a person *must* give attention to detail.

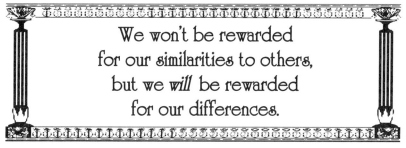

We won't be rewarded
for our **similarities** to others,
but we *will* be rewarded
for our **differences**.

In every situation you face in life, keep thinking about the details. What are the little particulars that other people don't see or pay attention to? Whatever those details are, be attentive to taking care of them. Remember, your difference will bring value to you, not the things you do the same as other people.

In Psalm 105:19, the Bible tells us, **"Until the time that his word came to pass, the word of the Lord tested him [Joseph]."** We, too, will be tested continually — not just by the devil, but by God. Are we going to hold on, or are we going to let go? What are we going to do? Joseph's example tells us what to do: We must never let go of our larger vision, but at the same time, we must stay faithful and attentive to the details that will help bring our vision to pass.

What was the difference between Joseph and Saul? Nothing but attention to detail. When God says something, we don't change it. When our employer says something, we don't change it. When any authority figure says something, we don't change it. We may appeal, but even in our appeal we don't willfully change our assignment. We do what is required, staying attentive to the details.

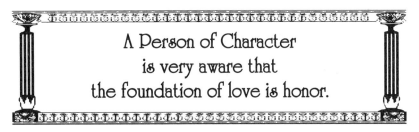

A Person of Character
is very aware that
the foundation of love is honor.

Jesus said it like this in Luke 6:46: **"But why do you call Me 'Lord, Lord,' and not do the things which I say?"**

Many Christians say the words, "Oh, yes, I believe in You, Jesus"; then they proceed to follow their own agenda as they go about their day. But Jesus responds, "Whether or not you believe in Me isn't the question. The question is, if you believe, why don't you do what I say?"

Then in John 14:15 (*NIV*), Jesus said the same thing a little differently: **"If you love me, you will obey what I command."**

Notice that Jesus does *not* say, "Well, I understand if you love Me but don't do what I say. I realize that even though you don't want to give Me your full attention, you still love Me. I know your heart."

Yet many Christians assume that this is exactly how God thinks! They say, "God knows my heart," and then they quote First Samuel 16:7 to prove it: "**...Man looks at the outward appearance, but the Lord looks at the heart.**" However, that scripture was never meant to be an escape valve for bad behavior!

We need to be very careful about what we hear in this life (Mark 4:24). Personally, I want to hear only what God is saying to me, because the information I take in and the kind of thoughts I entertain will determine the outcome of my actions and my life. That means I must agree with Jesus when He tells me that I cannot love Him unless I do what He says.

In my natural mind, I can still love Jesus and not conform to what He says. But in Jesus' mind, there is no love without compliance. Whatever I'm conforming to is what I am setting my affections upon and being attentive to.

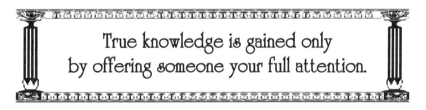

True knowledge is gained only
by offering someone your full attention.

We can skim the surface and gain some knowledge about any subject. However, our value regarding that knowledge is measured only by the degree of our attentiveness to learn more.

Attentiveness always implies deep concentration. A person with undeveloped attentiveness only skims over the subject being discussed. He doesn't really hear what the other person wants him to hear.

I remember a man who once told me, "I never raise my voice when I talk to people. I whisper."

"Why do you do that?" I asked.

"Because when you whisper, people have to give you their undivided attention to hear what you are saying!"

When I heard that, I thought, *This man may have come up with a good idea for teaching people to pay attention!*

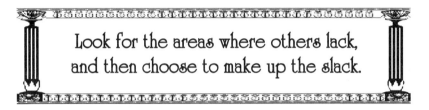

Look for the areas where others lack, and then choose to make up the slack.

Without fail, every minister who has ever come through our church doors has said to me, "No one has ever done for me what you have done for me."

Why is that true? Because I look to see what other people haven't done, and then I make up the difference. My value is not in what I do the same as everyone else. My value is in what I do differently than others.

You have no idea how it warms a person's heart to realize that you've observed him carefully enough to know the things he likes and the things he doesn't. It means so much to someone when you see the areas where he lacks and you make up the difference.

An employee blesses his superior beyond words when he listens intently to the directive given and then carries it out to the last detail without complaint or procrastination. This is the person who receives promotions and favor in the workplace. The employer relaxes when he hands out an assignment to this employee, knowing that there is no need to wonder whether or not he is going to do his job right.

An employee who fits this description is a rare find for a person in authority. So many people complete almost 90 percent of a given assignment and then just give up and quit, never finishing what they started.

But it isn't how we start the race that matters; it's how we finish it. Every one of us is a great starter, but very few of us really know how to finish.

And where does the breakdown usually lie when people fail to finish what they have been assigned to do? *In their lack of attention to detail.*

You can see why attentiveness is the key that determines how far a person will be promoted in every area of life!

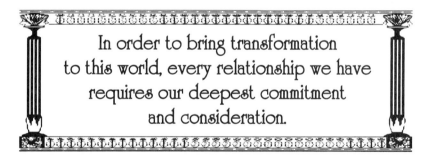

In order to bring transformation to this world, every relationship we have requires our deepest commitment and consideration.

I have to consider my relationships. One of the greatest mistakes I could ever make is to assume that people can handle whatever I have on my heart to tell them. Before I ever speak, I have to consider who they are, what they're facing, and where they are in their spiritual walk.

I especially have to consider my wife Linda. In each situation we face together, I have to think about what it means to her and what I should protect her from so she doesn't have to deal with it. While Linda is attending to the details of *my* life, I must also be attentive to her specific needs. And in every conversation, I must be attentive to hear what she *doesn't* say as much as what she *does*.

Let's talk about how you can develop attentiveness in your various relationships, whether at home, on the job, or with those who are over you in the Lord.

First, when someone addresses you, don't keep doing three things at the same time. Don't allow yourself to be preoccupied. Put down what you're doing; face the person; look in his eyes; and give him your full attention.

Second, don't allow your relationships to remain meaningless and superficial. Care enough to find out what the other person is facing; then help him solve his problem. As you listen to him, stay attentive to hear what he is *not* saying as well as what he *is* saying, for *your rewards in life are in direct proportion to the problems that you solve for others.*

Third, if someone over you in authority is giving you an instruction, don't be casual about it. Always give your superior the idea that you're poised to get up and do exactly what he asked you to do as soon as he finishes speaking.

This kind of attentiveness is such a rare quality in today's society. For instance, I remember the day Linda and I went out for lunch at a certain restaurant with a missionary and two pastors. Three of us asked for the same menu item with variations. But when the waitress came with our meals, not one of us got what we asked for!

That kind of thing happens quite often these days because people are so preoccupied. They're not truly listening. They don't ask questions. And then when they do something wrong, they often don't say, "I'm sorry — we'll do this over again at no charge." Instead, they say, "Oops! Well, you have a great attitude, so this will be all right, won't it?" In other words, they expect someone else to accept and pay for their inferior work just because that other person happens to have a good attitude!

But that is not the way *you* are supposed to live. God has called you to be attentive to detail and a continual learner. Be a person who is always interested in what other people are saying. Manage your time in a way that shows those with whom you have relationship how important they are to you.

Let me tell you something about life. Relationships are the only thing you will ever keep from this life to the next. Cars rust; money stays here. *Nothing* matters except relationships. So don't allow yourself to be quick to break them; in fact, do everything in your power to keep them!

God isn't interested in running the Church like a business; rather, He runs it like a family. Therefore, fight *for* your relationships, not *against* them. Give them your attention. Take notes. When you hear the way someone thinks, write it down. If something is important enough for that person to bring up in a conversation with you, it is important enough for you to write down. That's what James was talking about when he said, **"So then, my beloved brethren, let every man BE SWIFT TO HEAR, slow to speak..."** (James 1:19).

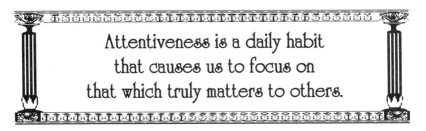

Attentiveness is a daily habit
that causes us to focus on
that which truly matters to others.

Concentration requires every part of our being. Since we can only be attentive to one thing at a time, it is vital that we stop focusing on things that don't matter and choose instead to focus on the most important things of life, including the relationships God has given us.

The word "attention" implies a consistent choice to concentrate. In order to be attentive to a particular person, we must choose to gain the full picture of what that person is communicating with us. We must know what he wants and desires. We must give him our undivided attention and gain the inner picture that only God can give us.

This choice of attentiveness is to be applied to every area of our lives. It doesn't work to demonstrate attentiveness on the job but not in our marriages or in our role as parents. But as we consistently choose to concentrate on what is most important not only to us but also to others — paying close attention to the details that make all the difference — we will put ourselves on the road to promotion in every single endeavor we undertake!

Principles for Attentiveness: Your One-Way Ticket to Promotion

✯ The game of life is won or lost in the details.

✯ Attentiveness ensures that the assignment is completed before saying, "Mission accomplished."

✯ Promotion is summoned to your life the moment you give attention to detail.

✯ The Person of Character is more attentive to God than to the voice of pleasure.

✯ The Person of Character knows that life is won or lost in the attention to detail.

✯ We won't be rewarded for our similarities to others, but we *will* be rewarded for our differences.

✯ A Person of Character is very aware that the foundation of love is honor.

✯ True knowledge is gained only by offering someone your full attention.

✯ Look for the areas where others lack, and then choose to make up the slack.

✯ In order to bring transformation to this world, every relationship we have requires our deepest commitment and consideration.

✯ Attentiveness is a daily habit that causes us to focus on that which truly matters to others.

<u>NOTES:</u>

CHAPTER THIRTEEN

BEING INDISPENSABLE IN THE NEW MILLENIUM

I am interested in the way you and I face this new millennium we have just embarked upon. I want us to be known as the most valuable people anyone can find to work with, rely on, and relate to on a daily basis. But to achieve that goal, we must become indispensable to those around us — not only in the workplace, but also in our homes, in our churches, in our careers, in our relationships, and in every other arena of life.

How do we become indispensable? First, we must focus on eliminating the unprofitable things that have hindered us in the past. Then we must begin to build into our lives certain key ingredients that are both profitable and essential to people of godly character.

With this in mind, I want to share some keys that will help you in your quest to become invaluable to the people around you. These guidelines will change your life if you will take them seriously and act on them as the Lord leads you.

1. *Step out of every unprofitable relationship that threatens your relationship with God.*

If those relationships haven't bitten you yet, they most assuredly will if you stay in them! You have to separate yourself now from unprofitable people so that when the time comes for the hammer of consequence to fall on their lives, you will be far away, enjoying the blessings of God.

2. *Eliminate every unprofitable attitude from your life.*

In Philippians 2, the apostle Paul is attempting to tell us how to live and how *not* to live our lives as children of God. Then he comes to verse 14 (*AMP*) and gives us crucial instruction regarding what *not* to do:

Do all things without grumbling and fault-finding and complaining [against God] and questioning and doubting [among yourselves].

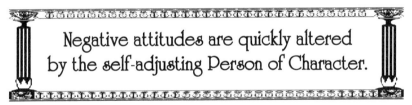

Negative attitudes are quickly altered by the self-adjusting Person of Character.

Most people (including Christians) whom we meet along the road of life spend a great deal of time violating this scripture. They are usually doing one of four things: murmuring, complaining, fault-finding, or grumbling.

They may start by murmuring under their breath. If you ask them if anything is wrong, they'll say, "No, nothing is really wrong." But is anything really right in their lives? No, nothing is really right. So they just keep murmuring, until finally their murmuring becomes more vocal and they start voicing their complaints.

The children of Israel were a good example of this kind of murmuring and complaining. They didn't like life in the wilderness, so they began to talk about how great it was to live in Egypt. Never mind that God had delivered them from slavery and had supernaturally taken care of them every step of the way. And so what if God had been raining down manna from Heaven every day to feed them and give them nourishment? The Israelites were tired of manna — they wanted some meat!

On and on the people murmured and complained — all the way to the moment of consequence when they ran head-on into judgment for their unprofitable attitudes and words.

Many Christians today make a similar mistake of harboring a complaining attitude. For instance, they may say, "I've been trying this 'doing the Word' stuff for a while now, and I'll tell you what — it was better back when I was in bondage to the world!

"At least back then, I could think whatever I wanted to think and say whatever I wanted to say. Back then, people weren't always nagging me about my confession. They weren't talking to me about straightening out my life. I just want to be able to do what I want to do without caring about what anyone else thinks about it!" On and on these people complain, allowing themselves to become more and more negative by the minute.

After a long bout of complaining, people often start finding fault with others in order to take the pressure off themselves. In other words, by finding fault in the life of another, they are attempting to distract someone else from grumbling about *their* lives.

Another reason people grumble and find fault with others is that they are discouraged about themselves. Because they don't have anything positive going on in their lives, the only way they can feel better about themselves is by tearing down someone else.

No one finds fault with other people unless they have faults themselves that they don't want to deal with. But the Bible warns that a person is in danger of being judged himself when he judges and finds fault with others:

> **Therefore you are inexcusable, O man, whoever you are who judge, for in whatever you judge another you condemn yourself; for you who judge practice the same things.**
>
> **Romans 2:1**

Jesus sends out a similar message in Matthew 7:1: **"Judge not, that you be not judged."** He goes on to tell us that we need to get that 2' x 4' beam out of our own eye before we pick up a magnifying glass and a pair of tweezers and attempt to surgically remove the speck we can't even see from our brother's eye (vv. 2-5)!

God's message is clear: We are to work on eliminating our own wrong attitudes, and leave it to Him to work in the lives of everyone else!

3. *Build profitable character qualities into your life, such as integrity, honesty, and a sense of honor.*

We have already talked quite a bit about honesty and integrity. However, I want to take the subject a little further in this context of becoming indispensable to others.

I don't know about you, but one thing I would love to have in my life is more honest people — people who actually are who they claim to be so I could believe what they say. Proverbs 20:6 (*NAS*) says it best: **"Many a man** proclaims his own loyalty, but who can find a trustworthy man?"

All of us want people of integrity in our lives — people who are faithful to who they say that they are. Such a quality is a priceless commodity in this world.

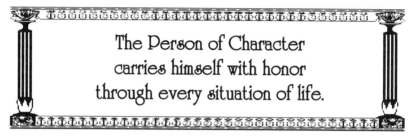

The Person of Character
carries himself with honor
through every situation of life.

The person of integrity is also an honorable individual. When he says something, it is as good as gold as far as everyone else is concerned. There is no mixture in what he says — only a pure, undefiled wholeness. And because he is a person of honor, he will not take advantage of a situation for his own benefit. He knows that there is much more to life than what he can accumulate for himself.

There must be a sense of honor that accompanies you wherever you go in life. Honor must cover all your dealings with other people and the way you carry yourself in every situation. If anyone is ever going to be upset with you, let it be over your honesty and your stance of honor. Don't ever let someone be upset with you because you took them to the cleaners again after they decided to trust you one more time.

Be honorable in all you do. *Never* break the principle of honor. As you live in this manner, people will begin to recognize you as someone who isn't looking out for his own benefit but for *God's* benefit in every situation. They will see that doing the honorable thing means more to you than making sure you get blessed yourself.

Let's talk about being a person of honor in the workplace for a moment. Colossians 3:22 refers to this issue:

Bondservants, obey in all things your masters according to the flesh, not with eyeservice, as men-pleasers, but in sincerity of heart, fearing God.

Of course, if a superior tells us to do something wrong, we have to say, "With great respect, I have to say no. I can't do that." However, if we have already been living our lives honorably before that superior, he will understand our response. More than likely, he will even be afraid to ask us to do something that is out of character for us.

On the other hand, if we have *not* been living our lives honorably before our employer, we shouldn't expect much sympathy when we say, "I can't do that. That would be stealing." He is likely to reply, "Well, why can't you? You did it yesterday."

"What do you mean?"

"You had someone else punch in for you at eight o'clock, and you didn't show up until almost nine o'clock."

Or maybe he would say, "You spent twenty-five minutes on your fifteen-minute break."

Or perhaps this one hits close to home: "Yesterday you spent most of your time on the phone making personal phone calls."

Remember, we are to obey superiors in *all* things, even the seemingly little things.

"Oh, but my boss doesn't mind if I come in a little late or talk on the phone during work hours."

Let me help you with this — there is no employer who doesn't mind. There may be a boss who doesn't say anything, but every boss cares about how honorably his employees act in the workplace.

Verse 23 goes on to say, **"And whatever you do, do it heartily, as to the Lord and not to men."** Notice that both these verses talk about doing something unto the *Lord*, not unto *another person*. That is the key. Whatever we do, we are to do honorably as an act of love unto the Lord whom we serve.

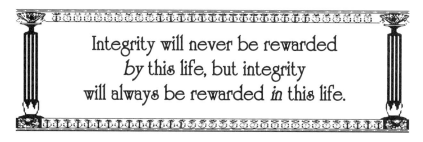

Integrity will never be rewarded
by this life, but integrity
will always be rewarded *in* this life.

When we walk in honor, God will honor us. As we live honorably in our place of business or in any other field of endeavor, we will find that we are highly sought after because honor is such a rare quality. However, we shouldn't expect everyone we meet to be happy with us. Some people will actually turn on us because of our integrity.

But that's all right. Regardless of what other people do, my goal is to be an honorable person. I am not honorable because I think it will do anything for me. I am honorable because I live my life before God.

You should also choose to live your life as an honorable person. Then when you walk in a room, a sense of respect will greet you among those present. Why? Because the people will know that when you walked into that room, honesty walked in with you.

First Peter 2:12,15 says it well:

> **Having your conduct honorable among the Gentiles, that when they speak against you as evildoers, they may, by your good works which they observe, glorify God in the day of visitation....**
>
> **For this is the will of God, that by doing good you may put to silence the ignorance of foolish men.**

It is by doing good that you will put to silence the ignorance of people who come against you. Your part is only to do what is right in the sight of God and in the sight of men, living your life with uncompromising honor.

Verse 17 describes this honorable lifestyle, exhorting us to **"honor all people. Love the brotherhood. Fear God. Honor the king."** In the coming days, this is the only way we will be able to truly live the Christian life. Until now, we as believers have been largely playing spiritual games. Perhaps we have gotten away with fudging on His principles in the past. But now is the time to ask the Holy Spirit to purify us and to help us eliminate the sloppy lifestyle we have allowed just because it's "easier" to live that way. It is time for us to live in the fear of God.

It is so important that we walk in the reverent fear of God on a daily basis, no matter what situation we find ourselves in. Yes, we live in a generation that has no fear of God. But remember, we do not choose to act honorably for other people anyway. We act the way we act because we live our lives before *God.*

4. *Make profitable choices that will lead you toward God's destination for your life.*

In Deuteronomy 30:19, the Bible sets forth a principle regarding our God-given ability to *choose:*

> **I call heaven and earth as witnesses today against you, that I have set before you life and death, blessing and cursing; therefore choose life, that both you and your descendants may live.**

We have the ability to choose the direction we go in every arena of life. But we also have the responsibility to choose *God's* way in every decision we face.

Let's take the selection of a job as an example. We need to choose to allow God to lead us to the job that is right for us at the present time.

Most people have a problem with the job they currently have. They wish they had another job. They are constantly thinking, *I wish I was doing something else that I like.*

But often the problem isn't the job. It is a sign of the times — a spirit of discontent that is present in this world today. People who feel this way might very likely feel the same way in a different job position.

So what does the Word say pertaining to this matter of job selection? Well, Matthew 6:13 tells us that the Lord will not lead us into temptation. In this context, that means He will not lead us into a job position where we are going to be dealing with temptation all the time.

"But the only kind of job I can get is tending bar."

No, the Lord won't lead you to a place where you will be tempted. He also won't lead you to a place where you're going to be continually unhappy. If you are complaining about your present job all the time, perhaps God didn't lead you there. Stay alert in your spirit, for you may have a short window of an opportunity to find out how to get where you need to go.

Whatever job God leads us to, we must then choose to *win* at that job. In fact, we must be determined to win in *every* area of life, for that is God's desire for us.

That's why Paul said in Philippians 4:13, **"I can do ALL things through Christ who strengthens me."** And in First Corinthians 15:57, he said, **"But thanks be to God, who gives us the victory through our Lord Jesus Christ."**

You can do *all* things through Christ. You have the victory!

"But I don't know if I can do it."

You *can* do it! There is nothing that is too great for you to do. God's answer to you is *yes*. It isn't no or maybe. God doesn't say, "Well, I don't know if you can. Maybe someone else can, but you can't." Second Corinthians 1:20 applies to you, just as it applies to every other believer:

> **For all the promises of God in Him are Yes, and in Him Amen, to the glory of God through us.**

All God's promises are *yes* to you. Everything you can put your hand to will prosper. Your job will prosper. The place of business will prosper just because you're there, just because you showed up on the scene. The people you do business with will get more business just because they're doing business with you.

Isn't that wonderful to know? People get blessed just by associating with you! And in every situation, *you win!*

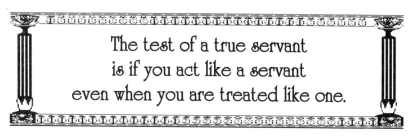

The test of a true servant
is if you act like a servant
even when you are treated like one.

We must also choose to be servants at our jobs. Of course, that also applies to every other arena of life. But it isn't always easy to choose servanthood; after all, most of us grew up catering to our flesh that loves to *be* served.

Jesus talked about the importance of servanthood in Matthew 23. First, He talked about the religious leaders who expected to be served rather than to serve others:

> **For they bind heavy burdens, hard to bear, and lay them on men's shoulders; but they themselves will not move them with one of their fingers.**
>
> **Matthew 23:4**

Then Jesus said, "But it isn't supposed to be that way with you."

> **But he who is greatest among you shall be your servant.**
> **And whoever exalts himself will be humbled, and he who humbles himself will be exalted.**
>
> **Matthew 23:11,12**

What you need to understand is this: If you will choose to make yourself a servant in any job or relationship you have in life, there is only one way you can go, and that is *up*. But if you attempt to position yourself as someone other than a servant, the only thing you will ever be is disappointed. Why? Because you thought you were someone Jesus didn't make you to be.

The greatest way to live your life is in the service of others. The more you are promoted by God, the more you will realize this and grow to love your position as "servant of all."

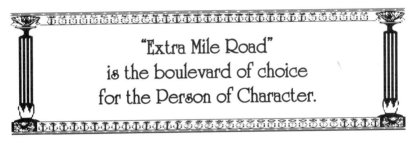

"Extra Mile Road"
is the boulevard of choice
for the Person of Character.

Another choice you must make at your job is to go the extra mile. In Matthew 5:41, Jesus tells us the principle: **"And whoever compels you to go one mile, go with him two."**

I have noticed something over the years about this subject of going the extra mile. When people begin to understand this principle, they will start doing extra things at their job, in their home, etc. The problem is, they get distracted by the "extra mile" and never finish what they were instructed to do in the first place!

Don't "go the extra mile" until you are done with what you are responsible for. That is how you make sure that you stay valuable to your superior. Do your job as unto the Lord, but do it quickly and efficiently. That way you will be able to do extra things for your superior in the amount of time it takes others to finish their normal responsibilities.

Remember, your superior is looking for problem-solvers. He asks questions such as: "What kind of problems does this individual solve? What kind of assets does he bring to the table? Is it a benefit or is it more of a hassle to have this person around?"

You need to know how to go beyond being a hard worker. Get to a place where you're not only doing what you are paid to do, but you are always finding a way to put icing on your superior's cake for him. That is how you can become extremely valuable in this new millennium — not only in the workplace, but in *every* area of life!

One more thing about becoming indispensable in the workplace: Determine never to pick up a bad attitude about your wages. If you want to go in and negotiate with your superior about a raise in pay, that is what you need to do. Meanwhile, you must fulfill with excellence the agreement you originally made with your employer. Keep your word. It is imperative for you to do so as a person of character.

"Well, yes, but those other employees make more than I do, and they have the same job!"

Now, wait a minute. That is one of those areas that isn't your responsibility; therefore, you shouldn't even have an opinion about it.

I'm all for people making good wages. I don't sit around and think, *He makes too much money. I don't think he's worth it.* I just say, "Hallelujah! I'm going to be faithful over little, and God is going to put me in charge over much. I am *not* going to move off God's principles just so I can make more mammon in this world. He set those principles down in His Word for me to live by!"

All these keys are important as we make our way through this new millennium. They represent God's way of making us valuable to the people we work with, live with, and interact with every day of our lives. And in the workplace, these keys can make us indispensable to those companies that are right now undergoing tremendous internal changes.

Many company leaders are thinking, *Who is going to stay with us, and who are we going to let go?* But you can make sure you are never even considered for that dreaded "lay-off list."

In the workplace, at home, in your church, in your relationships — wherever you are, just focus on bringing great value to the table as a person of honor and integrity. Choose to be a problem-solver who always goes the extra mile to serve!

PRINCIPLES FOR BEING INDISPENSABLE IN THE NEW MILLENIUM

- ☆ **Negative attitudes are quickly altered by the self-adjusting Person of Character.**

- ☆ **The Person of Character carries himself with honor through every situation of life.**

- ☆ **Integrity will never be rewarded *by* this life, but integrity will always be rewarded *in* this life.**

- ☆ **The test of a true servant is if you act like a servant even when you are treated like one.**

- ☆ **"Extra Mile Road" is the boulevard of choice for the Person of Character.**

NOTES:

CHAPTER FOURTEEN

DISCRETION:
THE FINISHING SCHOOL
FOR YOUR CHARACTER

Let's say you have worked hard to develop the character traits we have already talked about. You are ready to say, "Integrity, self-control, obedience, and compassion are qualities that I can honestly say I possess." But what can you do to make sure all these qualities are firmly fixed in your life? Is there one more quality that supplies the finishing sheen to your life when you are walking in the character of God?

The answer is *yes*, and the character trait is called *discretion*. Discretion is like the finishing school for your character. It is also the invisible glue that holds all the other elements of godly character together and keeps them permanently set inside your heart.

Someone might be a person of great truth, but if he doesn't understand discretion, he will become so brash that no one will be able to tolerate him. Someone else might be a person of great integrity. But unless he is also a person of discretion, he will become a person of great arrogance. In this way, discretion becomes the governor of all the other character traits that we must develop in our lives.

Discretion has so many facets and is so deeply planted in the core of each possessor that it cannot be easily defined with a simple statement of "this is what it is." Let's look at a number of different definitions as we try to encompass the meaning of this word.

The dictionary defines "discretion" as *being careful about what one says or does* or *the ability to keep silent.*

The dictionary also says that this quality is *regulated by one's own choice.* For instance, when the law says that something is "left up to one's discretion," that means it is left up to a person's choice. You cannot decide what another person's discretion is, for it has to do with his own conclusion to the question, *How do I think this situation should be approached?*

You are a person of discretion because you *choose* to be a person of discretion. However, discretion isn't a character trait that you either possess or you don't. Rather, it is a quality that lives in degrees inside every person.

Other words that help fill out the meaning of the word "discretion" are *calculating; careful; considerate; guarded; safe; precaution; foresight; forethought; restraint;* and *common sense.*

People of discretion are calculated, careful, and considerate. They are safe to be around. They are people of precaution who will test the integrity of a situation before they ever go into it.

A person of discretion possesses:

- the wisdom to avoid damaging attitudes, words, and actions.

- the ability to give insightful counsel to others.

- a God-given perception of the nature and the meaning of things that results in sound judgment and wise decision-making.

- the ability to discern spiritual truth and to apply it to human disposition and to human conduct.

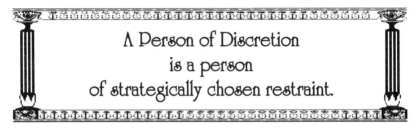

A Person of Discretion
is a person
of strategically chosen restraint.

Can discretion be learned? Yes, it *can* be learned, and the best way to do it is by keeping our mouths shut! As Proverbs 17:28 (*NIV*) says, **"Even a fool is thought wise if he keeps silent, and discerning if he holds his tongue."**

At one time or another, every one of us have wondered why certain people act the way they do. This is especially true when we encounter individuals who always seem to say abrasive and offensive things to others without understanding how the other party is perceiving them. What is the source of such poor behavior? A lack of discretion.

On the other hand, a person of discretion understands how to accurately discern a situation so that he says no more than he is asked to say. At times he even conveys his heart with nothing more than a look, for he uses his words very sparingly. As a result, when he finally does choose to speak, his words tend to carry greater weight among those who hear than do the words of those who voice their opinions with great abandon.

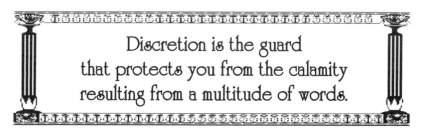

Discretion is the guard
that protects you from the calamity
resulting from a multitude of words.

Someone I esteem very greatly once said to me, "I don't ever have to wonder whether I should take you into a particular situation or to meet certain people, because I know you'll never hurt me." I considered that a very high compliment, because it let me know that discretion was operating in my life.

A person of discretion can talk to everyone in the room without telling all he knows, because only a fool speaks his whole mind: **"A fool uttereth all his mind: but a wise man keepeth it in till afterwards"** (Prov. 29:11 *KJV*). However, that doesn't mean a person of discretion is a secretive person. He is actually a warm, open, loving person, someone who genuinely cares for people. He just has the wisdom to know what to say and what *not* to say in any given situation.

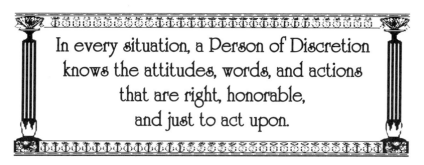

In every situation, a Person of Discretion
knows the attitudes, words, and actions
that are right, honorable,
and just to act upon.

A person of discretion also knows what *not* to do in the life of another. He knows how far he can go in a person's life when it comes to speaking the truth in love before he risks causing offense or breaking the person's spirit.

People sometimes tell me, "Oh, you can tell me the truth, Pastor Robb. Go ahead — tell me whatever is on your heart to say to me."

But there are times I have to reply, "No, I can't tell you the truth, because you don't want to know the truth. You want me to tell you what you want to hear. You're looking for someone to agree with you and tell you that you're okay."

Why don't I just blurt out the truth without concerning myself with the possible fall-out of offense or hurt emotions? Because I seek to be a person of discretion, and that means I must know how to avoid stepping over the line in another person's life. My only concern is that my own attitudes and words fit the need of the moment and are perceived as honorable and pleasing to the Lord.

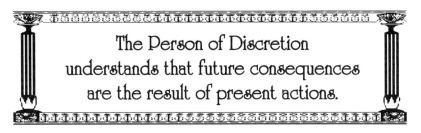

The Person of Discretion understands that future consequences are the result of present actions.

The person of discretion is a person of foresight. He seriously considers the things he should not do because of long-term consequences. He understands that, in the long run, some actions will cause more pain than the present problems they try to alleviate.

Individuals who lack discretion don't think that way. They just want to get rid of the pain they are feeling in the present, and they don't really care about the consequences they might suffer in the future. They think, *If I can just get the pressure off me today by doing this, who cares about what might happen to me in five years?*

A person of discretion is also a person of forethought. He thinks about his decisions in ten-year time frames. He ponders, *What is this decision going to cost me in the long run?* Based on the answer to that question, he then decides if the price is worth the long-term pain.

And if the road to excellence gets tough, the person of discretion understands that he can't just perform a spiritual abortion to make things easier on himself. He is looking for long-term pleasure and is therefore willing to endure short-term pain.

Some people attempt to have spiritual abortions every day for selfish motives. They have an attitude that continually says, "It's all about me." They think, *It doesn't matter what I do, so I'll just get rid of this relationship. How I treat this situation isn't the issue. After all, I have to take care of myself!*

When a person starts thinking like that, it's only a matter of time before he reaps a negative harvest. But that harvest won't return at a time when it's convenient for him. It will always come at a time when he doesn't want it to show up in his life, because the devil isn't interested in giving a person a choice in the timing of his consequences. If the enemy has his way, that harvest will come at a time when the person thinks, *Oh, God, I just can't take the pressure of this right now!*

Discretion also includes forethought when it comes to relationships with other people. A person of discretion thinks, *I'm not going to say that because if I do, this person might take it wrong and get offended.* Or he thinks, *If I say this, I'll give people the wrong idea about what I really mean, so I'm not going to say it.*

A person of discretion will put himself in someone else's position; then from that position, he will make a decision that pertains to him because of what it will mean to that other person. This kind of forethought is very rare and therefore a quality that is highly sought after. When you meet someone like that, he will always bring a smile to your face because he is such a delight to be around.

In my own life, forethought has to be a part of my daily existence. I realize that if I ever backslid, many of my church members would also backslide. If I suddenly chose to leave my church tomorrow, the church might not continue to exist.

That is part of the reason I pursue excellence the way I do. I realize that the work I have started will not live unless I continue to live for God in the midst of it. Therefore, I cannot think about short-term comforts for my flesh. I have to continually choose to do the right thing for the long-term good of the people I'm called to serve.

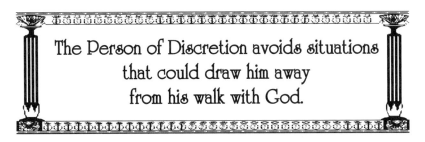

The Person of Discretion avoids situations that could draw him away from his walk with God.

In your pursuit of godly character, you need to know how to detour around people who will attempt to destroy your life if you give them the opportunity.

In Proverbs 5:1-4, David tells his son Solomon that discretion is the quality a person has to cultivate in order to avoid this kind of danger in his life:

> **"My son, pay attention to my wisdom; lend your ear to my understanding,**
>
> **That you may preserve discretion, and your lips may keep knowledge.**
>
> **For the lips of an immoral woman drip honey, and her mouth is smoother than oil;**
>
> **But in the end she is bitter as wormwood, sharp as a two-edged sword."**

The Hebrew word for discretion in verse 2 is the word *mezimmah*. It refers to *the ability to devise innovative, witty, insightful plans.* So how does this word fit in this context?

David tells his son in verse 4 that in the end, the immoral woman's words are as bitter as wormwood — a deadly poison — and as dangerous as a snakebite. In other words, David was saying, "Solomon, when an immoral woman attempts to draw you away from your relationship with God and into sin, remember that the ultimate harvest she offers you is death."

This Hebrew word for discretion, then, has to do with your ability to detour around people like the immoral woman mentioned here — any individual who would like to find access to your life and destroy who you are.

A person of discretion looks at a potentially danger-ous situation and sees where that path leads. Then he thinks, *I know that within eighteen months, that will destroy my family, so I'm not going that direction!*

A man who lacks discretion doesn't think that way. For instance, he might say, "My wife doesn't like to go to church, and I don't want to make a big issue of it."

But that husband better get on his wife's case and tell her, "As for me and my house, we're going to serve God! So get ready for church and start worshiping Jesus, Sweetie, because a house divided against itself cannot stand!"

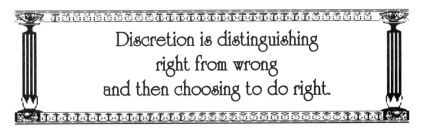

Discretion is distinguishing
right from wrong
and then choosing to do right.

I know people who have the ability to discern the difference between right and wrong, but they don't choose what is right. I have asked people like that, "Now, please help me understand. How did you come up with that answer when you know what God says is the right thing to do?"

"Well, it's all because they did this to me..."

Don't ever let that be your excuse for making the wrong choice. The moment you attribute your choices to anyone else's actions is the moment you have allowed your life to get out of your control. You must *never* give up control, for the outcome of your life is determined by the decisions you make.

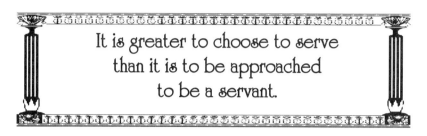

It is greater to choose to serve
than it is to be approached
to be a servant.

Let's look back at Proverbs 5:1,2 (*KJV*) for a moment. Notice what it says:

My son, attend unto my wisdom, and bow thine ear to my understanding:
That thou mayest regard discretion, and that thy lips may keep knowledge.

The word "regard" there is interesting, because most people *don't* really regard discretion. They may want to be discreet about their own private matters, but they *don't* want to be discreet about the private matters of others.

Personally, I do regard discretion. That's why I hardly ever ask a person to do something for me. If I ever asked a person to do something for me, he would be assured of one thing — that he is greatly trusted in my life.

But why *don't* I ask others to do things for me? Because I would rather consider what another person needs than for him to consider my needs.

I choose to keep myself far out in front in this arena. I do things for other people before it is ever expected. That way no one can ever say that I didn't keep my word or that I didn't do what I said I was going to do. All they can say is, "Hey, thanks for taking care of that."

The person of discretion understands the importance of serving others first. He does what would have been expected before it was ever asked for. Because he continually remains in the servant's role, he has people chasing him, trying to figure out what his next step will be. That is a *much* better position to be in than to hear people say all the time, "You didn't do that right"!

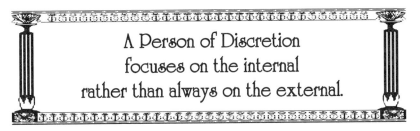

A Person of Discretion focuses on the internal rather than always on the external.

A person of discretion focuses on what other people don't focus on. He concentrates on what is happening inside people rather than what he sees on the outside.

Many Christians will tell you that things are going great in their lives. Then all of a sudden, you won't see them for three or four months. And when you finally do see them again, you find out their lives are a wreck!

But still they will protest, "Oh, no, we're really doing fine."

"You're really doing fine? What about those bankruptcy papers you have in your hand?"

Believers who fit this description desperately need a reality check regarding their walk with God. Meanwhile, a person of discretion is able to look beyond the external and discern what is working on the inside of the other person, beyond what the natural eye can see. And because he focuses on the internal, he is better able to help move the external circumstances to a higher plane.

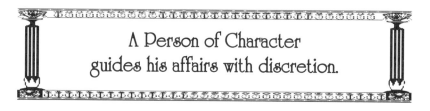

A Person of Character guides his affairs with discretion.

We looked at Psalm 112 earlier, but now I want to focus on a phrase in verse 5:

A good man deals graciously and lends; he will guide his affairs with discretion.

What does it mean when a person "guides his affairs with discretion"? He considers future consequences. He exercises foresight as he continually thinks about what is going on inside the situation he is facing.

The word "discretion" here is the Hebrew word *mishpat*, which means *giving a judgment* or *making a verdict*. The person of discretion guides his affairs with judgment. He makes a verdict, and he doesn't backtrack on it later. He cannot be persuaded to change his mind once he knows what to do. He says, "I don't want to hear anymore about that issue. I have made up my mind, and that's the end of it."

Let me give you an example of what it means to guide one's affairs with discretion. I may enter into an agreement with one person that I wouldn't even consider doing with another person. Why? Because I will not obligate an individual to keep his word who has no capacity for keeping his word.

For instance, God may speak to me about certain people to whom I have lent money, and I will tell them, "Brother, listen, I want you to forget about the money you borrowed from me. It's fine. Consider the matter closed."

On the other hand, there may be other people whose debt I will not forgive. It might even look like I *should* release them from their debt obligation, but I won't do it. Why not? It's very simple. Because that is exactly what they planned for me to do. They were just waiting for me to let them off the hook, but I'm not going to do it! If I did, I would just be giving in to their lack of faithfulness. No, people like that have to come to the place where they keep their word. All I'm doing is guiding my affairs with discretion.

When we keep lending money to people who don't pay us back, we demonstrate a lack of discretion. Yes, the psalmist says, **"A good man deals graciously and lends...."** But then he adds, **"...he will guide his affairs with discretion."**

The man of character doesn't lend to people who don't pay back the debt. Otherwise, he wouldn't be lending; he'd be *giving*. He understands that one doesn't lend something to someone who doesn't have the opportunity nor the wherewithal to pay him back.

We have lent to people unwisely. We have even given to people who have acted foolishly all their lives, soaking off anyone they can find who lacks the discretion to say *no*. These people will eventually come to the place where they don't have any more money and no one is left to borrow from. At that point, they're going to get knocked up the side of the head, and it won't be pretty. We would be wiser to allow them to get hit a little more quickly so that life's hard lessons won't hurt them as badly. And certainly our pocketbook wouldn't get drained as badly as well!

Psalm 112:6,7 tells us the reward of the person who guides his affairs with discretion:

> **Surely he will never be shaken; the righteous will be in everlasting remembrance.**
> **He will not be afraid of evil tidings; his heart is steadfast, trusting in the Lord.**

This man will never be afraid of receiving bad news. Bad news just doesn't bother him. Why not? Because he isn't hiding anything. He isn't trying to escape from a bad decision. He has guided his affairs with discretion, so bad news doesn't get to him. Even in the worst of times, he knows that God will make the midnight hour seem like noon and bring him out into the light of victory. And in the end, his life will be exalted with honor because he walked in discretion through every situation of life (v. 9).

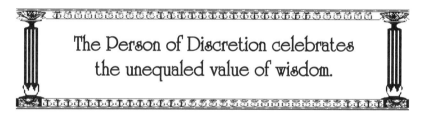

The Person of Discretion celebrates the unequaled value of wisdom.

To treasure something is to guard it, to cherish it, and to delight in it. In Proverbs 3:21-24, the Bible tells us this:

> **My son, let them not depart from your eyes —**
> **keep sound wisdom and discretion;**
> **So they will be life to your soul and grace to your neck.**
> **Then you will walk safely in your way, and your foot will not stumble.**

When you lie down, you will not be afraid; yes, you will lie down and your sleep will be sweet.

It is possible to be a very bright person and yet not be very wise. However, a person of discretion *is* a very wise individual. I didn't say he has a lot of brains, but he does know how to guide his affairs with wisdom.

Discretion will produce treasures in a person's life. However, if a person treasures finances more than he treasures wisdom, that person won't be able to sleep well at night. Only discretion will give him peace as he rests in the knowledge that he has done the right thing.

That's why we don't have to spend our energies on protecting what the world considers to be treasures. All we have to do is guard and protect this quality of discretion in our lives.

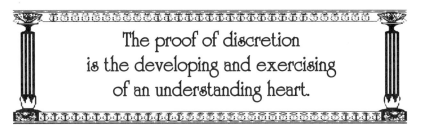

The proof of discretion
is the developing and exercising
of an understanding heart.

Proverbs 2:11 tells us one of the treasures discretion produces — an understanding heart:

Discretion will preserve you; understanding will keep you.

An understanding heart is a listening heart. It is also an obedient heart.

Solomon, the author of the book of Proverbs, possessed this treasure of understanding. When he was a young man who had just assumed the throne from his father, Solomon asked God for an understanding heart so he would be able to lead His people.

Solomon knew he had to have every possible resource in order to lead God's people well and wisely. And he was smart enough to understand that if he asked God for an understanding heart, he would receive not only the understanding heart, but everything else that was necessary for him to complete his job unto perfection.

God was pleased with Solomon's request for wisdom. And in the end, Solomon became the greatest king of Israel, surpassing all who came before and after him in the breadth of his wisdom, his wealth, and his power.

Proverbs 1:1-6 (*NLT*) outlines the purpose for which Solomon wrote the book of Proverbs. This purpose centered around the same treasure that Solomon had petitioned God for years earlier — an understanding heart.

These are the proverbs of Solomon, David's son, king of Israel.

The purpose of these proverbs is to teach people wisdom and discipline, and to help them understand wise sayings.

Through these proverbs, people will receive instruction in discipline, good conduct, and doing what is right, just, and fair.

These proverbs will make the simpleminded clever. They will give knowledge and purpose to young people.

Let those who are wise listen to these proverbs and become even wiser. And let those who understand receive guidance

by exploring the depth of meaning in these proverbs, parables, wise sayings, and riddles.

Proverbs 4:7 (*KJV*) shows how important it is that we pursue this particular treasure:

Wisdom is the principal thing; therefore get wisdom: and with all thy getting get understanding.

Understanding is a gift from God, but it comes to us through His Word. It isn't something we can obtain just by hanging around our local church. Only by diligently getting into God's Word can we develop an understanding heart.

I have known people who hung around the church a great deal, and all they got was religious! Others just received a bunch of head knowledge. But then there are those who come to church, and it is obvious that something has touched them deeply and transformed their lives. Understanding has begun to enter their hearts.

When that happens, harshness and arrogance begins to leave people's lives. They aren't so judgmental anymore. They don't push so hard any longer; they aren't as driven as before. They become more interested in *demonstrating* their faith through their actions than they are in *talking* about their faith. All of this comes as a result of *getting understanding* through a steady diet of God's Word.

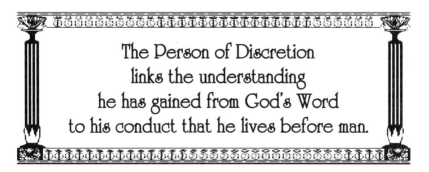

The Person of Discretion
links the understanding
he has gained from God's Word
to his conduct that he lives before man.

God is the Source of wisdom and an understanding heart. This is the message of Proverbs 2:6:

For the Lord gives wisdom; from His mouth come knowledge and understanding.

If you have spent much time at all studying God's Word, you know much more than you realize. You're a lot smarter than you think you are! But you have to keep in mind that *knowing* something is not what makes a difference in your life. It is *acting on* what you know that will make the difference.

Psalm 49:3 (*NIV*) says, **"My mouth will speak words of wisdom; the utterance from my heart will give understanding."** Years ago, I started listening to what I was saying to other people. At times I would even walk around with a tape recorder so that later I could listen to what I said. Sometimes I'd think, *Wow, that was actually really good! I think I'll listen to that again!* Understanding was coming out of my mouth that I didn't even realize I possessed. My life wasn't yet up to the level of the wisdom I had gained from the Word.

We must link our understanding to our conduct. We cannot allow ourselves to speak what we know of God's wisdom without being willing to act on it ourselves.

I want to say something else along this line: *Don't ever listen to a person who doesn't do what he says.* Someone like that has nothing to lose in giving you advice. But if his wisdom and understanding isn't good enough for him, don't let it be good enough for you.

Only listen to a person who is willing to risk everything he is for that which is right and true in life. A person like that will put everything he is on the line in order to get the right thing to happen in your life. That is the person you want to talk to in order to gain understanding.

And if you *are* in error in any area of your life, understanding will correct you, teaching you how to stop doing wrong and begin to do what is right: **"They also that erred in spirit shall come to understanding, and they that murmured shall learn doctrine"** (Isa. 29:24 *KJV*).

We just discussed the fact that understanding is a gift from God. But Proverbs 19:14 (*NLT*) takes this a little further.

> **Parents can provide their sons with an inheritance of houses and wealth; but only the Lord can give an understanding wife.**

Here we see that understanding is God's gift to the woman for her marriage. Only He can bring a man's wife to understanding.

There are so few women in this world who even *want* to understand their husbands. That's why it's so important for the godly wife to seek to be God's gift to her husband by pursuing understanding in the marriage relationship.

Too many Christian couples spend their married lives arguing with one another. Finally, after being married for thirty years, they get to the point where they just decide to put up with each other for the rest of their lives because they don't want to start over again in another relationship.

I cannot adequately express to you the value of an understanding wife. Personally, I couldn't handle it if I had to spend each day justifying myself to my wife —

who I was as a person, what I was doing every minute of the day, why I thought the way I thought.

I don't need another mother who is always asking me, "Why weren't you home on time? Who were you talking to on the telephone? Where were you this afternoon?" I need a wife who tells me, "I'm for you. I'm with you. I agree with your decision on that." And sometimes I need a wife who says, "I support you on that decision, even though I don't agree. Help me understand the way you think."

That is so much better than suffering through a daily argument or "bucking of the heads" in the home!

Husband, there is no alternative but for you to become the man of God and lead your family. If you are not the man of God of your home, your home will fail. Wife, if you don't become understanding, your home will fail. And when the parents fail to take their roles in the home, their children are the ones who pay the price of their flesh.

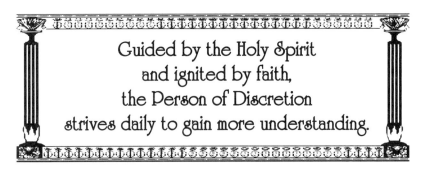

Guided by the Holy Spirit
and ignited by faith,
the Person of Discretion
strives daily to gain more understanding.

How do we gain understanding? The first way we do that is *through faith*. Hebrews 11:3 *KJV* presents this principle:

Through faith we understand that the worlds were framed by the word of God, so that things

which are seen were not made of things which do appear.

James 1:5 tells us that God gives us understanding when we ask:

If any of you lacks wisdom, let him ask of God, who gives to all liberally and without reproach, and it will be given to him.

Do you need understanding about a particular subject? God says, "If you lack wisdom, just ask of Me, for I give wisdom to all men liberally and without reproach." That means God isn't going to get mad at you, even if you continually ask Him for understanding. All you have to do is pray, "God, I need understanding in this situation. Please help me understand. I'm asking You to tell me what this is all about."

I actually look more for understanding in a situation than I look for the answer. The answer means that closure is now available to a particular situation, whereas understanding is something I can take into all areas of life.

We also gain understanding through the Spirit of God.

Now we have received, not the spirit of the world, but the Spirit who is from God, that we might know the things that have been freely given to us by God.

1 Corinthians 2:12

But the Helper, the Holy Spirit, whom the Father will send in My name, He will teach you all things, and bring to your remembrance all things that I said to you.

John 14:26

The Holy Spirit's job is to bring things back to your remembrance so you can better understand. Why? Because the principal thing in life is to get wisdom, and in all your getting, to get understanding.

Understanding comes as you begin to pursue God and to pray, "God, I need understanding. Please bring back to my remembrance what You showed me before." God will often reveal in little glimpses the things you need to know. When you see one of those small glimpses, you need to pray, "God, please bring that back to me. I need to see that again and again until I finally get it!"

John 16:13-15 has more to say about the Holy Spirit's role in giving us understanding:

However, when He, the Spirit of truth, has come, He will guide you into all truth; for He will not speak on His own authority, but whatever He hears He will speak; and He will tell you things to come.

He will glorify Me, for He will take of what is Mine and declare it to you.

All things that the Father has are Mine. Therefore I said that He will take of Mine and declare it to you.

The Holy Spirit's responsibility and assignment is to guide you into greater understanding regarding God's perspective of the situations you face in life. In Ephesians 1:17 (*NIV*), the apostle Paul prays that this role of the Holy Spirit would be fulfilled in our lives:

I keep asking that the God of our Lord Jesus Christ, the glorious Father, may give you the Spirit of wisdom and revelation, so that you may know him better.

We need wisdom so we can know God better. We also need understanding so we can see the situations we face from a divine perspective, not just from a human point of view. If we look at our lives through our own perspective, we will never understand it, for truth lies only in what God has to say about any given subject.

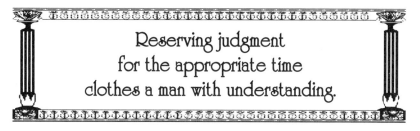

Reserving judgment
for the appropriate time
clothes a man with understanding.

A person of discretion is a person of wisdom, insight, wise counsel, and understanding; therefore, he does not judge by what he sees.

Don't look at situations as they seem to be, for people can make things look the way they want them to look. That's why God said to the prophet Samuel when he was choosing the new king of Israel, **"...For the Lord does not see as man sees; for man looks at the outward appearance, but the Lord looks at the heart"** (1 Sam. 16:7).

Christians have the idea that this verse means God doesn't care about the way things look. But He never said that. He says, "I look upon a person's heart. That's how I judge."

A person of understanding therefore understands that he cannot look only at the outward appearance to discern the truth of a situation. This same principle is found in Isaiah 11:3, in reference to the coming Messiah:

His delight is in the fear of the Lord, and He shall not judge by the sight of His eyes, nor decide by the hearing of His ears.

In order to guide your affairs with discretion, you need to know why things are said and why people do the things they do. But you won't understand these things using your natural reasoning abilities. That is why you must never judge by the seeing of your eyes, nor decide by the hearing of your ears. As Jesus said in John 7:24, **"Do not judge according to appearance, but judge with righteous judgment."** A righteous judgment is only possible when you ask God for understanding through His Word.

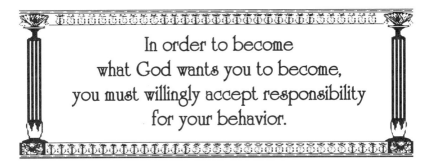

In order to become
what God wants you to become,
you must willingly accept responsibility
for your behavior.

A person of understanding realizes that he must be corrected at times because it is vital that he become whole in every area of his life. However, most Christians don't ever want to be rebuked. They resent it when someone confronts them with something they need to change in their lives. They don't realize that if they live without chastisement, they are nothing but illegitimate sons (Heb. 12:8).

Proverbs 17:10 (*KJV*) says, **"A reproof entereth more into a wise man than a hundred stripes into a fool."** That is an interesting comparison. A man of understanding receives reproof more readily than a fool does who has been whipped a hundred times!

Proverbs 19:25 says, **"Strike a scoffer, and the simple will become wary; rebuke one who has understanding, and he will discern knowledge."** If you reprove a person who has understanding, he will grow in knowledge through the correction. He understands that in order to become what God wants him to become, there will be times when he must be rebuked.

I decided long ago that no one needs to hit *me* with a hundred stripes. I'm a fast learner! I'm willing to get with the program right away. I have certain individuals over me in life who can rebuke me anytime they feel the need. No matter what they say, I will immediately comply with their wishes, no questions asked. I know I'm not above being dealt with in correction. I have to have someone in my life who helps me get my little wheels back on the track all the time!

However, that doesn't mean we can put the responsibility of the outcome of our lives on those who are over us in authority. We must always be willing to take responsibility for the outcome of our lives if we're ever going to gain understanding from God. Only as we are willing to take responsibility *for* our lives will we be able to gain understanding *about* our lives.

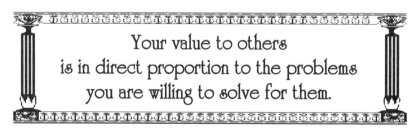

Your value to others
is in direct proportion to the problems
you are willing to solve for them.

We don't have to try to get along with someone if we're willing to solve his problem. He will accept us no matter who we are as long as we are willing to solve a problem for him.

This makes life very simple. When we walk in wisdom with people, we don't need to try to figure out their individual personalities. All we need is to understand that "the greatest among you is the servant of all" (Mark 10:44).

What do you do when you want to obtain favor from those who can help you grow in understanding? Proverbs 18:16 gives us a clue: **"A man's gift makes room for him, and brings him before great men."**

The greater the men are before whom you come, the greater the wisdom that will be deposited in your life. However, it will only be the wisdom you are able to embrace that will *keep* you in the presence of great men. A gift will get you in front of great men, but a gift will not *keep* you there.

Whether people smile or frown when we walk into a room is in direct proportion to the problems we solve. People will either think, *Here comes a solution*, or they'll think, *Oh, no — here comes that problem again!*

You see, we are either solving problems or creating problems every day of our lives. We cannot be neutral.

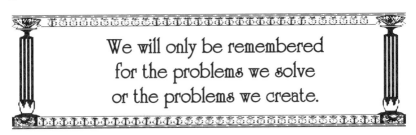

We will only be remembered
for the problems we solve
or the problems we create.

If we would sit back and evaluate our past perform-ance in the different areas of life, more than likely we would discover that we have been solving less problems than we thought we were. If so, we need to start making the needed adjustments right away. The moment we create more problems than we solve, we have put our-selves in a position to become unnecessary.

For instance, if a person has a chronic bad attitude in the workplace, it is only a matter of time before he is replaced. He has now lit the fuse on the outcome of his position in that job.

How can I say that? It's very simple. It is unnatural for a businessperson to maintain a painful relationship. As soon as he can find someone who will do the job with no pain, he will get rid of the painful relationship. So it is up to that person to become a problem-*solver* instead of a problem-*creator* — and the same principle holds true in every area of life.

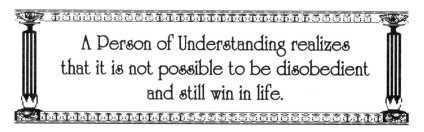

A Person of Understanding realizes that it is not possible to be disobedient and still win in life.

What are the results of developing an understanding heart? *First, we learn to walk in obedience before God.* As we discussed earlier, obedience is an absolutely crucial ingredient of our character, for it is the cornerstone of our foundation in God.

It's just a fact that disobedience will not bless us. The world exalts the notion of "I did it my way!" But if we insist on doing it our way, God will just look for someone to bless and to use for His purposes.

I learned this principle early on in my Christian walk. If God said green was blue, I'd say, "Isn't that blue beautiful, Lord?" I would *not* say, "Lord, you made a mistake. That blue is not blue. That blue is green."

No, I'm not going to argue with God about anything. If He says that lying is wrong at all times, then lying is wrong at all times. If He says that a man's gift makes room for him, then that's the way it is. Someone might say, "God, that isn't fair to some people." But I am not going to change God's principles because they seem unfair or difficult to follow. My only concern is that I get better at obeying those principles every day of my life.

Nehemiah 10:28,29 presents an important requirement of obedience to God:

> **Now the rest of the people — the priests, the Levites, the gatekeepers, the singers, the Nethinim, and all those who had separated themselves from the peoples of the lands to the Law of God, their wives, their sons, and their daughters, everyone who had knowledge and understanding —**
>
> **these joined with their brethren, their nobles, and entered into a curse and an oath to walk in God's Law, which was given by Moses the servant of God, and to observe and do all the commandments of the Lord our Lord, and His ordinances and His statutes.**

The people of God who had understanding separated themselves from anyone who might draw them into violating the laws of God.

We, too, need to separate ourselves from people and situations that could draw us away from God. In order to make sure our foundation is strong, we must dismantle our lives, cutting out anything that hurts us spiritually, and then put our lives back together again according to the principles of God's Word. If we fail to do so, we put ourselves in danger of ultimately walking away from Him.

That is what happened to Solomon. Solomon became very successful and well-known as king of Israel because he possessed wisdom and understanding and discretion. However, by the end of his life, Solomon had lost his discretion. Why? Because he did not separate himself from immorality; instead, he allowed it to draw him away from wisdom — a tragic end for a king who had once been so great.

Understand this: Whatever we do with our bodies will eventually be manifested in our minds. We can't say, "I worship Jesus" and then go out and party with the world. If we worship Jesus, we worship Him twenty-four hours, seven days a week.

Too many people have the attitude, "Everything is okay because I'm forgiven. After all, the Bible says all things are lawful for me!" But they leave off the rest of that verse that says, "**...But not all things are profitable...**" and "**...I will not be mastered by anything**" (1 Cor. 6:12 *NAS*).

The truth is, although we are free in Jesus, we are *not* free to do what we want to do, because we have been bought with the precious blood of Jesus. Once we belonged to the devil and did what the devil wanted us to do. But if we belong to God, we are called to live in holiness.

"But I thought God was forgiving."

God *is* loving and merciful and very forgiving. However, He isn't stupid, nor is He casual about sin. We shouldn't think that we can act like the devil's crowd and then climb right back up on His lap without facing any consequences for what we have done. Throughout His Word, the message is proclaimed that He will not bless disobedience.

Separation from whatever draws us away from God is a requirement of obedience that reaps eternal benefits — and understanding is at the top of the list. This is the message of Psalm 119:100: **"I understand more than the ancients because I keep Your precepts."**

Older people should possess more wisdom than the younger generations. However, in this modern society, that isn't necessarily true. This verse says that if we will hold on to and obey the precepts and principles of God's Word, He will give us more understanding than everyone around us. We'll even gain more understanding than those who are older than us in years but have not lived their lives in obedience to God's Word.

When we live a life of obedience, we also reap the benefits of sensible living. Job 28:28 says, **"And to man He said, 'Behold, the fear of the Lord, that is wisdom, and to depart from evil is understanding.'"** Sensible living includes walking through life in the fear of the Lord. In other words, when the Word says something to us, we immediately bow down before its truth and say, "I will obey." We *don't* balk and say, "Well, that's just someone's interpretation."

When God's Word is spoken, it doesn't matter whether we agree or disagree with it or whether we like or dislike the person who said it. We submit to the truth because it isn't the word of a man that we fear; it is the Word of *God*. We embrace God's Word even in the midst of disagreement because we refuse to displease the holy God whom we serve.

Another aspect of sensible living is found in Proverbs 11:12:

> **He who is devoid of wisdom despises his neighbor, but a man of understanding holds his peace.**

We need to keep our mouths shut when it comes to speaking negatively about other people. When someone wants to know what we think of a certain person, we don't need to say anything if the answer is negative. The other person can hear more from what we don't say than he can ever hear from what we do say. All he has to do is listen to the volumes of silence!

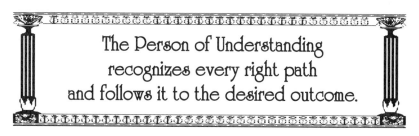

The Person of Understanding
recognizes every right path
and follows it to the desired outcome.

The second result of developing an understanding heart is *the ability to know the right path to take in any given situation*. Psalm 119:104 says, **"Through Your precepts I get understanding; therefore I hate every false way."** Verse 128 says something similar: **"Therefore all Your precepts concerning all things I consider to be right; I hate every false way."** In other words, the psalmist is saying to God, "In every situation, I consider Your precepts to be right. I follow Your way of doing things and hate every other way that has nothing to do with what You have said is true."

That is the reason we must separate ourselves from people who make deals with one another in order to make things work. We set ourselves up for failure when we link ourselves to such individuals by making a deal, because the moment they want out of the deal, our lives will fall. But if we will determine to believe God and build our lives only on His precepts, then we will still be standing even when others fall.

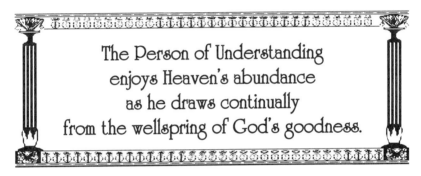

The Person of Understanding
enjoys Heaven's abundance
as he draws continually
from the wellspring of God's goodness.

The third result of an understanding heart is *the enjoyment of a good life.* Psalm 119:144 says, **"The righteousness of Your testimonies is everlasting; give me understanding, and I shall live."** An understanding of God's Word is the first step toward enjoying life according to *His* definition of abundant living.

Proverbs 16:22 says, **"Understanding is a wellspring of life to him who has it...."** This is why it is so important to pursue understanding — because an understanding heart allows the wellspring of God's life to continually build up, refresh, and renew the person who possesses it.

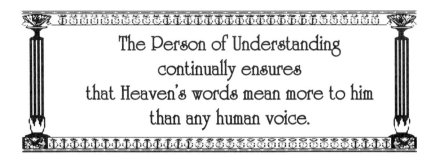

The Person of Understanding
continually ensures
that Heaven's words mean more to him
than any human voice.

We've seen some of the results of developing an understanding heart. But what are the results of a *lack* of understanding? The primary result is *foolish behavior.* A person who lacks understanding commits stupid errors of judgment that can adversely affect the outcome of his life.

For instance, Proverbs 6:32 says that a man void of understanding commits adultery. Proverbs 7:7 talks about the same thing: **"And saw among the simple, I perceived among the youths, a young man devoid of understanding"** (v. 7). This passage of Scripture goes on to reveal that a person who is devoid of understanding is easily seduced away from God, not realizing the serious consequences of his actions: **"...As a bird hastens to the snare, he did not know it would cost his life"** (v. 23).

Why is a person who lacks understanding so easily pulled away from God's Word? Because he starts listening to other people and believing what *they* say over what *God* says. The only thing that keep any believer from falling into that trap and backsliding is by making sure that God's Word means more to him than the words of any other.

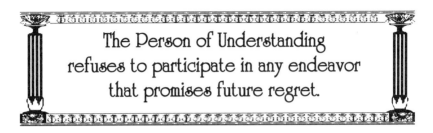

The Person of Understanding
refuses to participate in any endeavor
that promises future regret.

Another example of the kind of foolish behavior produced by a lack of understanding is found in Proverbs 17:18:

A man devoid of understanding shakes hands in a pledge, and becomes surety for his friend.

This is talking about cosigning a loan for someone. Don't let yourself get into that kind of contract. If you don't have the money to give the person, don't cosign for him. You may as well just say, "Let me take out this loan on my own and pay for it myself."

You can rest assured that the devil *wants* to make Proverbs 17:18 come to pass in your life. He wants you to be so void of understanding that you shake hands in a pledge and become surety for your friend. Then as soon as you do, he will smack your friend with adverse circumstances that keep him from being able to pay the debt. And although you may be thinking, *Oh, no, this guy would never back out on me*, in the end you will find that you have lost your friend.

Don't let that happen. Tell the person who has asked you to cosign for him, "Listen, I'll give you every penny I have to spare, Brother, but I cannot cosign for you. I will not make a commitment with someone who may not be able to keep it."

Another example of foolish behavior is the person who allows idleness to lead to ruin in his life. Proverbs 24:30,31 talks about this kind of person:

> **I went by the field of the lazy man, and by the vineyard of the man devoid of understanding;**
> **And there it was, all overgrown with thorns; its surface was covered with nettles; its stone wall was broken down.**

This man was too lazy to keep the cares of this present life from choking out the Word and making his life of no effect for the Kingdom of God. The Bible says that this is one more clear indicator of a person who lacks an understanding heart.

The bottom line is this: God had a very good reason for His command in Proverbs 4:7: **"...In all your getting, GET UNDERSTANDING."** An understanding heart is the key to experiencing God's best in life and to reaching the destiny He has ordained for us. But an understanding heart only comes as we develop the quality of discretion in our lives.

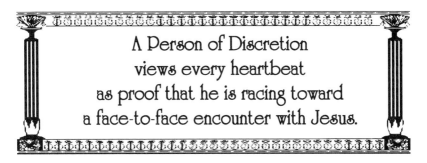

A Person of Discretion
views every heartbeat
as proof that he is racing toward
a face-to-face encounter with Jesus.

You have to fight to keep your commitment to God in this life, because as soon as God begins to promote you, the devil is going to say, "Do you want the promotion, or do you want God?" Most people will go for the promotion if they have to choose. But I say, "No, I don't want the promotion; I'll just take God."

"Yes, but you have the money now. You can buy a boat and spend all your free time out on the water having a good time!"

I don't care. I'll give the money away so someone else has the money for a boat. Why? Because God means more to me than a boat or anything else the world can offer me.

This is the divine perspective that discretion teaches us. We have to continually keep in mind that we are in a race toward the day when we stand face-to-face with Jesus. On that day, our material possessions aren't going to mean a thing. People can bury us with those possessions, but we can't take them with us.

What about the person who chooses his promotion over his relationship with God? When he dies, the question won't be, "Did he take his boat with him?" The only question people will ask is, "To whom did he leave his boat in his will?" That person gave up his relationship with God to get that boat, and in the end, someone else will get it for nothing! Now, *that* is foolish behavior!

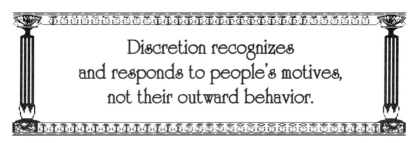

Discretion recognizes
and responds to people's motives,
not their outward behavior.

Do you ever wonder why people do what they do or say what they say? I do. I love to watch people. I like to find out what a person's method of operation is and then watch to see how he acts from that "M.O." in various situations.

People are funny that way. So often they use the same routine on everyone they relate to in life. Knowing that to be true, a person of discretion recognizes and responds to a person's *motives*, not necessarily to what a person *does*.

The following is a common scenario in my life: A person comes to me and says, "Pastor, this is the reason I'm thinking what I'm thinking."

I reply, "No that's not true."

"Oh, yes, Pastor, that's the reason I'm doing this."

"No, it isn't. Now, I believe that you believe what you're saying because I don't think you want to lie to me. But the truth is, you're lying to yourself."

A few months later after everything has blown up in the person's face, he comes by and says, "You know what, Pastor? You were right."

I reply, "Well, if you had just listened the first time, you wouldn't have had to go through all this pain."

You might ask, "Is your ability to recognize a person's motives some kind of spiritual gift?" No, it isn't. It's just common sense and an exercise of discretion.

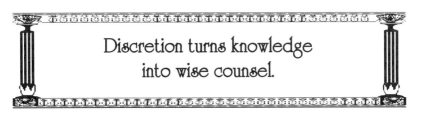

Discretion turns knowledge
into wise counsel.

Let's look at Proverbs 1:2-4 (*KJV*) once more. These are the verses where Solomon sets forth the reason the Holy Spirit inspired him to write the book of Proverbs:

> **To know wisdom and instruction; to perceive the words of understanding;**
> **To receive the instruction of wisdom, justice, and judgment, and equity;**
> **To give subtilty to the simple, to the young man knowledge and discretion.**

The word in verse 4 translated "discretion" is the Hebrew word *mezzimah*, which emphasizes the subtlety and insight of the counsel that is given in the book of Proverbs.

I know about the depth of insight in this book, because I listen to the book of Proverbs on tape almost every day. More than likely, that is why it amazes me so much when people persist in doing foolish things that can only hurt them in the long run.

People who do that often rationalize, "Well, yes, but this will take the pressure off me *today*, and that's what I need!"

I remember the time I made a decision for my family that was designed to relieve present pressure. I lived to regret that decision, for it only caused us an unnecessary dose of future pain.

I decided that we were going to take out a bill consolidation loan. If I had left things the way they were, it would have taken me only two more months to pay off everything. Then we would have been free from the intense pressure of not having enough that we had been living under for twenty-two months.

But all of a sudden someone came to me and said, "We'll help you with your debts by consolidating them in one loan and giving you one monthly payment."

I thought, *Eureka, the Lord has given us an answer!* I even had all my Christian friends convinced that this opportunity came from God. So I went in there and signed on the dotted line, and they consolidated my bills. Immediately my monthly payments went way down, and I didn't feel any pressure anymore. At least, I didn't feel any pressure for about two months. But then came the day when I would have been free from debt if I had just kept on paying my bills according to my earlier method. That day came and went, and I was still paying!

Instead of freeing myself from the pressure of debt, I had only multiplied it. It took me two more years to pay off my debts. My situation reminded me of the Israelites' forty days of doubt that gave them forty years in the wilderness. Because I had two months of pressure that I was unwilling to put up with, I had given myself two more years of pain.

That is why I find it so helpful to listen to the book of Proverbs every day while I'm praying in the Spirit — because I've had to deal with the fruit of my own foolishness! Everything good in my life can be traced back to a principle or precept that the book of Proverbs gave me.

I'm not real smart. I don't have an edge over anyone else. I just see something in the Book and I do it, and it makes me look good. It's no big deal. Anyone can do the same thing I do. If a person would just listen and meditate on the book of Proverbs on a regular basis with a determination to do whatever he hears, life would start becoming very different in a very short time.

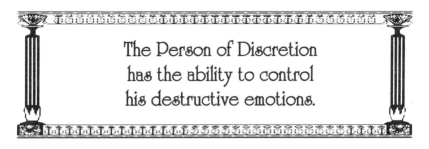

The Person of Discretion has the ability to control his destructive emotions.

Discretion includes the ability to control our destructive emotions. The truth is, our emotions have gotten us into more trouble than our bodies could ever get us out of!

For instance, a boy tells a girl that he loves her, and her emotions get all involved. Nine months later, she has a love child! Then she finds out that the love he proclaimed isn't love anymore. However, she still has a love child who will be with her for life.

Don't live for what a person says at his best. Live according to what he says at his worst. Watch and see how he treats other people, and don't think you'll be any different. Be a person of forethought who thinks, *What's the worst that a person with this character can ever do to me?* That is much wiser than thinking, *What's the best he can do for me if he's having a good day and comes through with some of his promises?*

Here is another thing about controlling emotions: A person may have wisdom in giving counsel to others, yet lack the ability to control his own emotions.

I know a lot of people like that. When they come to me with a problem, I ask them, "Well, what would you tell a person if he came to you with the same problem?" They easily rattle off what the Word says to do in that situation.

I reply, "Do that, and you'll be free."

"Yes, but..."

I tell them, "'Yes, but' is what other people tell you because they don't control their negative emotions of fear, bitterness, low self-esteem, or frustration. But you know the answer. You know what to do. Just do it, and you'll be free."

Proverbs 19:11 talks about the connection between discretion and the ability to control one's negative emotions:

The discretion of a man makes him slow to anger, and his glory is to overlook a transgression.

The word here for "discretion" is *sekel*, which just means *intelligence* or *prudence*. It is *prudent* and *intelligent* for us to hold back our anger and overlook a transgression!

On the other hand, it is important to know when to speak and confront an issue. Too often we overlook things we shouldn't overlook and refuse to tackle issues we should tackle. That isn't prudent at all; remember, we will never change anything in life that we are unwilling to confront.

Wife, let me tell you something about your husband. You need to make him confront you about *you*. Why? Because he doesn't want to confront you. He knows that after he confronts you, he has shot all his bullets. There's nowhere left for him to go. Therefore, you need to encourage him to confront you about you so you can become all God has called you to be.

Some women say, "Well, no man is ever going to confront *me!*"

It is that kind of attitude that will cause tomorrow to be just another day of defeat, for nothing will change until we are willing to uproot any bad seeds that are producing a negative harvest.

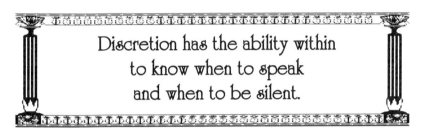

> Discretion has the ability within
> to know when to speak
> and when to be silent.

A person of discretion knows when to get involved in a situation because he understands the jurisdiction of the people who are in his life. If they are within *his* jurisdiction of authority, he considers the possibility of confronting the issue. If they are not in his jurisdiction, he doesn't allow himself to have an opinion about it.

This is what Proverbs 18:13 refers to when it says, **"He who answers a matter before he hears it, it is folly and shame to him."** Unless a matter is under my jurisdiction and my responsibility, I will not know everything I need to know to make a decision. Therefore, I won't allow myself to have an opinion about it.

The problem is, many people don't follow this principle. They neglect what God has made them personally responsible for; meanwhile, they spend all their energies forming opinions about what *someone else* is responsible for.

The person of discretion doesn't do that. He stays out of other people's business. He only has an opinion about the things God has made *him* responsible for. He understands that if he took the time to have an opinion about someone else's jurisdiction, he wouldn't be taking care of what belongs to him. Therefore, he never attempts to take authority over something he is not responsible for. This is a very good example of *sekel* — intelligence!

Proverbs 26:17 tells us, **"He who passes by and meddles in a quarrel not his own is like one who takes a dog by the ears."** If you grab a dog by the ears, he is going to bite you. And if you stop and meddle with a quarrel that you're not responsible for, you are going to get bitten as well.

For instance, be intelligent enough to never get between blood relatives. You may be 100-percent right, but you'll still end up as the bad guy. Don't even think that you won't! I know, because I've been smacked around a time or two over that issue!

Just exercise your discretion as you decide what to do in a given situation. Be intelligent about it, and remember, it is a man's glory to overlook a transgression. Learn when to say something and when not to. Know which battles to pick and which ones to pass up. As you develop this aspect of discretion in your life and refuse to pick up a battle for which you are not responsible, you will avoid unnecessary grief and keep yourself on the path that transforms you from glory to glory in Christ.

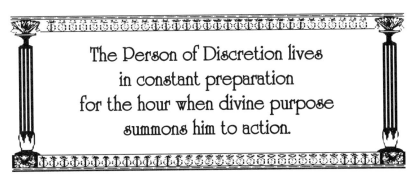

The Person of Discretion lives
in constant preparation
for the hour when divine purpose
summons him to action.

So are you willing to go through the "finishing school" of discretion? It isn't always easy, but it is the key to firmly establishing all the other traits of godly character in your life. If you decide to pursue this finishing school of character, you will take your place among a small remnant of God's people, for very few possess this particular trait. I'm telling you, God has plenty of room for your name on His "people of discretion" plaque!

As you commit yourself to the pursuit of excellent character, realize this: Two people inside you are being trained right now. The first is the king or queen God made you to be; the second is the warrior who lives within. The warrior's role is to beat off everything that would try to keep the king or queen from ever assuming his or her throne.

You must stop anything that would get in the way of your reigning in life, for Jesus Christ paid the ultimate price for you to do just that. To that end, you must guard your pursuit of godly character at all costs.

One of our past presidents said, "Great men and women do not just happen." He was right — greatness does *not* just happen. There are unseen years of discipline and character development that equip people for leadership in an hour of need.

During the Second World War, the King of England called for Winston Churchill to have an audience with him.

When Churchill stood before the king, the king asked him, "Winston, do you know why I've called you here?"

He said, "No, Your Highness. I have no idea why you've called me here."

The king replied, "Winston, go and form a great, new government."

Winston later related, "In a moment's time, I knew I had been born for this hour. This was the reason I came to this earth. Every moment of my life up to this time had only been in preparation for what was about to happen."

Churchill was the Prime Minister of England throughout World War II. During those years, he became one of the greatest and most inspiring leaders of our time. But right after the war ended, Churchill was defeated in an election.

I was watching a documentary about Churchill on television awhile back, and a man stated how glad he was that Winston Churchill had been defeated after World War II. I turned and asked someone whose opinion I hold dear, "Why is it that people didn't care for Winston Churchill after the war?"

My friend responded, "Great men can only be tolerated for short moments in time."

I can see the truth in that statement. The standards of great men are too high for most people. What they desire out of life is so great that they can only be tolerated for short spans by those who are content with mediocrity.

Within *you* lies the seed of greatness. However, it is in the times of preparation that you build your character and your potential for becoming all God created you to be. Now is the time when you must prepare for your hour, whenever that hour may come.

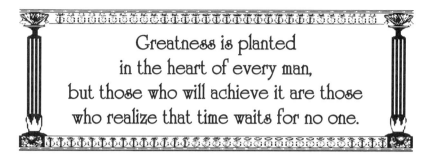

Greatness is planted
in the heart of every man,
but those who will achieve it are those
who realize that time waits for no one.

Personally, I'm convinced that my hour hasn't come yet. I haven't yet entered into God's ultimate destiny for my life. But I know that every moment must be in preparation for that hour. Every moment, I must get ready. Every moment, I must take it on the chin if needed and then rise up again to keep walking in the character of God.

That is your responsibility as well. Even when you feel like you have been wronged, take it on the chin once again. Choose to forgive and to walk in love, even if you have to do it a thousand times a day.

Just keep developing your character in the fear of God, for your hour *is* coming when you will be called upon to fulfill your God-ordained purpose on this earth. When that hour comes, you will need every ounce of godly character you have ever developed over the years.

So where does that leave you in this present hour? With a very important goal to focus on: *Whatever the cost, you must build a character that will last forever.* The outcome of your life and the lives of those you love depend on it!

PRINCIPLES FOR DISCRETION:
THE FINISHING SCHOOL
FOR YOUR CHARACTER

✯ A Person of Discretion is a person of strategically chosen restraint.

✯ Discretion is the guard that protects you from the calamity resulting from a multitude of words.

✯ In every situation, a Person of Discretion knows the attitudes, words, and actions that are right, honorable, and just to act upon.

✯ The Person of Discretion understands that future consequences are the result of present actions.

✯ The Person of Discretion avoids situations that could draw him away from his walk with God.

✯ Discretion is distinguishing right from wrong and then choosing to do right.

✯ It is greater to choose to serve than it is to be approached to be a servant.

✯ A Person of Discretion focuses on the internal rather than always on the external.

✯ A Person of Character guides his affairs with discretion.

✯ The Person of Discretion celebrates the unequaled value of wisdom.

✯ The proof of discretion is the developing and exercising of an understanding heart.

✯ The Person of Discretion links the understanding he has gained from God's Word to his conduct that he lives before man.

✯ Guided by the Holy Spirit and ignited by faith, the Person of Discretion strives daily to gain more understanding.

✯ Reserving judgment for the appropriate time clothes a man with understanding.

✯ In order to become what God wants you to become, you must willingly accept responsibility for your behavior.

✯ Your value to others is in direct proportion to the problems you are willing to solve for them.

✯ We will only be remembered for the problems we solve or the problems we create.

✯ A Person of Understanding realizes that it is not possible to be disobedient and still win in life.

✯ The Person of Understanding recognizes every right path and follows it to the desired outcome.

✯ The Person of Understanding enjoys Heaven's abundance as he draws continually from the wellspring of God's goodness.

✳ The Person of Understanding continually ensures that Heaven's words mean more to him than any human voice.

✳ The Person of Understanding refuses to participate in any endeavor that promises future regret.

✳ A Person of Discretion views every heartbeat as proof that he is racing toward a face-to-face encounter with Jesus.

✳ Discretion recognizes and responds to people's motives, not their outward behavior.

✳ Discretion turns knowledge into wise counsel.

✳ The Person of Discretion has the ability to control his destructive emotions.

✳ Discretion has the ability within to know when to speak and when to be silent.

✳ The Person of Discretion lives in constant preparation for the hour when divine purpose summons him to action.

✳ Greatness is planted in the heart of every man, but those who will achieve it are those who realize that time waits for no one.

NOTES:

_____

_____

_____

_____

NOTES:

_____

_____

_____

_____

_____

_____

_____

_____

_____

_____

_____

_____

_____

_____

_____

_____

_____

_____

_____

_____

_____

_____

_____

_____

Prayer of Commitment

Father, in the Name of Jesus, I confess to You that I need to deal with me. I make a commitment to get rid of every ungodly trait that has built a faulty foundation in my life. From this day forward, I choose to embrace Your principles and to live my life through Your eyes, not through mine.

I ask You to forgive me for the self-centeredness I have allowed in my life in an attempt to protect myself, Lord. Thank You for forgiving me and cleansing me by the blood of Jesus so that I can live free from guilt and shame.

Holy Spirit, I give You full right to change me into a new person. Take every self-centered bone out of my body, Lord, and drench me with Your compassion for others. Soften my heart so that I may be pleasing to You as I help erase the pain that others are facing.

I believe that I will walk free from every area of deception and bondage from this moment forward. Today I choose to start taking steps of integrity and truth as I pursue a life of godly character in every area of my life. In Jesus' Name, amen.

QUOTATIONS ON CHARACTER

More men fail through lack of purpose than through lack of talent. — *Billy Sunday*

Great minds have purposes. Others have wishes. — *Washington Irving*

An unused life is an early death. — *Unknown*

Purpose is the engine, the power that drives and directs our lives. — *John R. Noe*

Most time is wasted not in hours but in minutes. A bucket with a small hole in the bottom gets just as empty as a bucket that is deliberately emptied. — *Paul J. Meyer*

You are rewarded for your accomplishments, not for your intentions. — *Robb Thompson*

If you are not a good example, you will be a tragic warning. — *Robb Thompson*

Men decide their habits; their habits decide their future. — *Mike Murdock*

Never complain about what you permit. — *Mike Murdock*

Sow an action and you reap a habit; sow a habit and you reap character; sow character and you reap a destiny. — *Charles Reade*

The only thing that walks back from the tomb with the mourners and refuses to be buried is the character of a man. — *J. R. Miller*

God does not give you integrity; rather, you develop it, cultivate it, seek it out, and chisel it out from the granite of your being. — *Unknown*

God can never bless exaggerations. — *Smith Wigglesworth*

Talent without discipline is like an octopus on roller skates. There is plenty of movement, but you never know if it's going forward, sideways, or backwards. — *H. Jackson Brown*

Life is a grindstone. Whether it grinds you down or polishes you depends on what you are made of. — *Unknown*

The true test of a servant is if we act like one when we are treated like one. — *Unknown*

To be right too soon is to be wrong. — *Emperor Hardin*

Believability is more than mere words; it is the integrity of the individual. — *Ed Cole*

Never relinquish your God-given authority for pseudo-harmony. — *Robb Thompson*

Character is nurtured when we bow our knee to godly authority. — *Robb Thompson*

The measure of success is not whether you have a tough problem to deal with, but whether it's the same one you had last year. — *Former Secretary of State John Dulles*

The absence of character is often more visible that its presence. — *Unknown*

What we do on some great occasion will probably depend on what we already are; and what we will be is a result of previous years of self-discipline. — *Oxford University Professor H.P Liddon*

Leadership is the potent combination of strategy and character. But if you must be without one, be without strategy. — *General Norman Schwarzkopf*

Believability is more than mere words, it is the integrity of the individual. — *Ed Cole*

When one has integrity, there is an absence of hypocrisy. He or she is personally reliable, financially accountable, and privately clean...innocent of impure motives. — *Charles Swindoll*

Power is like a mighty river. As long as it keeps its course, it is a useful thing of beauty. But when it floods its banks, it brings a great destruction. — *John Maxwell*

Money doesn't change men; it merely unmasks them. If a man is naturally selfish or arrogant or greedy, the money brings that out, that is all. — *Henry Ford*

No other profession is expected to model morality as is a minister. — *Drs. Trull and Carter*

There is no dignity quite so impressive and no independence quite so important as living within your means. — *President Calvin Coolidge*

It is only the strongest of men that can ever avoid the seductive power of an understanding woman. — *Robb Thompson*

When we dilute God's absolutes, we reduce their potency. — *Robb Thompson*

Principles should not change with time or polls. — *President George W. Bush*

There are two kinds of people who never achieve much in their lifetime: the person who won't do what he is told and the one who does no more than he is told. — *Andrew Carnegie*

In life we must always underpromise and overperform. — *Robb Thompson*

Excellence is doing a common thing in an uncommon way. — *Booker T. Washington*

People forget how fast you did a job but always remember how well you did it. — *Howard W. Newton*

Don't be afraid to give up the good for the great. — *Kenny Rogers*

The quality of a person's life is in direct proportion to their commitment to excellence, regardless of their chosen field of endeavor. — *Vince Lombardi*

Always do more than is required of you. — *General George S. Patton*

Superiority is doing things little better than anybody else can do them. — *Orison Swelt Marden*

We are judged by what we finish, not by what we start. — *Unknown*

OTHER BOOKS BY ROBB THOMPSON

Victory Over Fear

The Winning Decision

You Are Healed

Marriage From God's Perspective

The Great Exchange:
Your Thoughts for God's Thoughts

Winning the Heart of God

Shattered Dreams

Excellence in Ministry

Excellence in the Workplace

The Endless Pursuit of Excellence

Excellence in Attitude

Excellence in Marriage

Excellence in Seed, Time, and Harvest

For a complete listing
of additional products
by Robb Thompson, please call:

1-877-WIN-LIFE
(1-877-946-5433)

You can also visit us on the web at:
www.winninginlife.org

ABOUT THE AUTHOR

For almost two decades, Robb Thompson has pastored the congregation of Family Harvest Church in Tinley Park, Illinois, reaching out to the Chicago area with a practical, easily understood message of "Walking in Excellence." A hallmark of his exciting ministry has been his ability to teach Christians how to act on God's Word and move out in faith so they can become people of excellence and *winners* in this life. Today Robb Thompson's teaching ministry continues to grow through books, tapes, and the ever-expanding television program, "Winning in Life," as he ministers to people throughout the United States and around the world.

To contact Robb Thompson, please write:

Robb Thompson

P. O. Box 558009 Chicago, Illinois 60655

Please include your prayer requests

and comments when you write.